WALKING TO VICTORY

ADAM GILCHRIST

WALKING TO VICTORY

A personal story of the Ashes and World Cup
campaigns, 2002–03

Edited by **Mark Whittaker**

MACMILLAN
Pan Macmillan Australia

The Australian Cricket Board (ACB) changed its name to Cricket Australia
on 1 July 2003. As the events in this book occur prior to that date, the
organisation is referred to by its former name throughout.

First published 2003 in Macmillan by Pan Macmillan Australia Pty Limited
St Martins Tower, 31 Market Street, Sydney

National Library of Australia
Cataloguing-in-Publication data:

Gilchrist, Adam, 1971- .
Walking to victory: a personal story of the Ashes and
World Cup campaigns, 2002–03

ISBN 0 7329 1138 9.

1. Test matches (Cricket) – Great Britain. 2. Test matches
(Cricket) – Australia. 3. Cricket players – Australia – Anecdotes.
4. World Series Cricket. I. Title.

796.35865

Text design by Nada Backovic
Printed in Australia by McPherson's Printing Group

FOREWORD

It is a little-known fact that cricket has a higher incidence of suicide amongst its players than any other sport.

I once asked the celebrated cricket columnist, Peter Roebuck (himself, a former English county captain), why this was so. He mused that it was probably because cricketers spend so long in the field with only their thoughts to keep them company that, perhaps, too much introspection led the unwary down dark paths.

He may be right. While hardly suicidal, one only needs look at Australia's last four captains — Waugh (taciturn), Taylor (laconic), Border (grumpy) and Hughes (teary) — to see the toll that cricket can take on a man.

And let's face it, if ever a sport was designed to send a man mad, it's cricket.

Beyond the solitary nature of so public a trial, consider the many variables a batsman has to contend with: humidity, moisture, breed of grass, length of grass, prevailing winds, cloud cover, available light, trajectory, velocity, spin, swing, bounce, age of the ball, self-expectation, human fallibility, sledging, heckling and psychological intimidation. And that's just from the non-strikers end.

Is it any wonder, then, that most modern-day cricketers are a mass of neuroses and clichés clinging desperately to whatever life-raft they can fashion out of career statistics?

All of which begs the question: if this is true, where in the hell did Adam Gilchrist come from?

Adam Gilchrist. The man with the Cheshire cat smile. Gilly. Who walked when he was given not out. In the World Cup. Uncomplicated Adam Gilchrist. Who whacks a ball over the rope and into the pavilion just as easily as he makes a joke about his batting in India ('I had so many zeros they thought I was sponsored by Telstra'). Gilchrist, A. With the highest Test match average of any current Australian cricketer (even though he bats at 7), who somehow manages to be modest about it and look sincere at the same time.

By rights, Adam Gilchrist should have died 40 years ago — with his swashbuckling batting and his old-fashioned sense of cricket as a game, now enshrined in legend as an example of 'the kind of cricketer they don't make any more'.

Is he real, or is he a robot put together by the ACB to try and counter the less-than-family-friendly image of some of Australia's other cricketers?

He is real. And I speak from personal experience. In the summer of 2002–03, I spent a day as Assistant Coach of the Australian Cricket Team, during the fifth Test against England, courtesy of an auction for the Malcolm Sargent Cancer Fund For Children.

Riding in on the team bus, slips practice, bowling in the nets, making jokes about Matt Hayden's haemorrhoids — I did everything that the Australian cricket team did. This gave me a unique opportunity to see them up close and with their clichés down.

From the easy humour of Jason Gillespie, through to the almost frightening intensity of Justin Langer, they ran the whole range of personalities. The one thing that bound them together: their fiercely competitive nature. Gilly was no exception, but it was a quiet conversation we had while he was waiting to bat that showed me the true nature of the man.

Not for Gilly, talk of catches held or bowlers faced. For an hour, as others played cards, or watched the game, or were attended to by the physio, we spoke about the challenges and joys of fatherhood.

That Gilly should be besotted with his son, Harry, did not set him apart from the rest of the team. That he would spend an hour on the subject in the dressing room while waiting to bat in a Test, did.

Here was a man who had life in perspective. And it showed. That afternoon, he went out and belted a century, helping Steve Waugh to his famous 102 not out in the process.

In *Walking to Victory*, Adam has attempted to transcend the clichés forced on modern cricketers by a rampant media and a restrictive ACB. He talks, with candour and feeling, about matters with which most cricketers would feel uncomfortable. Subjects such as rumours that he was not the father of his child. And the powerful political protest of Zimbabwean captain Andy Flower.

It is typical Adam Gilchrist. Memorable. Thoughtful. Decent.

The man may be quite a champion. More importantly, the champion is quite a man.

Andrew Denton

CONTENTS

ACKNOWLEDGEMENTS

To Tom Gilliatt and all the crew at Pan Macmillan, a huge thank you for your efforts in making this account of the Ashes and World Cup come to fruition.

Mark Whittaker, thanks for everything, mate. Your contribution to this book has been nothing short of outstanding, and I have appreciated your guidance and the expertise you happily shared with me. Thanks to you as well, Amy.

To Hamish Blair, sincere thanks for all your help and effort with the photos that appear in the book.

Axe, you are an extraordinary friend, and one that Mel, Harry and I are very lucky to have. Thanks for your invaluable input and suggestions, and for sharing the journey.

Mel and Harry, thanks for being who you are. For riding the roller-coaster of life with me and for always being there, unconditionally.

PROLOGUE

Here we go again. For the second time in as many weeks I'm set and cruising against the Sri Lankans. My opening partner, Matty Hayden, and I have survived a few probing overs and are still scoring at nearly six an over. The wonderful tingle which signals that a big innings is on the way surges through my body. But suddenly, I'm stranded down on one knee after attempting a sweep off the bowling of Aravinda de Silva. Urgent cries of 'Catch it!' come from the Sri Lankans as they anticipate their first wicket.

I have no idea where the ball is, only that I'd got an edge so thick I'm sure the whole crowd has heard, and it has shot off my pad … somewhere. I stand, confused, trying to find it. Then a sickening realisation hits me: the ball is safely in the keeper's gloves. *That's it. I'm gone.* My biggest chance to have an impact on this 2003 World Cup semi-final has passed.

As the Sri Lankan team start to show their jubilation, I look at the umpire, Rudi Koetzen. He shakes his head. Not out. It's a stunning reprieve, but something inside me says: Go. *Walk.* And in one of those split-second decisions that can change the course of a game, or even a life, I find myself actually doing it. My legs are carrying me away from the place where I so want to be. The place where I still could be, but for that powerful impulse: Go. *Walk.* There's a dream-like, almost surreal quality to it. The dominant voice in my mind is calling for order as the many smaller voices jeer and jostle, looking for reasons for what I've just done.

The small ground of St George's Park in Port Elizabeth is erupting. The Sri Lankan supporters are crazy with joy. The local South Africans are just as happy. The Australian tour groups are still waving their flags. And as I realise what is going on around me, I ask myself: *Is it the crowd that's crazy, or is it me?*

I've just defied an unwritten rule in modern cricket. You never walk. Let the umpire make his decision and accept it, but never, ever rule yourself out. It's a tough enough game as it is.

But even during this lonely stroll against the grain, somewhere deep in the back of my mind, something is reminding me: *You're doing the right thing.*

Sweeping against Sri Lanka in the World Cup semi-final. Little did I know that this shot would create such interest and comment.

Or was it what I did after the shot? The lonely walk off, as the questions and doubts started to bounce around my mind.

I discard my gear in the back change rooms, grab a drink and join my team-mates in the viewing room. I'm starting to feel more comfortable with what has just happened.

That is, until the boys ask me whether I saw the umpire give me not out. I see their looks of bewilderment when I say, 'Yes.' And suddenly it hits me how widespread the effects of my decision could be. Already I feel somewhat alienated from my team-mates. They don't have to say anything more. It's a World Cup semi-final, for crying out loud! Of course they're pissed off with my sudden decision to form a closer relationship with my conscience. I wish someone would say something so that I could blab out some poor, nervous excuse, but no one does. We watch the rest of the innings in silence.

When you get a good start as an opener in one-day cricket, you feel like you're in total control of the show. You're the ringmaster. Just like today. When either of us gets out, we always feel like we've blown an opportunity and reduced the team's chances of winning. That feeling usually lasts until the next partnership gets going and the realisation kicks in that one of the many talented players in the middle order will pick up the whip and see us through.

But there's trouble today. Ricky Ponting is soon back in the pavilion. I get a hollow feeling in my stomach. *Have I started a collapse? Please, no.* Then Haydos is back with us, too. *Oh, shit!* I'm having a nightmare.

I keep telling myself that if we lose this game, it's not because I walked. But I'm not totally convinced.

Darren Lehmann does a fine job of stemming the tide before he, too, rejoins us. Worse is to follow when one-day cricket's ultimate lion tamer, Michael Bevan, is out first ball, caught behind, and we're staring into the ugly jaws of defeat and elimination from the tournament. Bevo storms into the shed, adamant that he hadn't got an edge to the ball. He goes out the back to let off steam away from prying eyes and ears, but his displeasure is clear to everyone.

That gets me thinking. Haven't I, too, been wrongly given out countless times? Shouldn't I have just taken today's decision as payback? It's not as though I haven't stood my ground in the past.

I look around at my team-mates. No one is saying it, but I'm sure I know what they are thinking. I'm thinking it, too. *I've blown the World Cup with a self-righteous brain explosion.* I can feel the millions of eyes of a cricket-mad nation boring into the back of my head. *What have I done?*

As I sit there and watch our dreams crumble in the biggest tournament of all, my mind goes back to the previous Australian summer and the Ashes series, when certain events changed the way I would view cricket forever.

PART 1

THE ASHES, 2002–03

Chapter One

THE BAGGY GREEN

I remember the passion that I felt going into my first Ashes Test in England in 2001. I was inspired by thoughts of the hundreds of clashes that had taken place between Australia and the Mother Country over the previous 120-odd years. I felt awed to be following in the footsteps of household names like Grace and Armstrong, Jardine and Bradman, Chappell and Brearly. And of more recent times, Waugh and Warne. Like any Australian cricketer, or most young Aussie boys, that was the cricket series I wanted on my resume. It was a milestone that I self-consciously ticked off in my mind. *I'm playing an Ashes Test.*

I enjoyed it so much I spilt two catches in the first ten overs.

But that was 2001. Now, in November 2002, we were squaring up against the English again, only this time it was on our turf.

Having started my last Ashes campaign in horrific fashion, I was really keen to get the series off to a good start with some quality preparation. But no, it wasn't to be. What's that they say about the best-laid plans?

Five days before the Brisbane Test was to begin, I was in Sydney filming a commercial for the Australian Cricket Board's Test match sponsor, Orange, with Matt Hayden and Damien Martyn. During the shoot, I leaned on the coffee bar and felt something strange on my elbow. It looked like a pimple, but it seemed like an odd spot for the unwanted guest. I didn't pay it much more attention.

We flew to Brisbane the next day and I reckon we signed between 700 and 800 items — bats, shirts, all sorts of memorabilia. To sign the shirts, we sat in a line and about 16 staff moved along the line, stretching a shirt out in front of us. We'd produce our best signature, or something resembling it, and they'd move on. Signing, signing, signing for hours.

We didn't do any training that day, but my elbow was starting to ache a little. I mentioned it to Errol Alcott, our physiotherapist. 'Hooter', as he is known, immediately said I should head straight to hospital and get on an IV drip with antibiotics.

I was surprised by his urgency, but, with all due respect for his 19 years of touring experience, suggested that I would monitor the elbow during the night. He didn't push it.

By the next morning, the joint was swollen and really, really sore. I tried to pick up my son Harrison, but I couldn't fully bend or straighten my arm. It had swollen even more by the time I showed it to Hooter again before training. It was now around the size of a tennis ball and seemed to be getting bigger by the minute. Off to hospital I went.

The doctor didn't really know what it was. There was no cut on the skin where a germ could have got in, but he felt I should take a few repeats of antibiotics via a drip, which meant I was to stay in hospital for at least 24 hours.

So, that's how I found myself in hospital with a drip in my arm three days before the first Test was to begin. My chances of playing were getting slimmer with each minute that this strange thing continued to grow. It seemed to have a life of its own. I rued my earlier decision to ignore Errol's advice. I was also beginning to relive the nightmare of those two catches I had dropped back in 2001.

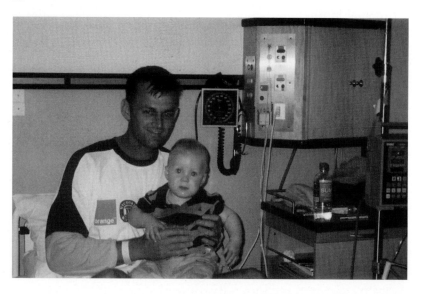

Harry visiting me in hospital. Not exactly the perfect preparation for an Ashes Test series.

A week earlier, we had arrived home from playing a series against Pakistan in Sri Lanka and the United Arab Emirates. As I lay in my hospital bed, I wondered if the trip had anything to do with my elbow. We had played in the most difficult conditions imaginable. Perhaps they had sapped my immune system.

The series was moved from Pakistan because of security fears. So, we played the first Test in Colombo, where we came close to being beaten, and then the next two in Sharjah, in the United Arab Emirates, where a modern, 30,000-seat stadium rises from the desert sands.

There was hardly anyone there, including many of Pakistan's stars, who had all come down with injuries. We had already been away for almost two months playing one-day cricket and there was definitely a feeling within the team of, 'Let's get this over with and get home for the big one, the Ashes.'

We lost the toss, I think, because I can't imagine Steve Waugh electing to bowl in those conditions. We walked on to the ground and heat shimmers rose from the lush green outfield. We knew it was going to be stinking hot, but nothing had prepared us for more than 50 degrees with 70 per cent humidity. There is no way to describe how that feels. You could try running around in a sauna fully clothed, I suppose.

It was clearly dangerous.

We tried to shut the conditions out of our minds and focus on the game, but it's just not possible. Within an hour, my whole kit — gloves, pads, everything — was drenched through. My shoes were squelching like I had just got out of a pool. Just watching the bowlers do their work was something to behold. Andy Bichel, in particular — the energy that he uses and the way he charges in. He never wavered. But all the bowlers put in.

I can't think of a game where I've wished more strongly that we'd bowl a team out in a session. And that's just about what we did. We had them nine wickets down at lunch, then came out and got the last wicket straight away. All out for 59. I've always had great respect for our bowlers and their efforts, but after getting us off that field so quickly, my fondness for them reached a new level.

Matt Hayden then went out and crafted a courageous century. It was an innings that I'll never forget, but it may be one that he'll never remember, such was his delirium when he came back in. It was an unbelievable performance.

We knocked them over for 53 on day two in exactly the same conditions. And it was all over. Had the Test gone on longer, it might have really messed with us.

The Pakistan bowlers often came off the field for 20 minutes after each spell, which is outside the spirit of the rules but was a very sensible thing to do to prevent heat exhaustion. After the first Test, we had a team discussion about whether we should do the same in the second match. Steve Waugh challenged us not only to shy away from that, but to push ourselves the other way. Tugga wanted us to make a statement to the Pakistanis that we wouldn't use the heat as an excuse. 'We're not going to crumble just because it's tough conditions. Let's continue to run between overs. In fact, let's even step it up a gear. Let's show these guys that we can handle it in these conditions.'

Batting with Matty Hayden against Pakistan in Sharjah, where he scored a brilliant century in stifling 50-degree heat.

It was a big ask, but it was symbolic of the way our captain thinks: never look for the easy way out, and never give the opposition the slightest hint that you're struggling.

The International Cricket Council (ICC) had minimal provision for extra drinks breaks or any slackening of the over-rate requirements. Thankfully, common sense prevailed and the match referee, Clive Lloyd, allowed both teams extra time at drinks and made subtle allowances for slower over rates.

Meanwhile, the English team had arrived in Australia and we had visions of them playing a couple of leisurely games in Perth and sitting by their hotel pool, totally invigorated for the Ashes.

The second Test, a week later, was easier. The temperature was only in the forties. Still, we weren't exactly calling for our long-sleeve pullovers. By that stage we had ice vests down at fine leg, and frozen wraps that we tied around our necks. It was the most sensational feeling to put them on, but then they'd be warm in five minutes. Our support staff were brilliant.

We knocked Pakistan over in quick time once again. Ricky Ponting scored a great 150, while Tugga got his first century in a while to get the critics off his back. The stadium echoed with emptiness, though, as Mark Waugh played his last innings for Australia.

Among the few who saw the Test was the crew from HMAS *Arunta*. They had been away from home for four months and we'd been away for two, so it was good to catch up with some Aussies. They invited us for a tour of their ship, and it was clear that the one person they really wanted to rub shoulders with was Steve Waugh. It's something we see all the time — the regard in which people hold him. Seven or eight of us were there, but Steve was the one they were in awe of.

And we were in awe of what *they* were doing. They had been patrolling the Gulf, enforcing the embargo on Iraq, so they had been living in a constant state of alert. They were on a six-month tour, living 12 bunks to a tiny room, with the ever-present fear that the next boat they stopped might be one huge fertiliser bomb.

I vowed then that the next time we were in some small hotel and the water pressure was lousy and the television didn't work, I wouldn't complain … too much.

While in Sharjah we caught up with the crew of the HMAS *Arunta*. Several of us were able to take a look on board in between tests against Pakistan.

This group of people really were an inspiration. Their dedication and commitment to the job was second to none. Meeting them certainly reinforced how much it means to represent your country overseas.

While we at first thought our preparation for the Ashes had been appalling, we were physically intact and mentally hardened. Brisbane could get pretty hot, but nothing was going to worry us after what we'd just survived. Or so I thought until my elbow blew up.

I definitely had too much time to think in that hospital bed. The antibiotics kicked in after a few hours and everything started to seem more manageable. Yet, it was amazing how in a hospital gown and with this contraption hooked up to my arm, my mindset changed. I'd get up to go to the bathroom and be moving like an 80-year-old man, even though I was feeling 100 per cent fit except for the sore elbow.

It took me a while to realise that I wasn't terminally ill. Steve Waugh had something like it once, only his arm was swollen right up to the shoulder and he had to spend a few days in hospital.

I checked out after 24 hours. The doctor wanted to keep me in longer, but I had a Test match to prepare for and a couple of dropped catches to avoid.

There was massive interest in the series from the sports press, which had been starved of its footy for over a month by then and was just beginning to swing into its summer mode. But because nothing had actually happened yet, the coverage was quite speculative.

There were several reports that Shane Warne and Glenn McGrath had said we were going to win the series five-nil. You never know if these articles are an accurate representation of what the players actually said, but both Shane and Glenn have been known to drum up a bit of psychological warfare in the papers. Glenn will target a batsman and be happy to let him know about it. Warnie's the same, except that he'll target an entire batting order. It's in their characters to use that as a motivational tool and as a way to unsettle their opponents.

My view of the England team was that they had some outstanding cricketers. They'd had terrific results against other teams, even if they hadn't performed against Australia for over a decade. I remember that part of my nervousness back in 2001 came from not wanting to be part of the Australian team that handed the Ashes back after such a dominant period. I felt that same fear deep in my belly again this time. Particularly since they had guys like Michael Vaughan, who had some impressive recent statistics. Darren Gough, if he was fit, and Andy Caddick were always dangerous; but there was also a lot of big talk about their two young quicks, Simon Jones and Steve Harmison. We had reports from guys who had played county cricket that they were both very quick and very aggressive. So, there was an element of the unknown about the English.

That's why I was shocked by the number of people coming out and predicting a whitewash. I wasn't aiming for a clean sweep. At that stage, I would have been happy with one-nil and four wash-outs. Just so long as we didn't do to the Ashes what Dennis Connors did to the America's Cup — lose it. My attitude would change if we got to three-nil up. But that was still a long way off in early November 2002.

I didn't train on the Tuesday when I got out of hospital, but I had a light hit and a catch on the Wednesday, the day before the game was to start. It wasn't an ideal preparation, but my thinking was that I'd done enough foundation work leading into the series, so that a couple of practice sessions weren't going to matter. I'm not someone who has to do 50 catches the day before the game, 20 dives to my right, 20 dives to my left, and hit a hundred cut shots. I just try to relax so that when something like this elbow problem comes along, I'm not freaking out.

I don't buy into the argument that the first session of the first Test sets up the whole series. It obviously helps to get off to a good start, but it's simplistic to think that that's all there is.

Yes, I know that Michael Slater smoked Phil DeFreitas backward of point first ball of the opening Test back in 1994–95 in Brisbane, and that many people feel that set the tone for the series. But a bad ball, or even a bad session, surely can't signal that it's all over for the Poms and time for us to crack open the bubbly.

If the first hour at Edgbaston in 2001 — with my butter fingers — was the barometer of that series, we might as well have packed our bags for Heathrow. The beauty of Test cricket is that you can have a bad hour, session or day. There is ample time to repair the damage simply by returning to the basic principles: disciplined batting and bowling. I think we sometimes forget that, such is the pace with which we play the game.

Steve Waugh's a big thinker, and he never enters into any Test without putting a lot of time into our plans and goals. In team meetings, he'll occasionally talk about nailing the match, or even the series, but he always qualifies these statements by emphasising that we must focus on the process if we are to achieve these results. Discipline in bowling. Partnerships in batting.

In our meeting prior to the first Test he addressed us, like he always does, with only a few points written down. He conveyed them very simply and with little emotion. There's never a big rev-up from Tugga, but he certainly does motivate. What he says is always so relevant. Sometimes it may seem basic. You might have heard the same things from your under-11s coach, but that just reinforces how relevant it is. Stephen's leadership style is uncomplicated and direct. There's no doubt that he has that rare ability to inspire and motivate those around him, even when he's unaware that he's doing it. To me, that's the sign of a very special person.

He spoke about having belief in ourselves and trust in each other. And, like he often does, he asked us to think about the history we would be creating in this series. How we could join the history makers by winning the Ashes again for Australia. Generally, at the start of any series, Stephen will also make special mention of the baggy green cap. I know that everyone has heard the clichés about the pride and passion when we put it on, but that's what it's like. Honest! We're the luckiest blokes in the world whenever we take the field with that cap on our heads.

Chapter Two

THE GABBA EXPRESS

English captain Nasser Hussain won the toss and elected to bowl. He's not the first person to go to Brisbane, see a green tinge in the pitch and an overcast sky, and think, 'Let's have first crack at this.' Steve Waugh's done it a couple of times. My first Test was at the Gabba and Stephen won the toss and bowled. I've never been one to go and look at the pitch and say it's going to do this on day one or that on day five. I generally don't even look at the wicket before a match. I'm better off summing it all up when the action has begun.

The sun came out soon after the toss, but the wicket did play some awkward tricks. Justin Langer and Matt Hayden, however, got off to their usual solid start, cruising to 50 in the 12th over. The critics were already on Nasser's back. What made his call look so bad was the poor way his bowlers used the wicket. The first bouncer came after an hour and 40 minutes. On day one on a pitch you've elected to bowl on, a bit of intimidation might have been in order.

The only bowler to have an impact in the first session was the young Simon Jones, who got JL out for 32. He had probably dreamed of sending shivers down the spines of the Australians all summer long, and he achieved that with an awkward dive on the boundary after lunch. The sickening accident, which ruptured his knee and ended his tour, was replayed on TV ad nauseam.

The only intimidation going on out in the middle was from Matt Hayden. Being such a huge bloke, Haydos creates an imposing figure at the crease. He stands upright, puffs out his chest and just overawes the opposition. As he swatted the ball away this day, he grew larger and larger.

The Gabba had filled and there was a real vibe about the place as the local boy did good. The Barmy Army were in fine voice, too. They've become such a feature of recent seasons that their songs have become like the steel drums in the West Indies, boring into your head every waking moment. Even as Haydos and Ricky Ponting destroyed the English attack through the afternoon, the Barmy Army never shut up. It was like they thought they could stop this freight train with their vocal cords. They couldn't. The partnership swung through 100, 200, 250.

The only English bowler to look dangerous in the first session, Simon Jones's series ended with a freak knee injury before lunch on day one.

It was almost a surprise when Ricky got out late in the last session for 123, having put on 272 for the second wicket. The Army got something to sing about, but Haydos kept right on rolling to be 14 away from a double century at stumps.

At 2–364, we felt pretty good about the day. Most commentators were already declaring the Ashes over. I wasn't so sure. Tomorrow was a new day.

I don't think we showed any lack of respect the next day. Something had changed within the English. Haydos came out and played a couple of big, aggressive shots in the first few overs. We all settled into comfortable positions in the viewing room, preparing for another long day of dominance. Then, suddenly, Haydos gloved one down the leg side and was out, three short of his double ton.

That jolted us. To England's credit, they sensed vulnerability. Steve Waugh came in and we could tell they had plans for him.

Already, the critics were circling Stephen as though, at 37 years of age, his career was over. The media pundits sensed weakness, and Nasser wanted to expose it. Caddick was bowling much better this spell, digging them in short to Stephen with leg side fields set for it. They knew that he'd put away the hook and pull years ago, so it was going to be difficult for him to keep the score ticking over. I'm sure they felt that it would affect the rest of us as well, given the rate we like to score at. If they tied one of us up, it would build pressure on the rest.

With the bowlers bowling where they were meant to, it allowed Nasser to set very specific fields and to execute plans. All credit to them, they were playing good cricket. Marto went. Tugga hit seven in 71 minutes before getting out to Caddick, caught by Crawley at short backward square, bringing me to the crease at 5–408.

I don't think my most fruitful innings have come in these circumstances. I don't know if I'm too relaxed, or if I'm thinking too much about being aggressive to take us up to a declaration. If I walk in at 5–90, my first instinct is survival. Which, in a strange way, usually causes me to be more aggressive anyway. The bowlers and fields are more attacking, so the fours come easier. Walking in at 5–400, the field is defensive. I think they had a plan for me, too — to bowl wide and make me come at them. It was fine by me if their plan was to bowl exactly into my scoring areas — wide outside off stump. I just had to bide my time. Get my eye in.

I chased the second ball and spooned it straight to gully.

I've really got to change my thinking in those scenarios and remember that 400 is a good score, but it's not a match winner. We'd suddenly lost four wickets for 37. Fortunately, Warnie put on a dazzling little half-century, dragging us up to 492 all out. Otherwise, the day would have been a complete disaster. They had taken 8–128 for the day. The momentum was all theirs.

The two great hopes of English cricket, Michael Vaughan and Marcus Trescothick, came out to bat. Having already played a series against Trescothick, we were more interested in seeing Vaughan. We'd heard a lot about him. He was the big name that Glenn McGrath had decided to target this summer. This was the first showdown.

Pigeon bowls what we term 'back of the length' — fractionally shorter than a lot of people. It's an undriveable length, but too full to pull. Well, almost.

From the start, Vaughan showed his intentions. He rocked back and pulled one away. Soon after, he rocked back and pulled another. Then another. Others have tried this, but few have succeeded. I sensed immediately that we were up against quality. There was something about Vaughan's balance and composure. Pigeon went for 23 runs in his first four overs before Tugga gave him a short break.

When he came back, Vaughan went to pick up where he had left off, raising his bat as if to pull before he seemed to back out of the shot. Too late. He got an inside edge through to me and he was gone for 33 off 36 balls. First points to Pigeon in that contest, but only just. An interesting summer loomed.

That little battle took the focus away from Trescothick. He had raps on him just as big as Vaughan and he was still going at the other end, albeit a bit slower. He and Butcher took the Poms to stumps at 1–158. So,

England had dominated day two and we had a lot to think about. That first-session theory was being well and truly tested.

Whenever we have a bad session or a bad day, we always come back to the processes we have to go through to turn it around. There's not a lot of in-depth analysis. Stephen's leadership style is to keep it basic and unemotional. There's no snarling. So, we went out the next day with the simple plan to do the basics: bowl a line and length; believe in each other and trust that it will work.

Trescothick started the day driving two consecutive deliveries back past Pigeon. He doesn't like that, Glenn, but it's amazing how often he'll bounce back from it. In no time at all, Butcher had edged him to Haydos in the gully. Five balls later, it was Trescothick to second slip.

The day looked like it might be ours, but Hussain and Crawley dug in and took them through to lunch, adding almost 100. The momentum, however, swung again after lunch. Hussain had just top-edged Jason Gillespie for six over the short boundary at fine leg to bring up his 50 when, a ball or two later, Dizzy produced a sharp leg cutter to have the England skipper caught behind. Alec Stewart went for a duck and their house came tumbling down. After sitting pretty on 3–268, 20 overs later they were 9–325, with Jones unable to bat. Our bowlers were ruthless. Similar to the way the English attack had turned their fortunes around on day two, our guys just bowled their line and length and reaped the rewards.

The Matt Hayden steam train got right back on track and rolled along into day four with another superb innings. When he brought up his second century, it felt like all the ins and outs of his career had been wiped clean. He'd spent such a long time in the wings waiting to get a second chance in Test cricket, all the disappointment seemed to disappear with his smile when he got that second ton and stood there with his arms raised to his home crowd.

He was caught and bowled soon after for 103, bringing his match total to exactly 300, and bringing me to the crease shortly before lunch. We were 359 in front, and Stephen had lifted me two places up the order to have a crack at getting us up to a declaration. But I was facing a dreaded pair and all I wanted was to get off the mark.

My last pair of ducks was in Calcutta, in that famous Test where we made India follow on and then not only lost the Test, but also the series. My previous innings of 122 in the first Test of that series was perhaps my best Test knock and I followed it up with 0, 0, 1 and 1. It was a huge crash. The sports psychologists would say that I shouldn't have been thinking about this as I approached the crease in Brisbane, some 18 months later, but I was.

And so was Nasser, I suspect. The fieldsmen, who had been scattered around the edges for Haydos, were brought in close to try and stop me getting off strike.

Mid-on had been left back near the fence, but just before the tall left-arm orthodox spinner, Ashley Giles, came in to bowl, Nasser stopped him and brought mid-on in close to further eliminate the chance of a single.

If he bowls the right delivery, I'm going over the top. I blocked the first ball, then the next one was the 'right delivery'. I was off the mark with a six. That eased the nerves and I was away.

The day Haydos owned Test cricket. Back to back centuries in a home Test for the big Queenslander.

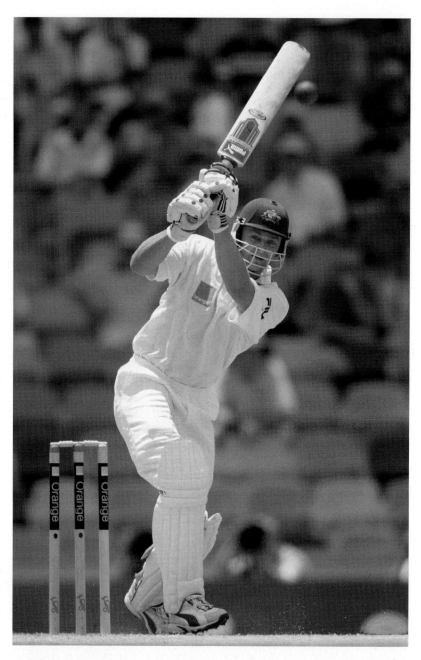

Having avoided the dreaded 'pair' after my first innings duck at the Gabba, I was able to hit out before a declaration in the second dig.

Tugga joined me soon after, but again they hammered him with short balls and again he toughed it out for a while before going cheaply, although unselfishly, in an attempt to raise the scoring rate as a declaration loomed. One sensed the media pressure building around our skipper. Darren Lehmann and I added a quick 50 before Tugga called us in well before tea, declaring with a lead of 463.

Gillespie got Trescothick in the first over, and McGrath got Vaughan in the second. Round two to Pigeon. But what summed up that innings was the 16th over, just after tea. Hussain and Butcher were putting up a stiff resistance for the third wicket. Hussain on strike facing McGrath. Pigeon sent down a couple of perfect length balls, just outside off, in what we call 'the corridor of uncertainty'. You could tell Hussain was tempted to play at them, but he let them go, let them go. The next three deliveries were identical. Hussain sort of fidgeted, didn't play, didn't play, didn't play, then finally on the sixth ball — same line, same length — he could hold back no more and pushed at it. Straight to Ricky at second slip.

Steve Bucknor, the well-travelled West Indian umpire, said later that it was the best over of Test bowling he'd seen. A pretty big rap from a guy who has seen a lot of Test cricket. I was amazed by how ruthless and clinical all the bowlers were. I hardly took a ball down leg side the entire second innings.

About the only ball that did come down the leg side was bowled three balls after Hussain's dismissal. Warnie sent down a leg break, which pitched outside leg but just didn't spin, shooting straight on. A bit of laziness on my behalf meant I missed it. The ball raced away and hit the bowler's marker where Dizzy began his run-up. I think that put some doubt in the batsmen's minds. Justin Langer scooted around from backward square, dived and returned it to me. I turned and threw it at the bowler's-end stumps. Direct hit and Crawley was out by a foot. That was the way the momentum was going. Four for 34.

A straight throw from the keeper and we can sense a win. Running out John Crawley at the Gabba.

Alec Stewart came in and, like me, was facing a pair. Warnie gave him a short ball outside off stump second ball. He cut it hard straight into Haydos's chest. It bounced up and the big Queenslander caught it on the third attempt. Unbelievable luck. Everything Haydos touched turned to gold. But that was the sort of afternoon it was. Haydos hurled it into the air as everyone ran in in amazement, and the ball came down right on to Alec Stewart's shoulder. He'd just got his first pair in a long and distinguished Test career and then suffered that indignity. The great thwack on the shoulder took him by surprise, but I think he soon realised it was an accident. Just one of those days.

That was the moment we sniffed the possibility of a victory that night. The vibe built on itself. It almost felt like it was out of our control.

In Sharjah, we had bowled Pakistan out in one Test match for 50-odd in each innings, but you don't expect that sort of thing to happen too often. The bowlers, however, were ruthless once more.

And suddenly, at ten past four, it was all over. They were 9–79. We'd won by 384.

We expected to see the Poms in our rooms for a drink afterwards. In international cricket these days, no one mixes after each day's play like they used to. If you've been in the field all day, you've got stretching, warm downs, ice baths, assessment and monitoring. There's an hour's worth of things to do.

But after a Test, we like to get together with our opponents and have a chat and reflect on the game. The tradition is that the losing team comes into the winning team's rooms, so we sat back and enjoyed a cold one, waiting for them to appear. I was keen to catch up with Alec Stewart, who I really get on well with. When, after a while, they hadn't shown up, I went to their rooms to find Alec, but the place was just about empty.

It had been announced that the English pace spearhead, Darren Gough, would be heading home. His chronic knee injury wasn't going to get any better. As if it wasn't bad enough for them already, news filtered through that Brett Lee had just bagged five wickets for New South Wales against Tasmania, giving him ten wickets for that match. So, while their bowling was looking increasingly impoverished, we had this embarrassment of riches.

Binga, struggling for form, had been picked as 12th man for the first Test, but the selectors decided to release him to play in the Pura Cup. It was a decision that didn't sit easily with some players. Australian cricket has always had the philosophy that if you're picked in the 12, you give 100 per cent to make sure the team has every opportunity to play well, be it by changing bats and gloves or running drinks out.

Let the celebrations begin. A win in Brisbane and the perfect start to my first home Ashes campaign.

In England, they release the 12th man all the time and just have some local bloke doing the chores; but not in Australia.

Ironically, it was Andy Bichel being picked as 12th man for a whole lot of Tests in a row the previous summer that prompted the rethink with Binga. A fast bowler can lose condition pretty quickly if he doesn't play enough. So, now Binga was starting to breathe fire again and it was Bic's spot that was under pressure, even though he'd performed very well in the Brisbane Test.

In the ten days between Tests, Tugga went out and hit 135 for New South Wales against South Australia. Binga took another ten-wicket haul in that game, too. Meanwhile, Martin Love was hitting 201 not out for Australia A against England, on top of the 250 he'd hit against them for Queensland. Like Binga, he couldn't crack the Test team either.

Even though there was a bit of a cloud over Dizzy's fitness, the Poms couldn't take a trick. Harmison broke Ashley Giles's wrist while bowling to him in the nets the day before the second Test. And on top of losing Gough and Jones, Andrew Flintoff still hadn't recovered from a hernia operation, and Harmison had shin splints.

Apart from Jones's injury, I didn't feel sorry for them. They'd come out here carrying injured players in the hope that they'd be all right. Obviously, Jones's injury couldn't be foreseen, but on any tour you're going to lose players through broken fingers and rolled ankles, or even split webbing in the hands. Those injuries are inevitable and they can put pressure on an otherwise healthy squad. The English selectors gambled and lost.

I don't envy the selector's job. Eighteen months earlier, as a selector on tour, I was involved in one of the toughest decisions I'd ever had to make — the dropping of Michael Slater. Since then, we'd all seen the results. A lot of things hadn't gone well for Slats and it wasn't easy now to look back, knowing that we'd played a part in altering his life so much. The trauma of it still bothered me. Anyway, it was all going to come out now, because in the days before the Adelaide Test we were due to shoot a television commercial together. It would be the first time we'd caught up since that England tour. We had a lot to talk about.

One of the toughest issues I've had to deal with in my career so far. Steve Waugh and I talk with Michael Slater after dropping him from the team in England in 2001.

The toss that Nasser would love to have again. Skippers Steve Waugh and Nasser Hussain get the Ashes series off and running on 7 November 2002.

Michael Vaughan in full flight during the first Test at the Gabba, giving us a taste of things to come.

Passion, pride … and plenty of pints! England's Barmy Army are fantastic for the game.

The Flying Pigeon. Although slightly out of position, Glenn McGrath's recovery to take this catch during the second Test in Adelaide was nothing short of amazing.

Michael Vaughan and our team await the third umpire's decision on Justin Langer's claimed catch during the second Test. My mind began to tick, and the seeds were planted for my actions later on in the World Cup.

Mr Reliable. Andy Bichel knocks over Nasser Hussain in the last over of the day during the second Test in Adelaide.

Chapter Three

TIGHTENING THE GRIP
IN ADELAIDE

Like any player who is dropped, Slats took it pretty hard. What made matters worse was the public scrutiny his every action was under, particularly in his personal life. There was also talk that our friendship had been stretched because I was a selector on tour.

Through the next Australian summer, 2001–02, our paths didn't really cross. We rang each other once or twice, but it was never the right time to discuss anything in great depth. So, the talk started playing on my mind. Like when I was in hospital, it's amazing what your mind will have you believe if you let it. Slats and I have always been great mates, stemming back to junior cricket in New South Wales country, but not seeing him for so long, the doubts started to fester.

Then, in about March 2002, someone drew a connection between Slats being dropped and my withdrawal from a one-day international in Sydney to be with Mel soon after the birth of our first child, Harrison. This heartless person — and to this day I wouldn't have a clue who it was or why they did it — posted their theory on a website called Cricket365, alleging an involvement between Slats and my wife, and questioning Harrison's paternity. The email got passed around at an unbelievable rate and it seemed that everyone had read it or heard about it by the time I was first made aware of it.

I was touring South Africa when my manager and close friend, Stephen ('Axe') Atkinson, rang me early one morning and told me the news. I felt sick in the stomach. It was the start of the toughest period of my life. Mel was at home with three-month-old Harry, so we couldn't even be there for each other. Whatever I suffered, it was many times worse for Mel — having her integrity abused like that when she's not even a public figure. She had trouble sleeping, and it made these early days of motherhood — spent almost as a single mother — so much more difficult. Thankfully, Mel's mum, Carol, flew across the country to Perth to help her through it. We also have a wonderful group of family and friends who always seem to be there for us in tough times. The strength that Mel showed in shutting out the pain and remaining totally committed to our little boy was extraordinary.

What hurt me the most was hearing and feeling just how much it was hurting her. We spent long nights on the phone, totally helpless. It was the worst time.

Upon reflection, it was such a ridiculous rumour that we should have been able to laugh it off; but when you're living it, it cuts deep into your heart.

What made it even worse was that it involved Slats. I already had this perception that there might have been friction between us. He and I discussed the email on the phone, but we never had a chance to catch up and talk about the other matters.

My emotional rollercoaster ride came to a climax during the first Test against South Africa. The email had made it to South Africa and there were banners at the ground that made reference to it. Sections of the crowd yelled out abusive taunts about Slats, Mel and me.

Somehow, I was able to shut it out and score a century in the first innings. I was then totally overcome with a wave of emotions and thoughts only of Mel and Harry; about all the drama they had endured as a result of their being my wife and my child. I felt so sorry for them, and yet I was proud of Mel and Harry, and of the fantastic support group around them that kept us going. I was also proud of my team-mates and grateful for their solid support. On reaching my ton, I didn't know whether to jump for joy or give a determined 'up yours' to the crowd and whomever it was that had started the rumour. In the end, I had no control over my reaction. I simply ran off the wicket, raised my bat to acknowledge the team and the support staff, felt the emotions bubble up and squatted with my head down. It was the first time I remember crying on a cricket field.

Mel and I launched a legal action against Cricket365. We mentioned our intentions to Slats. I mean, it was Mel and he who had been most seriously defamed in all this. But he declined the option of joining the suit. Axe handled the legal side of things, because I was still trying to play Test cricket. Cricket365 settled quickly. They had no choice.

What had happened was that a young employee of theirs had picked up this email off their public noticeboard, decided it looked interesting and shot it out to all of their subscribers via the website's newsletter. That was how the rumour spread so quickly and why they were so culpable.

Over the following months, I wondered why Slats hadn't joined us in the legal action, so that was one of the things I wanted to discuss with him in Adelaide this day. We filmed the advertisement and then, walking back from the ground to the hotel, we dived into it and opened right up. We talked about the email and the damage it had done to all of us. He told me he'd had a lot going on in his life at that time. He was in and out of the New South Wales team. He was getting a lot of negative press coverage. He didn't need any more on his plate. But now, nine months later, his life had settled down. He asked about our legal team and seemed keen to pursue the matter.

As we strolled back to the hotel, it really felt like I was closing that chapter of my life. However, I was still worried about where our friendship stood after the selection business. Slats made it pretty clear that most of the trouble there was in my mind. He admitted that for a while he had been very disappointed with Tugga and me. He had found it hard to understand how it was all meant to gel together; we were such close friends, but suddenly we were passing judgment on his career. He quickly stressed that he now had no problem with it and didn't bear any grudge. He was aware of 'talk' around that I was pissed off with him also, so it seemed that we had both just worried about the rumours, instead of finding out the truth and moving on.

We must have made quite a sight for the curious folk of Adelaide, slowing to a dawdle, deep in open and honest conversation. But it was a huge relief. We knocked the issues on the head and got them out of our lives for good. We really did have a strong friendship, and still do now. So, it's pleasing to have come out the other side of all that.

The Adelaide Test is my favourite every year. Adelaide holds many special memories for me. It's where I got my first first-class 100, and my second, too — 189 not out in the Sheffield Shield final back in 1995–96. It's where I captained Australia for the first time, and it's just an absolutely beautiful ground with a perfect pitch. It's really special. I love the way Adelaide embraces the Test match. It's a real social event. The atmosphere pours out of the place like in no other Australian city.

Les Burdett, the groundsman there, is a fantastic bloke, too. We have become good friends, and he has given me a lot of advice for a pitch up in Lismore, where I grew up. An oval there was named after me, and Les came up free of charge to have a look at it and suggest ways of turning the old concrete wicket into turf.

So, the first day at Adelaide is always high on my agenda.

It was very early in the piece. Michael Vaughan had just hit Andy Bichel for six to move up to 19. He was looking dangerous until he spooned a delivery to Justin Langer at backward point. JL claimed the catch, but Vaughan didn't budge.

I was certain it was a fair catch.

The umpire sent the matter up to the third umpire, but that didn't sit easily with me. I believe that we as players have to get back to trusting the word of the fielder, and at least hearing them out. But this sort of thing has become the norm, as players have realised that the technology isn't good enough to prove what has happened.

The third umpire ruled that it was inconclusive and, therefore, not out. I was frustrated not to have dismissed Vaughan, because he was the danger man; but more than that, it saddened me that cricket had come to this, and there was no obvious solution.

A couple of seasons earlier, Justin Langer edged a ball against the West Indies in Sydney and it was the same type of close call for the fielder at slip, Brian Lara. The appeal was referred to the third umpire, but only after JL had asked Brian directly if he felt he had caught the ball. Brian said he wasn't sure, so it went upstairs. People often refer to that incident as a scenario that favoured JL and say that he should take the good with the bad. They don't mention that he had asked the fielder and was prepared to take his word for it.

Not long after the Vaughan incident, a situation arose that potentially could bury my theory on these scenarios. Trescothick hit one back to Andy Bichel, who also claimed the catch in his follow through. I had a perfect view of that one and I felt straight away that it had bounced. All of us behind the wicket did. Bic was about the only one who went up. He genuinely thought he had caught it, although most of us were shaking our heads. Before we knew it, the third umpire was called on again.

In this case, in my perfect world, I believe the batsman should still ask the fieldsman if he genuinely thinks he caught it. If he says 'yes', but his team-mates know it didn't carry, as we knew this one hadn't, hopefully they would have the integrity to speak up. The umpires would still be able to overrule it. It's not a foolproof system, but it adds sportsmanship and accountability in these sometimes 'spiritless, professional' times.

It's a vexed issue, but, on reflection, I have no doubt that the seeds of my actions in the World Cup semi-final were planted on this day in Adelaide. They would have a summer to grow and toughen under the light of more such conflicts.

After his let-off, Vaughan didn't give us much in the way of chances again. It was the first time we had seen him compile a long innings, and his timing, composure and balance were memorable. He looked the complete batsman. He copped an absolute cracker from Dizzy that came up and hit him on the point of the shoulder. He dropped his bat and crouched in pain, but when he got up again he seemed unfazed. He had shots all around the wicket against all types of bowling. We would see it again on a more regular basis through the summer, but that innings had a real impact on me. I remember thinking: *This is a class act.*

He reached 150 in the last session as he and Butcher saw off the second new ball and steered the English towards a very respectable day. It had been a pretty thankless one for us.

Last over of the day, Tugga tossed the ball to Bic, who hadn't bowled for some time and hadn't had time to warm up fully. You often see the captain toss

Although he scored an outstanding century on day one in Adelaide, Michael Vaughan had a few uneasy moments.

a part-timer the ball for the last over in the hope of breaking up a partnership, but never a frontline bowler. And so Andy came in from the Torrens River end and bowled a nicely pitched delivery, just wide of off stump, but tight enough for Vaughan to feel the need to play at it. He edged the ball to first slip where the ever reliable Shane Warne held on to a fine catch.

Vaughan was out for 177.

I later asked Stephen why he went to Bic for that last over.

'Well, I know he's the sort of guy who's going to be ready to bowl right from the first ball,' Tugga said. 'He's not going to need an over and a half to get revved up. Bic'll charge in from the first ball of any spell. And I thought if Vaughan saw a part-timer come on, he'd be a bit wary, but seeing an unwarmed-up quick who he's been facing all day, I thought he'd relax. He might just think: "Right, I'm through here. This guy's not going to be on song from the start."'

It was terrific captaincy and a tremendous effort by Bic to produce the goods.

Suddenly, at 4–295, the day didn't seem so bad.

We came out next morning wanting to put the squeeze on, knowing that if we bowled a tight line and built pressure, we could get them out for under 400. On the 17th ball of the morning, Dizzy had Butcher edging to me without having added to his overnight score of 22. Dizzy, wicketless overnight, then upped the tempo on Craig White. A few overs later he came in to White and had him playing and missing at these perfect length balls, all of them not quite driveable. Last ball of the over, he dug in a bouncer. White had a crack at it and was caught at fine leg. It was like McGrath's over to Hussain in the first Test. A real working over, frustrating them until they could take it no more.

Dizzy took four for ten that morning, and Warnie got the other two to have England all out for 342. Once again, the bowlers produced the goods.

While our batsmen have achieved some great things in recent years, I can't help thinking the real reason for our success has been the intensity of our bowlers and their ability to build pressure. They really do suffocate the opposition. And they complement each other well, so the varying styles give you options on different wickets.

When I think of the great West Indies teams of the 1980s, I think first of the bowlers. Of course, their batting was also full of great names like Richards, Lloyd, Haynes and Greenidge, and like them, our batting complements the bowling group in that we've been able to score our runs quickly enough to give the bowlers the time to dismiss the opposition twice.

Winning Test cricket is all about getting 20 wickets. More pressure comes from a quality bowling attack than from big totals, I think. Looking at the English attack in Adelaide, they had 353 Test wickets between them. Ours had 1140.

Having said that, Haydos and JL went out and made another 100 opening stand and that never hurts your chances, either. They both got out just short of 50. Ricky Ponting and Damien Martyn then dug out a gritty stand. Marto took a ball on the helmet off Caddick and another two in the upper body from Harmison. The Poms weren't laying down, but Marto and Punter just chugged on into day three. It was really workmanlike, quite a different sort of partnership from what we usually play, but they were adapting to the conditions.

Marto was out for 95 (off 229 balls) after lunch on the third day, so that was pretty disappointing, getting so close.

At 3–356, he and Punter had set up a brilliant platform for the rest of us to launch from. But suddenly all the fieldsmen were being brought back in close, most of them on the leg side. Steve Waugh had arrived at the crease and Nasser was working his plan.

Here was Tugga, one of the greatest run scorers in Test history, being treated like a bunny. When he got off strike, the field was fleeing back to the boundaries for Ricky, who was well over 100 by this. Nasser was giving him the singles to get Tugga back on strike. It was what you'd normally do to expose a tailender. No one said anything in the viewing rooms. I guess we were all squirming a bit, amazed that this was happening to someone of Tugga's stature.

I haven't spoken to Stephen about this, but it soon became apparent that he had come to a decision after the first Test: the way to counter their contempt was with more contempt. You treat a man like that, he's going to get aggressive. From the start of this innings, we could see that anything that was there to be hit was going to be hit. Hard.

We saw some amazing flashes of the bat. Tugga smoked a few cover drives and played some deft flicks off the legs, although he kept his hook and pull shots tucked away in his kit bag. This was our captain speaking. Although the actions of the English skipper must have dug into Tugga, he never let it show and all the while used it as motivation. Ricky was out for 154 (off 269) — his fourth century in the last five Tests. It was like he started his innings in Colombo and just hadn't stopped.

Darren Lehmann came in and, just like in the Brisbane Test, the first ball he faced was from his brother-in-law, Craig White. They are great mates and team-mates at Yorkshire. Boof is married to Craig's sister, Andrea. So, here was Boof, who has waited so long to get back into the Test

A captain on the attack. Nasser Hussain tried to pressure Steve Waugh with aggressive fields in Adelaide, but Tugga took up the challenge.

team — every time he walked out to bat, his family member was trying to take it all away from him.

And it was working, too. White got him for five, caught off a fairly wide ball. It was a pretty tough scenario for Boof in front of his home crowd and all.

That brought me in with Tugga, at 5–414. He was about 30-odd and going at almost a run a ball, but he was out soon after for 34.

With me, they stuck to their plan to bowl wide. And I was grappling with this bug of mine about missing out when we've already got a good total on the board. I was determined just to occupy the crease and let the bowling come to me. Somehow, I managed to do that and get a start. Warnie and I put on almost 50 together before Warnie went and Andy Bichel came to the crease early in the last session.

Bic just went off. We didn't realise it at the time, but it was the start of some amazing form that we would come to treasure in the autumn. He batted with such confidence that he totally controlled that partnership of 77 until he was bowled for 48 (off 56) by Hoggard.

Tugga wanted quick pre-declaration runs, so when Harmison sent down a bouncer I sort of scooped underneath it, hitting it down to fine leg and it just cleared the fieldsman for four. Next ball was another bouncer. I had premeditated one of those newfangled scoop shots where I tried to lift it with a straight bat over the keeper's head, but it clipped my glove and I was caught behind for 54 (off 67).

Stephen declared then at 9–552, 210 in front.

It had been an uncharacteristically slow inning by us, but it certainly showed that we were able to dig in and eke out runs when the pressure was on, and still end up with a big total.

With a 200-run deficit, the English were under immediate pressure.

Dizzy got Trescothick leg before for a duck in his first over, and Pigeon picked up Butcher next over. They were two wickets down off the first 15 balls.

Vaughan, however, took us on again. He and Hussain settled things down towards stumps. Once again, Tugga tossed the ball to Andy Bichel, totally cold, for the last over of the day. With long shadows stretched across the ground, he came steaming in as Tugga knew he would. First ball beat Hussain cold, and the second beat him colder, clipping the top of off stump on the way through. Three for 36. It was déjà vu.

Rain was forecast for the fourth day, so nothing short of that or a record innings by Vaughan was going to save them.

Bic got Robert Key first thing in the morning, but Vaughan and Stewart started to put together a handy partnership. The weather was looking more ominous and we started to get nervous. They were shaping as major obstacles until Vaughan swept Warnie and skied it to deep backward square.

It should have been the perfect trap. Warnie had been applying a lot of pressure throughout his spell, and now the ball was coming down exactly where Warnie had told Pigeon to stand. It should have been straight down his throat. The trouble was, Pigeon wasn't standing there.

Glenn had unintentionally drifted out of position to an area finer than where Warnie had placed him. Now with the ball plummeting from the heavens, he was doing some serious legwork to get back to where he should have been.

He had no chance. The ball was a certainty to go for four, but he dived, stretching his full two metres horizontally through the air. Superman. As he landed, I was trying to see where the ball was and who was backing him up in case it hadn't got to the rope. But there it was. In his hands. We would later see the TV replays as often as we'd seen Jones's knee injury because it was the most spectacular catch, bouncing as it did from one hand into the other. It was a freaky thing, and it may also have won us the Test.

Rain stopped us getting back on to the field after lunch for 20 minutes. There were two more stoppages through the afternoon, but all the while wickets were falling and they were all out for 159 at 3.48 pm.

Within half an hour, it started to pour. It rained all afternoon and was still raining when we flew out the following day. Without that catch of

Glenn McGrath's amazing catch in Adelaide was well appreciated by the team, and seemed to provide great humour for Dizzy.

Pigeon's, and with Vaughan still at the crease, we may well have been lumbered with a draw. Instead, we were up two-nil going into the Perth Test.

As the heavens opened up after the match, we had again expected to see the English team in our rooms for a drink, but once more they didn't show.

We were to learn that it was part of Nasser's plans. He didn't want his guys getting too chummy with us. That was pretty sad, but they felt they had to try a circuit breaker to get out of the pattern of losing. It was easy for us, coming into this as winners. I heard that Allan Border did something similar in 1989 when Australia won the Ashes back after a long spell as the easy beats, so I could see where they were coming from. But I still thought it was the wrong way to go. Particularly against a team like ours that had a bit of an aura about it and several big-name players like Waugh, Warne and McGrath. I would have thought it was a perfect way to break down a bit of that mystique.

My mind went back to when we played the West Indies two years earlier; we didn't see them until after we'd won the series five-nil. They came in and it was one of the most entertaining afternoons in a change room I've ever seen. Guys like Wavell Hinds and Mahendra Nagamootoo were absolutely hilarious. They should be stand-up comedians, those blokes. The discussions ranged from some of their guys asking for various tips on technique, to them totally taking the mickey out of us. After a long summer with virtually no contact between the two teams, we realised they were picking up on everything we did, and imitating our little quirks and mannerisms. Wavell Hinds imitated Slats batting and came out with a comment Slats had made three months earlier; it totally cracked everyone up.

I remember thinking, 'Geez, why didn't they do that after the first Test? Why didn't they come in and break down some of those barriers?' I don't know that we'd have changed our approach on the field, but if you've had an afternoon of getting to know more about each other, it can change your perspective of the people you are playing against. Dare I say it, you might even consider them as friends.

Anyway, I'd thought this after the Brisbane Test against England and now it looked like it definitely was English policy. I couldn't help thinking they were making a big mistake.

I had to respect Nasser's plans. He thought it could help them win the series and that's what he's there to do. But it would be a sad day if regular socialising was lost to the game forever. Professionalism and heavy scheduling are already taking so much from the traditions that I think it's up to the players to fight to keep what we can of the past.

Noticeably absent from the field in the second innings had been Matt Hayden. He had played through a great deal of discomfort for the whole Test, but it had become unbearable by the last day and he'd gone off to hospital for an operation on a delicate bout of haemorrhoids.

I would like to say that we were all mature about Matt's condition and sympathetic to the considerable pain he was in, but I can't. He copped plenty. Nothing goes unnoticed in our team and, on top of the pain, he had to endure the new name of 'Grape Boy'.

You had to feel for the big fella. He couldn't do anything other than lie on his bed. We all went and saw him at various times to see how he was going. And he wasn't going too well, but you just couldn't help but have a massive grin on your face. Funny, that.

When I told my wife, Mel, that Matt was feeling a bit flat, she rang room service and sent him up a nice bottle of red, knowing how much the big fella loves his wine. But her cheeky side couldn't be stopped and she asked for a small plate of red grapes to be delivered with it.

The third Test was starting five days after the second finished, so we had to fly off to Perth. It was good to be going home. Even though it's my adopted state, I do feel like Western Australia is home now. I was in the middle of a ten-month period where I would probably have just 25 nights in my own bed, so that made returning for a Test all the more special. The guys from the eastern states get to pop home all the time if, say, we have a three-day break between playing in Brisbane and Melbourne, but it's just too far to get back to Perth. So we West Australians spend more time in hotels. When the team's playing in your home state, you can stay with them at the hotel or you can stay at home. For me, there was never any question.

The team was now cruising at two-nil up in the series. The WACA, with its pace and bounce, was always going to work in our favour, especially given the English injury list, which had just had Andy Caddick's name added to it. There was a good feeling as we headed into the game with the opportunity to wrap up the series. The only question hanging over the team was what to do with the resurgent Brett 'Binga' Lee. The curator had predicted the fastest surface in years. Could the selectors not pick Australia's fastest bowler to play on the country's liveliest pitch? A bowler who had taken 20 wickets in his last two matches?

The trouble was, Bic was doing such good things, too. So often he's been in the side, done well, but still never quite cemented his spot. Someone will get injured and he'll step back in, give 100 per cent, then when they're fixed up he steps back out again. You would understand if there was a resentment, but I've never seen that from anyone in the Australian cricket team while I've been involved. Particularly in the fast bowling group, who have all been vying for spots in the team at various times. Guys are shattered to miss out as Brett was in both those games, but again, once you're back in, whether you're 11th or 12th man picked, it's unconditional support for the team. Before Bic there was Michael Kasprovicz and Damien Fleming, and then Binga, all vying for a spot. And if ever there was going to be a feud or a bit of jealousy, you could understand it, but if you throw that whole fast bowling group in a room together, anywhere, it's going to be a hilarious time. Players realise that at the end of the day they're not the one responsible for picking the teams. It's the selectors' job to do that.

This time, they came down on Binga's side. It was yet another setback for Bic but, in typical style, he took it all in his stride.

Chapter Four

OURS AGAIN IN 11 DAYS

The third Test was the first game on the newly redesigned WACA, so I really enjoyed running out on to the field and taking in all the changes to my home ground.

The oval had been made thinner, which brought the crowds in closer and gave them pleasant, grassy banks to sit on, rather than the concrete desert that used to stretch around the square of the wicket. It was now an ideal venue for Test cricket and the atmosphere was good on this first morning but, still, I think Perth as a city could embrace its Test match in an even more positive way. The way Adelaide seems to. They have an opportunity to create an aura around the Perth Test. I hope to talk to the WACA about how to get everyone involved and make it a real showcase event for the city.

Well, the bowlers soon tested out how the new wicket was playing and it was definitely fast. There have been a lot of complaints about WACA Tests only going for three days because the wicket is too lively. Certainly there was plenty of bounce this time around, but it was playing true. It was just going to be a case of who was better equipped to handle it.

We hadn't been on the field long when the wisdom of releasing the details of Haydos's delicate condition to the media was called into question. The Barmy Army picked up on it and they wouldn't let it go. Songs and chants. 'Haemorrhoids, haemorrhoids, give us a wave! Haemorrhoids, haemorrhoids, give us a wave!' They got into the theme of grapes as well.

Maybe it would have been easier if the press release had just said he had torn a 'glute' muscle. It can't be easy being in front of 30,000 people while such a personal condition is being mocked. (That sort of thing should be left to your 11 team-mates.) But Matt had a great sense of humour about it and a very thick skin. He certainly handled it better than I would have.

Trescothick and Vaughan both got good starts. Trescothick, in particular, seemed keen to break out. He had done very little business at all this series and he announced his intentions by hitting Dizzy for three fours in one over. Then I missed a catch off him that went between Warnie and me. It was one I should have taken.

I hadn't been happy with my keeping in Adelaide, either. I felt like I had no rhythm behind the stumps. I wasn't moving well, and missing that catch really brought that home to me. It was a technical thing, but my body was too high and my feet too far apart. I was planted and unable to manoeuvre into position, which was frustrating.

Binga came on first change, ripping in and getting the breakthrough on Trescothick for 34. It was good to see him charging in again full of confidence. He seemed like a new man.

The wickets came pretty freely after that. Pigeon had Vaughan caught behind for 34. The only batsman to hold us up was their number five, Robert Key. He had hit Warnie for a six over his head and was looking like a far more accomplished player than his record suggested. He had forced his way into the team with a big score against Australia A and was starting to get us frustrated.

They were seven wickets down for little more than 150 when Tugga threw Marto the ball to try and rustle something up in the last over before tea. Marto came along with his innocuous little medium pacers and it was obvious that Key had switched off. His mind was back in the change room already. Fourth ball, Key chopped him back on to his stumps. We went into the break confident that it was just a formality to close them out. And it was. We were batting an hour later, chasing 185.

A captain's dream. Damien Martyn celebrates Key's wicket in Perth after Waugh gave him the last over before tea break.

A bit of local knowledge can be a good thing, so before Justin Langer went out to bat he shared some of his wisdom. 'There's no way with the Fremantle Doctor blowing so strongly across the ground that you could get run out by a bloke fielding on the eastern fence,' he declared.

He went out to play a big innings in front of his home crowd and was looking good, going at a run a ball. One went out to Chris Silverwood on that eastern fence and JL took him on. Against the wind, the return came in like a tracer bullet right next to the bails and JL was out by a foot, for 19. JL's tip wasn't forgotten by the lads and we were more than happy to remind him of it at every opportunity, once he had settled down and stopped blushing. Anyway, Punter and Marto took us to stumps at 2–126, so we were looking all right.

Before the match on day two, I was out in the middle and noticed Ian Healy doing a pitch report for television. I went over and asked him how he saw the catch that I'd missed the previous day and what he thought of my keeping at the moment.

He felt I had to slow my hands down, yet at the same time maintain or even speed up my footwork. We had a good chat about it all. Heals has always been very forthcoming with help if ever I've required or requested it. He took the time to take me through some basics and just got me thinking more about foundation skills. Nothing fancy. There he was in his Channel Nine gear, hitting me catches, having me do some diving and catching drills. They were things that we should do day-in, day-out, but which I'd probably started to neglect a little. It's easy to do that when the circus rolls on. You're playing every day and you can feel like you don't need the fine tuning.

I walked off the field after that chat feeling a lot happier that I had a good grasp of what needed doing, and it saw my keeping improve to the level it needed to be in the hard months ahead. I hope Heals didn't get into trouble from Richie for being late back to work.

Harmison came out that morning and bowled an awful lot of bouncers. What I remember about Marto's innings was just a lot of ducking, diving and weaving before he was eventually out for 71, which would prove to be our top score. That brought me to the wicket at 5–264.

Tugga was in there playing with his new aggressive approach. We already had a good lead and they had the part-timer Mark Butcher bowling into the wind. I didn't consciously think, 'Right, I'm going to take him down here.' But I felt that if he pitched it up, with the breeze behind me, I'd try to hit straight. I managed to hit a six and a four and I can't remember how many I got off that over, but it got the adrenaline racing and I think in the end I wasn't able to rein it in. Like my hands in my keeping, I should have slowed my mind down.

Craig White came on and they set a trap for me. They put a couple of blokes back on the hook and set me up with a bouncer. I knew what they were doing, but I was in such an aggressive mind I went after it anyway. I hit it pretty well, but Tudor was under it right down on the rope. He started to celebrate, so I figured it was out. I began to walk off and I think it was Rudi Koertzen, one of the umpires, who said, 'Hang on a minute, we'll have a look at it.' He signalled to the third umpire to check that Tudor hadn't stepped on the rope.

I didn't see any need to look at anything, so I stopped walking to look for Nasser Hussain. He was getting quite animated about why I wasn't going off.

I went over to him. 'Is he saying he caught it?'

'Yes,' Nasser said.

'Did he touch the rope?' I asked.

'No, he didn't.'

'Well, that's enough for me. I'm going.'

But the umpires actually said, 'Wait there.'

When the replay came on the big screen, it clearly showed he hadn't touched the rope, so I went. It was another occasion where I felt it didn't need to go to the third umpire. Alex Tudor's word should have been good enough.

Anyway, I'd made 38 off 28 and Tugga was on the way to a solid 53. Based around the foundation of Marto's 71, everyone had got a good start and then the tail wagged and contributed another 150 after I was gone to post an impressive 456.

Talk about momentum.

We were 271 in front with 11 overs left to bowl at them that night. The batsmen had nothing to gain and the bowlers had nothing to fear. Tugga elevated Binga into the new-ball role, and he came out firing down lightning bolts. They were really quick that night. I think he intimidated Trescothick with a couple of short balls before he found a glove down the leg side to me.

We went in at stumps with England limping at 1–33. There was blood in the water.

The next morning they lost their nightwatchman Dawson, without adding to his overnight score. And they only managed to score their first run of the morning in the fourth over, so they weren't doing much. On the second-last ball of that over, Binga misfielded, the batsmen had a mix-up and we ran Vaughan out.

Very next ball, Pigeon got Butcher, LBW. He was so annoyed at getting out, and with the run-out fresh in his mind, he smacked the stumps with his bat. It was an interesting response, because it wasn't like a total dummy-spit at a poor decision. He was just so frustrated at what was happening to his team that he took it out on the stumps. Still, he dropped half his match payment for his trouble.

At 4–34, we now had the scent in our nostrils.

New with old. Though the WACA had undergone a facelift, the wicket was back to its fast and bouncy best.

It was a tight-knit group that celebrated retaining the Ashes at the WACA on 1 December 2002, after just 11 days of Test cricket.

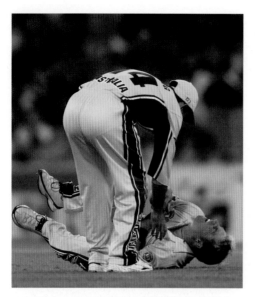

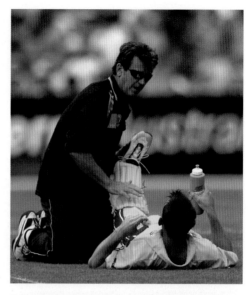

Major trouble for Warnie and the World Cup campaign. Shane Warne injures his shoulder during a one-day match against England at the MCG.

Fortunately, I've never had any serious injuries, but the minor groin strain I suffered during the one-dayer against England was enough to make me miss the next game in Perth.

Christmas in the spotlight. Harry and I sit for press photos on Christmas Day in Melbourne.

The Maestro. Matt Hayden's century on day one of the fourth Ashes Test in Melbourne was a masterpiece of aggression and entertainment.

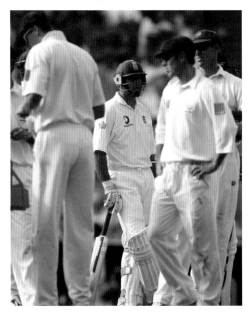

Standing around during the fourth Test while waiting for the third umpire to decide on a 'close' catch. This time it was off the bat of Nasser Hussain, and caught by Jason Gillespie.

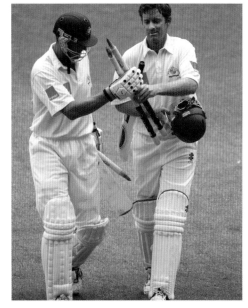

Martin Love and I share in the spoils of the Boxing Day win. Martin played his first Test as though it was his fiftieth, such was his composure.

Arms raised and head bowed. Steve Waugh in typical celebratory mode on reaching an emotional century in Sydney on 3 January 2003.

But Nasser Hussain stood against us for a while and batted well with Key to take them through lunch, and then with Alec Stewart to drag them into tea at 5–154. They were frustrating us, but the bowlers stuck to their game. Build the pressure and it will come.

Nasser really dug in and fought well. He was very courageous. He copped a barrage from Brett in one spell and stood up to take it on. He is certainly a gritty character.

Not long after tea, Warnie sent him down a leg break. He pushed forward and there was a big noise as it shot through to me. We appealed and he was out for 61 (off 170). He thought the noise was his bat hitting the ground, not the ball. After four hours in the middle, he wasn't too happy about leaving us this way.

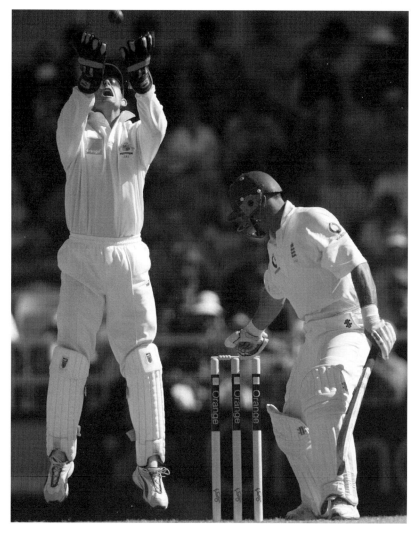

An unlucky captain. Although certain at the time, I was later informed that Nasser didn't hit the ball before being given out in Perth.

The TV cameras then showed him bashing some furniture in the change room. I'm no advocate for blokes hurling things around in there, but it's such an emotional game and there is so much riding on it, I don't see that it's in anyone's interest to focus on that and beam it around the world. Invariably, it's what makes the news. Your reaction on the field is public property, but once you're inside the sanctuary of the change room, it should be private.

There was talk that Nasser should have been penalised in some way, but there is no way I could agree with that. Thankfully, the match referee let it slide.

We later saw that Nasser hadn't hit the ball, so he appeared to cop a bad one. I can understand his frustration. Having said that, I'm sure that he would be the first to agree that he was the recipient of at least four favourable caught-behind decisions during that series and was happy to take them.

We were certainly seeing the benefits of Brett Lee having been allowed to go and get some wickets in domestic cricket. There weren't many blokes in our team who hadn't been dropped at some stage in their career and come back better players. With Brett, we would start to see some strong new leadership qualities emerge. This day, he was expensive compared to the other bowlers, but his psychological impact was huge. He provided a very distinctive weapon in our arsenal.

This was never more clear than when, with the second delivery of the new ball, he dug one in short to Alex Tudor. The ball got through the visor and you could hear it crack — leather on skull. It wasn't a pleasant noise, but what was more frightening was Tudor's reaction. He screamed and ran around, almost uncontrollably. Then he fell to the ground, flat on his back, and started quivering. His legs and hands shook. His eye started to swell on the spot and blood dripped on to the pitch. It was probably the ugliest incident of that type I've seen in my career.

I could see that Brett felt terrible. He can't stand the sight of his own blood, let alone someone else's. It might seem a bit weird that one of the world's most feared bowlers — a guy who tries to intimidate people for a living — was really taken aback by this. He was desperately concerned for Tudor's situation and had run straight to the injured batsman to help settle him.

Tudor was stretchered off — the first person to leave the WACA that way since Geoff Lawson's jaw was broken by Curtley Ambrose in 1988–89.

There was never any malice or ill feeling between the teams about what happened. Harmison came in to bat and, at around the second or third ball, Brett bowled him a bouncer that went clear over his head. The Barmy Army booed and got stuck right into Binga. I think the Barmy Army are quite astute cricket judges. They know and appreciate good cricket despite a perception that they are just drunken Pommies on a holiday. But I was a bit disappointed with their reaction to Brett's bouncer, because it's part and parcel of the game. I later read somewhere that the 'head' of the Barmy Army said that the only thing they'd done all tour that he regretted was to boo Brett that time.

The fact that Curtley took 'Henry' out all those years ago demonstrates that the old fast bowlers union has been long defunct. The old attitude of 'I won't bowl 'em at your head, so don't you bowl 'em at mine' is no longer relevant. There's too much at stake now. Batting standards among fast

A sickening blow to Alex Tudor that even had the man who inflicted it, Brett Lee, concerned.

bowlers have generally improved too, and there's a lot more protective gear. Binga cops plenty when he bats, and he can handle himself. Even Glenn McGrath, on the tour of the West Indies in 1995, just decided one day that he was going to stick it right up the West Indies' tail. His theory was, 'Well, I know I'm going to cop it when I get in, so I'm going to try and get a few while I can.'

Anyway, Binga bowled Harmison with a full toss soon after that. They were 8–223, but Chris Silverwood couldn't bat because of a bad ankle, and with Tudor retired hurt, it was all over. They were 48 runs shy of our total.

The Ashes had been wrapped up in only 11 days of cricket.

It was a great thrill to achieve victory in my first Ashes series in Australia. To have won it so quickly, though, was beyond our expectations. In the change room after all the presentations and a lap around the ground, the guys reflected on the game over a few beers. It was the first time we'd heard Steve Waugh say such a thing, but he actually said it wouldn't have been bad to have had a real dog fight on our hands; to feel like we'd earned the victory a bit more.

Prior to that, whenever we'd had a thumping victory, the attitude had always been: 'Who cares about the contest? We played well.' But sitting there, the feeling was … not hollow, but there was something missing. For a team that prides itself on being totally ruthless, there seemed to be a surprising agreement that a good scrap would have been more fulfilling.

We got into the celebration even though it was probably a bit more reserved than might have been expected. The joke around our room was that if the rule for the English team is they can't have a beer with us until the series is over, well, as far as we could see, it had just finished. Again, we didn't see them. That was disappointing, but I'm sure they were feeling pretty flat and weren't particularly in a mood to come bouncing in ready to have a few beers and a giggle with us.

I had a further discussion with Tugga about winning games so easily and it started me thinking about our place in history. Were we a freak team, or was the rest of the world struggling?

It's the first time I've really thought about it. I found it very hard to analyse where we stood, because I'm too close to it. Are we that good, or are we just a well-drilled, disciplined team playing an undisciplined opposition?

I don't know the answer. I know there are endless arguments comparing our team to the West Indies of 1984, or Ian Chappell's team of the mid-1970s, or Bradman's 1948 team. They are discussions that I don't give too much thought to, because they are irrelevant and we'll never know the answer. Keith Miller had said a few days before this that we were the best team he had seen, and that was a very nice compliment. I never got to meet Don Bradman, but whenever I've had anything to do with that era of player — Bill Brown, Arthur Morris — they've been very complimentary about us and our abilities. Maybe they are just gentlemen. I've had some good discussions with Bill Brown, who presented me with my Test cap. He is extremely flattering in his comments about us, and says that he is amazed by the skills in today's game. It's quite a thrill to hear that from legendary figures, because some former players are very staunch 'Our era was the best' types. They get better and better as their retirement rolls on. But the majority of that batch of very senior players has been so sincere and forth-coming with praise that I think it elevates their stature. I hope it's a lesson that I can take with me into my own retirement.

Chapter Five

TUGGA

We were still in the change room at the WACA, celebrating our Ashes victory, when word filtered through of the 30-man World Cup squad which would later be cut down to the final squad of 15. Within the player group, the news that Steve Waugh had been left out didn't really register as big news. We were resigned to the fact that the selectors, in leaving him out of the one-day team a year earlier, had decided he wouldn't be with us in South Africa. I'm sure, however, that it registered pretty strongly in Stephen's mind. There is no doubt that if you had to rank your best 30 one-day cricketers in Australia at the time, he would have been in most people's lists, mine included. But the selectors had decided to go a certain way, and if they didn't think he was in the top 15, there was no point putting him in the 30. Many believed it was a harsh call, no matter whether you're a fan of Stephen's or not, but it was the reality of the selection process and it will happen to all of us one day.

At that point there was a lot of confusion about whether players not in the 30 could still be added to the final list.

The time had come for us to walk away from Test cricket for a while and slot into the one-day mode. We had the limited-over series lined up against England and Sri Lanka.

Two days after fires ravaged Sydney and Pigeon was called over to Tugga's house to help save it from the inferno, New South Wales played England in a warm-up game. As though England didn't have enough to worry about already, Brett Lee broke spinner Jeremy Snape's right thumb with the very first ball the Englishman faced on the tour.

While England dealt with their 11th serious injury, that game really showcased Australia's embarrassment of riches. Slats got a century, and Tugga hit three sixes off five balls on his way to 30 off ten balls. There was plenty of life left in him yet, and there could be no doubt that he was still good enough to offer something in international one-day cricket.

The same can be said of his brother Mark. But by that stage, events had passed the brothers by and I don't think that anything they might have done would have changed the selectors' minds. That didn't stop *The Daily*

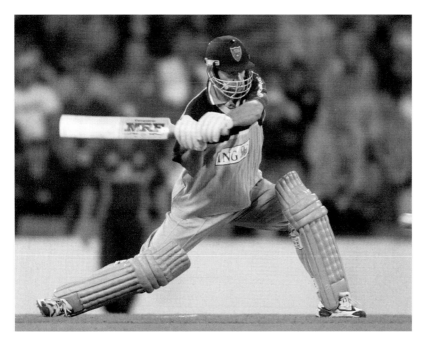

Although not named in the initial 30-man World Cup squad, Steve Waugh attempted to break in by weight of runs for New South Wales.

Telegraph leading the charge to have them reinstated. The whole business became quite rabid, and I don't think it was very constructive for the guys who were vying for the vacant spots in the final squad of 15 — Shane Watson, Michael Clark, Andrew Symonds and Ian Harvey. Ricky went so far as to tell Shane Watson that he had to put it all out of his mind. Not to think about the press coverage of Steve Waugh, but just to concentrate on being the best he could be.

We were trying to prepare for the VB series of one-dayers, and as part of that we had a practice match lined up against New South Wales. Tugga, of course, was going to be captaining his state team. The media hyped it up as his big chance to prove himself to the selectors. That story seemed to override everything else. Suddenly, he was going to force his way back in, overcoming all obstacles, proving everybody wrong. It was only ever meant to be a practice game, but now it had become 'Australia versus Steve Waugh', which didn't have a comfortable feel to it for anyone.

I must admit, I wasn't too disappointed when the drought broke in Sydney and the city got its first rain in months, which washed the game out without a ball being bowled. That game had the makings of those old Australia versus Australia A games; they just didn't feel natural. I played in one of them just after I'd replaced Ian Healy in the side. Heals was picked for Australia A. I got hammered by the Sydney crowd — they booed me mercilessly. So, I had some feeling for this predicament from the other side of the fence.

We soon learned that, contrary to what had been said earlier, no players from outside the squad of 30 could be included in the final 15, except to cover for injuries. So, all the fuss had been for nothing. That, of course, didn't make it any easier for Tugga, and it wouldn't have been easy to have the last nail drilled into your one-day coffin by an ICC technicality.

On commenting on the huge show of support for Stephen in my regular column for *The Australian* newspaper, I also touched on another issue that had annoyed me: the constant bagging of the selection panel. I wrote:

> It's wonderful that so many supporters have taken the opportunity to show Steve just how highly he is held in the people's hearts and minds by voicing their support of him. After all the courageous leader has done for this country on the field and within the greater general community, he is owed much loyalty and respect and it seems the public are obligingly providing that.
>
> Equally noticeable but more disappointingly has been the outrageous attacks and focus on the selection panel that is trying its best to perform the almost impossible task of fitting all the outstanding talent in the country into one 15-man squad.
>
> Whether it's selections at a local club side or picking the Australian one-day team, there are always going to be people who are disappointed at being left out; that's happened for well over one hundred years of cricket history and it won't be any different in the future.
>
> But to publicly admonish the selectors, Trevor Hohns in particular, hasn't made the situation any more pleasant and was done in bad taste.

I really did wonder what a certain newspaper's motivation was. I didn't understand how such a thing could get going the way it did. By the end of it, I think everyone was tired of it. I had a chat to Stephen about it and he said that he and his whole family were over it. 'I just want to be treated like any other player in the selectors' eyes,' he said.

Chapter Six

THE ONE-DAY SERIES

The one-day series had a different feel to it than usual. The first part was brought forward into mid-December 2002 so that we could shorten the summer calendar for the World Cup without having to move the icon events — the Boxing Day Test in Melbourne and the New Year's game in Sydney. We only had to get through three games before the Tests resumed.

The first game was in Sydney, where Knight and Trescothick got off to a run-a-ball opening stand of 101. We managed to bog them down in the middle, but they still looked pretty good at 2–205 after 41 overs. Then Darren 'Boof' Lehmann took three wickets in two overs, and Binga ripped through at the death to restrict them to 8–251 at the close.

Same as England, Haydos and I put on 101 for the first wicket, going at about seven an over. I hadn't been very happy with my one-day form. I was too hit-and-miss and I really wanted to work on my consistency. Before the VB series began, I had a good chat with Haydos about batting in the short game. He spoke about having the right tempo and pacing an innings along, but his main point was to just occupy the crease. 'With your game, all you've got to do is stay there,' he said. 'Don't think about scoring rates. It'll come.'

What he said was spot-on. I focused on staying there and the runs did come. We were travelling really well, but I ended up shanking one to deep mid-wicket and was caught on the fence for 53 off 50. I was a bit disappointed, because it was an option I didn't need to take. But we had the momentum and Haydos went on to get 98 off 92. Marto and Boof saw us home with five overs to spare. It was good to have maintained our dominance in the face of a respectable batting performance by England.

Half an hour after stumps, Ronnie Irani and several of the other one-day specialists came storming into our rooms. They had learned of the rule about not fraternising with the enemy, but they made a pact that they were going to do it anyway.

Ronnie's a character. I've known him since I toured England with the Australian under-19s in 1991. He was vice-captain of their under-19 team. We've bumped into each other around the world since then. Everyone gets on with Ronnie. He's a real lively guy who gives 100 per cent on the field and doesn't take a backward step.

Once Ronnie set the example, the whole England team drifted in — all except Nasser. It was a terrific hour and a half and, looking at the results, I don't think it hurt them.

The following day, Australia A played Sri Lanka and absolutely blew them off the park. The media focus by this time had very much shifted towards World Cup selection. The wire service AAP wrote: 'The World Cup aspirations of Australia A all-rounder Andrew Symonds are all but over after he failed to join in the run feast against Sri Lanka.' Jimmy Maher and Michael Clarke, however, both put on impressive innings and were looking good.

We headed off to Melbourne for a second game against England.

As we walked out to bat, the MCG had a totally different feel to it because there was a big hole where the grandstand that housed our change rooms used to be. As in Perth, we were walking out from a different side of the ground. It was really odd, having half the ground empty and looking straight into the city. Normally, you feel enclosed in the cauldron, but now there was a good strong breeze cutting through.

The wicket looked great for batting, but Haydos got out early. Ricky came in and was aggressive from the start. That enabled me to take my time and not feel the pressure to chase big shots. We went through 100 in exactly 100 balls, then lifted for the next 50. I got to my century off 92 balls and was really thrilled to make it. It had been at least 18 months since my previous one-day century and probably two seasons since I'd got one in Australia. Significantly, Ricky was at the other end. Out of my eight one-day hundreds, I would say he's been batting with me for six of them. He got to his century ten minutes later, so it was the second time we've both got hundreds together. He's a terrific guy to bat with, particularly in one-day cricket, because of his aggression and tempo and the way he takes challenges the bowlers.

I lifted my scoring rate after the century but was bowled by debutant James Anderson, with the first ball of his second spell, for 124 off 104. I was impressed with his bowling and thought he looked like a real talent. It was no surprise to see him go on and do very well at the World Cup.

I didn't know it at the time, but our partnership of 225 that night beat by one run the Australian record for the second wicket set by Dean Jones and Allan Border.

A few wickets fell after that, but we went on to 6–318, the highest ever by Australia against England.

The England innings was going completely to our script. The only batsman to put up a fight early on was Nick Knight. Following a century in Sydney,

Sharing tons with Ricky Ponting at the MCG. Punter has been at the other end for the majority of my one-day centuries.

he hit a good run-a-ball 70 before Warnie caught him off Shane Watson's bowling.

Soon after that, Warnie was bowling when a ball was driven straight. Warnie dived across to save the run, just as he had already done several times that evening. But he let us know instantly that something was wrong. He was writhing and screaming in agony. It was truly frightening to see his face contorted with pain. The guys tried to settle him, but he just kept rolling around, holding his arm and hunching up into a tight ball. I felt so helpless. It was obvious that he had popped his shoulder or done something very serious to it.

As Warnie was being stretchered off, I turned to Ricky. 'That could be his World Cup done.'

While our thoughts were on the big picture, Boof's brother-in-law, Craig White, who was batting, came over and asked: 'Can I drive his car home?' Warnie's silver Ferrari was parked out the back and had caught the eye of the English all-rounder.

White put on a pretty good innings as all else crumbled around him, and we had them all out for 229 in the 48th. Maybe he batted *too* well, because Warnie's brother came and got the car.

Certainly, by the end of the game, the long-term implications of Warnie's injury had sunk in. It was going to be hard work to win the World Cup without him, but I don't think anyone ever thought that it couldn't be done. One of the strengths of this era has been that whenever key players have been injured, someone has always stepped up and filled the void. The only question was, Who would it be?

I thought Stuart MacGill would be chosen in the Test team, but he had been excluded from the 30-man World Cup squad. So I thought the young Queenslander, Nathan Hauritz, would get the nod for the one-day-ers. Three days after Warnie's injury, however, my West Australian team-mate Brad Hogg was named. It would be his first international since his Test and one-day debut in India, six years earlier. At 31, Hoggie was no spring chicken, but I think his game had been refined in the intervening years. He had been doing good stuff for Western Australia and Australia A for a number of years. He was an attacking bowler, so we would have to see whether we had the luxury of using a guy who might go for a few runs but who could slow a team down by taking wickets. Time would tell.

We had a week between games, as England played Sri Lanka twice. I know they would have been looking forward to playing someone other than us. They had gone 13 games straight on tour without a win, so it must have felt good when they got two wins up against the Sri Lankans.

I had hurt my groin in Melbourne, so they rested me from our first match against the Sri Lankans at the WACA. Punter threw it open for whoever wanted to open in my place to stick up their hand. Boof volunteered, and I think it shows the flexibility of the side that he went on to hit 119 in setting up a huge win for us there.

We flew to Melbourne the next day to get ready for the Boxing Day Test, four days away.

The Steve Waugh issue had never gone away, but several sections of the media had very much grabbed the lead in the debate in calling for him to quit. Despite his 135 for New South Wales against South Australia, they argued that his average of 26.5 in the first three Tests was an indication that

In my absence, Darren Lehmann took the opportunity to open in Perth, and he scored an entertaining century against Sri Lanka.

he was past it. As real news dried up heading into Christmas, it was like Steve Waugh was the only story around.

He sat us down on Christmas Eve and made it very clear that all the issues surrounding him weren't to distract the team. His poise reminded me of how he carried himself in South Africa earlier in the year after he had been dropped from the one-day side. The team had to focus on the next two Tests, he said, and not for a moment was anyone to give emphasis to any one player.

There was going to be a lot of noise coming from outside the team, he warned, 'But I'm not making any decision on my future until after the Sydney Test.' We were to focus solely on joining Warwick Armstrong's team of 70 years earlier as the only ones to achieve a five-nil whitewash of England.

The first time I spent Christmas in Melbourne was in 1999. It was just Mel and me. We didn't have any family come down. There was a team lunch on Christmas Day, but it just didn't feel right. The team didn't seem that excited by it all, and I struggled with the concept that the media had to be there. *It's Christmas. Can't you just let us alone?* And, well … It just wasn't Christmas, to be honest.

The next year, however, the team seemed to embrace the whole thing a lot more. Mel and I got our parents to come down, and since then, Christmas in Melbourne has been fantastic. All the families are there these days, and as the team has got a bit older, there are lots of kids in the squad.

Christmas 2001 was a bit different, though. Harrison was born on 20 December and he had a few complications after the birth, so I was in Perth umming and ahhing about whether or not to play the Boxing Day Test. I ended up flying into Melbourne late on Christmas night.

So, this year was much more settled. We had our delightful little boy with us and were experiencing our first Christmas as our own family. Crown Casino puts on a big function room for the team. There's a games room for the kids with a bouncing castle, and Santa Claus makes a visit. Everyone embraces it now. We've all realised that, because we're on the road so much with each other, we're all family anyway, so everyone enjoys sharing that time of the year with all the kids and extended families.

Warnie had gone through the big operation on his shoulder, but he brought his wife and kids in and spent the day with us, so that was great. His recovery was looking better than expected, too, with the doctor saying he'd be right for the World Cup. That was a big relief.

There was an element of sadness, too. Boof was in hospital with an infected leg that had barrelled him the day after his century. He was actually quarantined, because the doctors couldn't figure out what had caused the infection. He couldn't even see his kids, so his wife Andrea and their twins Amy and Ethan were at the function with Mel and me.

The press were there for the first half-hour, in a room off to the side. They need their Christmas photos of the kids and us, and a few interviews. I realise now that it's part of our world. The Australian cricket team is a high-profile business, and people out there want to know what we do. So, we give them half an hour right at the start.

Dizzy and I made sure we grabbed Ethan and Amy and got them on TV giving their dad a wave in hospital. Boof was watching, so I think he appreciated it.

Dizzy and I with Boof's twins, Ethan and Amy, at our team Christmas lunch.

That night, Mel and I were walking back to the hotel from the casino when we bumped into Steve Harmison and Robert Key. We chatted briefly with them. They had been to a big lunch with something like 70 or 80 people — family and friends. But they were the only two who didn't have any family there. I felt a bit sad for them, particularly for Steve. His wife couldn't come out because she had just given birth to their second child. Steve had missed the birth. I spared a thought for them, because I know what it's like when you're travelling — you do have days and nights where you feel flat and a bit homesick.

The Christmas function is a relaxing way to lead into a Test match, and the whole city is in holiday mode. Melbourne is such a proud sporting town, you definitely feel the anticipation of a famous day in sport coming up. I think that unique feeling of a Boxing Day Test is spread Australia-wide. So many people are on holidays, they switch on the box and settle in to watch. It's what I was doing when I was a little tacka, and it's what I'll be doing when I'm not playing any more.

This year, it was Martin Love doing the last-minute rush into town, to replace Boof. While everyone was disappointed for Boof, it was certainly a just call-up for Lovie, purely on the stats that he had in the last month, not to mention his whole career where I think he had scored over 10,000 first-class runs averaging more than 50.

His debut for Queensland was in the Sheffield Shield final of 1992–93. I was playing for New South Wales and he walked in as a 19-year-old and got 40 odd. It was such a composed innings for a debutant, it looked like he had greatness written all over him. In 1995, I toured England with him in a Young Australian squad, where he scored a truckload of runs. I would never have believed that it would take him until he was 28 to debut for Australia.

The team was all assembled for the day. I remember standing for the national anthem, and a tingle ran up my spine. This is what I always thought Boxing Day Test matches would be like. I was standing next to Steve Waugh, it was a packed house of 64,000, Australia versus England, singing the national anthem. I felt more inspiration in that moment than I had on any of the previous three Boxing Days. The weather had a bit to do with it, because the others had been rain affected. This was a perfect sunny day, the childhood dream. The anthem finished and a big Melbourne roar went up. We were ready to go.

Chapter Seven

CHRISTMAS AND MIGRAINES IN MELBOURNE

We won the toss and batted. Matt Hayden should have been out the first ball he faced, top edging one straight over Harmison's head at fine leg, but the fieldsman was in too close and the ball went for four. They took ten off that over, and the vibe just swirled around the cauldron. So many people were there. The Barmy Army was huge. Their chants echoed about, more like English soccer than a sunny cricket ground. It was something to behold.

JL and Haydos both got starts, but Haydos was the one to demoralise the attack. His form had been so impenetrable of late, it was like he needed to invent different ways to keep himself interested. He was hitting balls in the air, challenging himself to land it on a hanky between two fieldsmen. It was just not the done thing on the first morning of a Test, but he was the maestro. When he got his hundred after lunch, he stood there with his arms wide open like a conductor finishing his concerto, bathing in the rapturous applause as he took a huge bow with a flourish of the baton.

And then he was gone for 102. Finito. Perfection had been achieved.

JL, who was still plugging away, stayed in as Ricky, then Marto, departed. In came Steve Waugh as the afternoon shadows lengthened. With all the speculation about his career — Will he retire? Will he be dropped? Will he be reinstated to the one-day team? — he came out with one very clear intention. To show that he still had it.

He weighed straight in and gave the crowd a run-a-ball feast of aggression. There were no batons here. This was heavy metal.

It was a courageous decision to be so aggressive, given what was riding on his form. Maybe he felt that if he wasn't able to play like that any more, he didn't want to be in the team anyway. And the crowd knew what was at stake, they knew what they were seeing, and they were in complete adulation. He went through 50 in 49 balls and on to stumps at 62 not out. While at the other end, there was JL, sitting on 146, quietly accumulating. Grinding away while others stole the limelight.

Early next morning, Tugga got an edge back to second slip, where Butcher dived low and gathered it in his hands. The only player not to appeal was Butcher. Tugga looked at him. 'Was it out?'

Butcher said he wasn't sure if it carried. So the decision went to the third umpire. Stephen later said that he just wanted to hear Butcher say he caught it. If he did, he was going to walk. I found it heartening that I wasn't alone with this bee in my bonnet. The video was inconclusive, so he was given not out. He played a lot more sedately on that second day and was out for 77.

Martin Love played solidly on debut to put on a 150 partnership with JL, before Justin was eventually out for exactly 250. The sheer bulk of his innings — the 11th-highest by an Australian — now dwarfed all the show-men who had gone before. He had set us up for a huge total. It was a fan-tastic effort, and typical of his career: grit and determination through tough periods; flair and aggression when the opportunities arose.

It was about 20 minutes before tea. We were 5–545, and I was coming in for a pre-declaration slog. Stephen said something about wanting us up towards 600 as quickly as possible, but it also seemed he might declare at any moment. It wasn't anybody's ideal batting situation, but I duly went out figur-ing I might as well have some fun, rather than noodle it around for 10 not out.

I noodled for a handful of deliveries before attempting to get the ball over the Great Southern Stand. I was clean bowled for one. Sometimes I forget that you don't have to get it through or over the stands. The rope will do fine.

Stephen declared straight away at 6–551.

We felt that we couldn't — or at least shouldn't — lose from there, but the game was far from won. It was a beautiful batting strip and we still had to bowl them out twice. Things began well. Pigeon bowled Vaughan in the seventh over, but when Binga came on at first change the Barmy Army had decided to call 'no ball' every time he bowled. They were call-ing him a chucker and giving all sorts of grief. It didn't seem to upset Brett at all, but it really got under my skin. Brett actually jokes with people about the speculation that he had a suspicious action, but I didn't like the rudeness of the crowd, just as I don't like it when the Australian crowd gives the Sri Lankan Muttiah Muralitharan a torrid time. And the Barmy Army kept on and on at it.

They weren't hurting Brett's pace. He bowled the equal-fastest deliv-ery in Australian Tests — 156.2 kilometres per hour — and averaged 149.9 kilometres per hour. When one thunderbolt got an edge from Trescothick to me, I gestured to the Barmy Army with a big fist pump and a *stick-that-up-ya* attitude, but I immediately realised I had to pull my head in. The emotions were running a little too high. As soon as you carry on like that,

The Barmy Army give their opinion on Brett Lee. The heckling fired me up more than Brett, I think.

you invariably have a moment of clarity and see just what an idiot you look like and that all you've done is let the hecklers know they've got to you.

As stumps loomed, England was in all sorts of trouble at 3–94. MacGill sent one down to Hussain who lofted it to deepish mid-on. Dizzy dived and got up claiming the catch. I didn't get a good view of it, but Dizzy was adamant. Hussain stood his ground to let it be adjudicated. Yet again, this unfortunate scenario had raised its head. Hussain was totally within his rights to do that, of course, but to me it was a missed opportunity for the England captain to make a statement about the spirit of the game. That was easy for me to say, and again, I hoped I'd be strong enough if I was in the same situation.

That night, in the press conference, JL made the comment that the Barmy Army were just overweight beer drinkers. He said they were a disgrace and that they didn't know anything about the game. Well, that ensured that he'd get a bit of airplay the next day and the Barmy Army absolutely went to town with it. They invented a few chants for him overnight, generally about his height, or lack of it, and right from the time we walked on to the ground for our warm-up they got stuck into him.

I think he regretted having said anything, and towards the end of the day he went down to see them, shook a few hands over the fence and had a bit of a laugh. It all ended up as light-hearted banter, but in the heat of the battle, it was very easy to lose perspective on what you should be laughing at.

Thirty-two thousand people turned up to see how quickly we'd rip through the Poms in the morning of day three. Indeed, it looked like it was going to be a total embarrassment for poor old England, who lost three wickets cheaply in the morning session and seemed to be totally shot at 6–118 after 42 overs. But their all-rounder, Craig White, dug in and held us off until he was left partnerless on 85, with England all out for 270 some 48 overs later.

They were 281 behind, and there was blood in the water, sure, but it had been a 90-over slog to get the first ten wickets. I thought Stephen would choose to bat for a couple of sessions, rather than enforce the follow on. It's the sort of decision you don't make until the last wicket falls, because if the last wicket drags on, it can change your outlook. When White had proved difficult to remove, I thought that would have changed his mind, but as we walked off the field, he said to me, 'We're going to bowl again.'

Inside the change room, when he had the whole team around, he said, 'I've decided. I think we should take it on … It'd be a really good challenge for us to try and go out there 'n knock 'em over again. If anyone's got a problem with it, speak up now because if in two hours' time they're none for 100 and we're doin' it tough, I don't wanna hear any complaints about it then.'

No one put their hand up.

'How are you guys going?' he asked, turning to the bowlers.

Everyone said they were fine to go.

This time around, Vaughan got going and with Hussain took them to stumps at 2–111. The next day he notched up his second hundred for the series, another brilliant innings of 145. None of the others made big scores but most got a few and, 120 overs later, they were all out for 387 — a lead of 106.

It had taken almost all of day four to take the last eight wickets. It was a brilliant effort by the bowlers, because it was still a good batting strip. Magilla bore the bulk of the workload and he got the breakthrough on Vaughan, taking 5–152 off his 48 overs.

Only 12,000 people had turned up on day four, and by the time the last English wicket fell — less than half an hour before stumps — the MCG was an echoing canyon.

Haydos and JL had to go out and survive two overs before the end of play, with the Barmy Army the only notable presence left. They survived that tense little stanza, but Haydos was out first ball the next morning.

I sensed a little flurry of nervousness spreading among the players after that. I was certainly sitting there with a bad feeling. *Please don't be one of those freak days where everything goes horribly wrong.* No one would ever say such a thing out loud.

JL and Punter seemed to get things under control, though, taking us up through 50, but then Ricky was out, caught behind down the leg side, and Marto was out for a third-ball duck. Three for 58.

The day was notable because it was the first fifth day of the series and, for the first time, the blood in the water was ours. Some 18,666 people had turned up to see it — half of them English, I'd guess. They were extremely loud.

Tugga strode to the crease and there was a part of every Australian, I think, that wanted to see him close the game out in a couple of overs. But it was clear from the beginning that something was wrong.

He was totally wobbly, playing and missing. We had no idea what was wrong until he asked for some migraine pills. Being a migraine sufferer myself, I don't know how he managed to score any with his vision blurred, but he struggled towards double figures. All valuable runs, in the circumstances.

Then he got a little nick to the keeper, but nobody appealed. We saw it on the TV replay and the Englishmen saw it too on the big screen. Suddenly they appealed, but too late. Not out.

No sympathy here, mate! Nasser Hussain watches over Steve Waugh, who suffered a terrible migraine before batting on the last day in Melbourne.

It looked like it wasn't going to matter, anyway. The next ball, Tugga hit a full-pitched delivery straight to Nasser Hussain at cover, and he took a really good catch. They went ape about it and Stephen had started to walk until they all realised it was a no-ball. He had to turn around and come back. The next ball was pitched up and he belted it straight back down the ground past the bowler for four. The amount of action and drama unfolding was incredible. They soon got Stephen for 14, and, while we were only four wickets down at the time, there was still a lot of tension. Small chases can be a nightmare and we continued to struggle. JL got a dicey LBW decision and there I was in the middle, teamed with Martin Love, to chase down 17 runs.

We got them soon enough, but it was a mighty relief. Just 50 more runs on the English total could have been very scary. Stephen's little innings and the incredible noise of the Barmy Army made it a really dramatic morning of cricket.

It was a hugely satisfying win, given that we'd had to work hard for it. It felt good to get back to the sheds before lunch to relax and enjoy it. Our hopes of a five-nil series were alive and well.

All through that game, during the lunch break, Channel Nine would have their cricket show on, and every day a different expert would pick his World Cup 15. Heals, Mark Taylor, Richie Benaud and Ian Chappell. They gave us some awkward moments, because a few of the guys who had aspirations to go to South Africa were being left out of these hypothetical squads, while the experts explained why. It wasn't like they had anyone sobbing, but it was inopportune. Everyone was quite aware of not discussing the World Cup selections.

As it panned out, it might have been better had Tugga retired hurt with that migraine. On the one hand, the guy had a rabid section of the media fighting for his reinstatement in the one-day team; on the other hand, he had a number of cricket writers circling overhead just waiting for a sign of weakness so that they could swoop down and poke out the eyes of his Test career. No matter how swashbuckling his first innings had been, the latter group seemed to perceive that one wobbly innings, batted with a thumping headache and blurred vision, constituted a cricket death. They had written a script — which they repeatedly referred to as 'the fairytale' — in which Steve Waugh's funeral was to be his home-town Test match. It would be perfect. A series whitewash, everyone in tears, dramatic eulogies. The only trouble was, the hero wasn't dead yet.

Anyway, that's how I perceived it.

Chapter Eight

PRESSURE COOKER AT THE SCG

It's become the norm for us to spend New Year's Eve with our families in the manager's suite at the Quay West hotel in The Rocks, so we've always got a spectacular view of the fireworks over the harbour. The city was buzzing with a festival feel, but we were in the middle of two Tests and everyone was tired. The Melbourne Test, which had finished the previous day, had left us feeling flat. Then the early fireworks were cancelled because of high winds, so that took a lot of the excitement out of it for the kids — and for a few of us adults, too. Mel and I went to bed immediately after seeing in 2003.

There were doubts about Dizzy's fitness. The media were reporting that he had withdrawn because of heel soreness after his 41 overs in Melbourne. But we were always pretty hopeful that he'd play. Pigeon, on the other hand, was struggling with some soreness around his back and was certain to miss the Sydney Test.

In all my Test career, I'd never played a game with both Pigeon and Warnie absent. In fact, the last time Australia played a Test where neither of their names featured was in November 1992, 118 Test matches previous. Thirty-one of those games were Ashes Tests, of which Australia had won 21.

You don't need statistics like that to know how important those two have been to Australian cricket, but here we were without them and I don't remember anyone showing any sort of panic. Our experience was that someone always stepped up.

Christmas/New Year's is a slow news time, so it allowed the media to spend a lot of energy poking at Steve Waugh. It filled a lot of talk-back radio. The whole country seemed to be locked in on the topic of our skipper's demise. We were probably the only cricket fans in the country not talking about it.

Stephen hadn't changed his manner in the slightest. He certainly wasn't giving away any secrets. I had no idea what his intentions were and what he was looking to achieve over the next few days. All I knew was that he was out to get that clean sweep for the record books. That's what he spoke about in our several meetings. Whenever there is something significant in the offing, he'll always say, 'This is a chance for us to create our own piece of history.'

As I looked around at the team, I could see the desire was there, but I wondered if we had the ability to carry it out. Back-to-back Tests are hard, but they're hard on both teams. The thing that gave England the edge was that they'd bowled their 146 overs on the Thursday and Friday, before we'd sent down 210 at them through Friday afternoon, and all day Saturday and Sunday. They'd had 21 overs on the Monday, but that was just a loosener. Then we had the scare of being 3–58, 5–90. The whole emotional and physical drain of that seemed to have left us pretty flat on the canvas.

This is all with 20/20 hindsight. I'm not saying it was Stephen's fault. He threw out the challenge and gave us the opportunity to speak up. None of us did. We had achieved a wonderful victory, but the simple fact was, we were tired. Now we were to go out on that Thursday, 2 January, and do it all again.

We had lost half of our first-string attack through injury, but that was nothing compared to what England had endured all summer. We liked to think of ourselves as a pretty good team and we knew that good teams lifted themselves off the canvas. That's what we were going to do.

We lost the toss and that was crucial, because our bowlers had to go straight into action. Still, there was certainly no feeling of fatigue as we walked into the huge match atmosphere of the SCG.

Adelaide may be my favourite Test, but Sydney's got a unique history and atmosphere to it as well. The Barmy Army was there in huge numbers again, creating such a different feel from that at the first Test match I ever saw live — Greg Chappell's 1983–84 Australia versus Pakistan. I had also seen some one-day games there in 1980–81, but my earliest memories of the SCG were of driving past it when we were up from Deniliquin — where I lived until I was 12 — visiting my grandparents in Maroubra, in the Eastern Suburbs. Whenever we went from their place to the city, we passed the cricket ground, with its huge grandstands and light towers, newly installed for World Series Cricket. I'd have my nose pressed to the window in wide-eyed wonder. Long before I ever went inside, I'd fallen in love with the idea of the place — the mystery of what was in there. I had also been in the crowd at the last-ever rugby league grand final played there — between Manly and Canberra in 1987 — so I'd seen it in all its moods.

So, here was Binga, elevated to open the bowling in his home town, and it was almost like the first crunching tackles of a league final where the crowd winces and groans with each blow. He had Vaughan playing and missing at some blistering outswing, then picked up an edge to have him caught behind for a duck in the third over. Next ball, he slammed one into Butcher's pads and there was a big appeal. Not out.

In the 14th, Bic found the edge of Trescothick's bat. I dived low and to the left, taking it in front of first slip. We had them on the run, but jubilation swung around pretty quickly because, soon after, an almost identical catch came back to me off Butcher who was sitting on about 20. I dived a little further than I needed to, so I kinked my arm slightly and the ball just didn't hit the glove in the right spot. Splat.

In those scenarios, I try not to analyse things too much because I've got to get up and get ready for the next ball, but when it's a player of Butcher's calibre I find myself praying that he gets out soon. When Butcher didn't, the spillage started to weigh heavily on me.

It must have been the same for Marto. He put down a tough one off Butcher in the gully, then Stuart MacGill missed a caught-and-bowled from Hussain, who was on six.

I can't put my finger on why we were dropping catches, but I know it was to cost us. Butcher and Hussain took the Poms through lunch, then got them to tea at 2–150. The last time England beat Australia, at Headingly in 2001, those two put on 181 for the third wicket.

Butcher grew in confidence through the last session, but on 97, he went to sweep Magilla and got a bottom edge on to his pad and up to Haydos. It was a fairly obvious bat-pad. Umpire Russell Tiffin, however, gave it not out. That added to the frustrations of a difficult day.

Dizzy got the breakthrough, though, getting one to lift, nicking Hussain's glove to have him caught behind, 75. Tugga bowled a few overs and bagged Key, then Butcher played on to Lee. Out for 124. We'd got a bit of momentum up in the late afternoon to have them 5–264 at stumps.

The next morning, the TV and radio personality Andrew Denton arrived as we were warming up. A cricket tragic, he had paid $5000 at a charity auction to be assistant coach for the first two days of the Test. The coach, John Buchanan, told him that if he was going to get the title, he had to play an active part in the team's preparation.

So, Andrew gathered us in a huddle this morning. I was expecting him to be hilarious, but he was quite serious and very passionate. He said how lucky he was to have been given the opportunity to be involved with us, and how privileged we were to do what we do. It was something we must never take for granted, he said. We must make sure we realised what we had achieved and never see winning the Ashes as just something we're expected to do. He felt that this group of players had already achieved greatness and would continue to do so. I guess he was referring to our chances of taking the series five-nil.

They were pretty serious words, which really came as a surprise. It's hard to capture now what it was like there, but I was very moved by it. I walked away feeling amazed that this guy who I have always respected would heap such praise on us. It was a special feeling that set us up for the day ahead. I don't know if it was fate or an accident that such remarkable Test cricket was about to unfold.

We had a lot of trouble removing Alec Stewart in the morning. They added 98 more before we got them all out, well after lunch, for 362. We came out determined to play our usual game but maybe we went too hard.

When Haydos was dismissed on the last ball of the sixth over, we were already 36 runs. When Punter followed eight balls later, we were 45. Then JL skied a hook shot and we were in the unusual position of being under pressure at 3–56.

I ran out the back into the change rooms to get my gear on — my whites and my thigh pad. I heard a roar go up, but I missed what I'm told was one of the biggest ovations you're likely to see, as Tugga strode out. It was obviously a huge moment in cricket history.

He never gave any indication of how he was thinking of playing it. At 3–56 there weren't too many options other than to knuckle down and build a partnership with Marto at the other end. And that's what they did to take us into tea, with Marto on four and Tugga on nine.

After tea, the captain started to play a few strokes. I remember seeing him hit a cover drive, then a flick off his pads for four. I looked around and sensed a certain anticipation in the crowd and in the change room. Big things were afoot. Stephen's momentum built and he reached his half-century in 61 balls.

Marto got out, then Lovie was back in the shed for a duck. Five for 150.

I'd been saying I batted best under these conditions. I hoped I was right.

My intention was to get in there and form a partnership with Stephen. We were in a dangerous situation, so survival was my main aim — even as Stephen adopted a fairly free-flowing style and the crowd worked itself up.

They were cheering his every move by this stage, but there was one ball which Tugga cut through point for four to go to 69 for which the applause lingered longer than usual. He came down the pitch towards me as the ball was being retrieved.

'Great shot,' I said. 'Head down now. Let's keep going.'

'That's 10,000, I think,' he said quietly.

I turned and was walking back to the bowler's end when the penny dropped. I went after him, by which time the big screen had announced it was his 10,000th Test run, joining Sunil Gavaskar and Allan Border in that elite club. So the crowd were applauding even harder now as I put out my hand.

'Well done,' I said. But there was no carry-on from him. He quickly acknowledged the crowd and walked back to start again. It seemed he had bigger targets on his mind.

I'd been going pretty slowly up to then, but Nasser decided to set his little trap for me with two fielders back deep on the leg and a third man in. He got Harmison, Caddick and, to a certain extent, Hoggard, to drop them in short.

Come on, Adam, I said to myself as the first few balls whizzed by my ear. *Don't get caught up in a hooking duel.* But the wicket was such that when they dug them in, I was seeing them pretty well. So, I played a few hooks and got a few boundaries. Unfortunately, that took away a bit of the strike and momentum from Stephen when he was up around the high 70s, early 80s.

It was down to the last few overs before stumps when I started to think he had an outside chance of getting a hundred that night. He hit a couple of boundaries and it really started to get tense. The crowd were right on to it. Every ball.

He squirted one out through the fourth slip-gully area past third man for four to take him into the low 90s and I thought that, with the few balls remaining in the day, he was still a chance. Suddenly, though, I was back on strike to face the last ball. It seemed like the end of the dream. Hoggard ran in and bowled a bouncer. It was the sort of delivery I'd been having a dip at, but because it was stumps I ducked it and went to walk off. Then I realised I'd miscalculated and there was still another over to come.

He has a genuine chance of getting a hundred here. I'd managed to give him the strike, too. Someone in the TV commentary — Heals, I think — apparently commented on what great team play it was on my part, leaving such a ball to give my captain the strike when I'd been whacking those balls all afternoon. Little did he know it was just an error of judgment.

The crowd, by this stage, were in a frenzy. They wanted to see their version of the fairytale.

Stephen was on 95. He blocked the first three balls and his opportunity seemed to be slipping away. He got on to the fourth ball with a cover drive and we ran three. So, with two balls left, he was on 98, but I was on strike. Forty thousand people were praying for me to get a single.

Fortunately for me, Dawson floated a ball up, so I ran down and bumped it into a vacant mid-wicket area. I was the most relieved person in the SCG as we crossed for that run. I'd done my bit, now it was up to him. Nasser took forever to set his field. Tugga came down to me. 'Make sure you're backing up.' The crowd were going off and the suspense was killing me as Nasser shuffled his men.

It was ironic that, throughout the series, Nasser had been giving Tugga singles on the last ball of the over to get him on strike for the next round of bumpers. Yet, here he was desperately trying to deprive him of the easy ones. I tried to guess what shot Stephen would play. *He'll go the slog sweep*, I thought.

I think Nasser thought that, too. He directed Dawson to bowl it straight and full so that if Tugga missed, he was a good LBW chance.

The ball came in quickish and straight, but veered slightly to off. Tugger absolutely creamed it. As soon as he connected that cover drive, I could tell it was heading to the fence. There was an almighty roar and all the emotion of a month of debilitating debate bubbled over. Among it all, I could tell that Stephen was pretty pumped, but he's a cool customer and didn't get too carried away. I was jumping around, excited as a little kid. It seriously felt like I'd been the one who had achieved something that day. I was swept up in the wave of support and just rode it.

A huge chunk of the emotion out there was for the big 'up yours' this innings gave to the doubters. *Stick that up your fairytale ending.*

It had certainly been a fairytale ending, but not to Stephen's career. It was a perfect day of Test cricket.

Steve Waugh writes the end to a perfect script as he scores that memorable ton in Sydney.

As Stephen led the way into the change room, the atmosphere was equal to when we won the 1999 World Cup. Stephen and Mark's father, Roger, came into the rooms and was pretty emotional. Then Stephen's wife Lynette and Rosie, their daughter, turned up looking quite teary. The feelings ran thick in the air. The significance of the moment was lost on no one.

Unfortunately, Mark had left the ground. I think he had a night out at the trots organised, and Tugga knows what Junior rates higher when the choice is between an afternoon watching cricket or the races. I'm pretty sure he heard the ton come up on the radio.

Andrew Denton was still there, being absolutely hilarious. He thought he was the luckiest man in the world to have jagged this. The writer, Thomas Keneally, arrived. He's a lovely bloke and a great supporter of our team. He was bouncing around in his bubbly way. Prime Minister John Howard was in there pretty quick-smart, too, enjoying it all.

When I went back to my hotel that night, Mum and Dad were there with Mel. It was plain to see from their excitement that the innings had really affected people. Dad lives and breathes cricket. He said it was one of only two times that the game had made him cry. I must ask him what the other occasion was.

The press reaction was hugely favourable and all of it thoroughly deserved. I'm not sure if they had changed their opinions or if they just had to report what they saw, but Stephen got a lot of credit for that innings.

The next day, we drove to the ground an hour and a half before play. Normally, there aren't many people around at that time, but as we walked from the minibus, people were clapping and cheering. Two or three TV cameras recorded Stephen's every move. Reporters asked us about our reactions to the previous day's events. A thousand people watched us warming up in the nets, where normally we'd get a few hundred. The feeling was terrific. I think everyone was thrilled to know that they were a part of something special — from the team, through to Andrew Denton and the paying customers who had come back for more.

There was an air of expectation as Tugga and I went out to bat. Most of the 40,800 crowd was already there. There weren't many empty seats. The adrenaline was still throbbing from yesterday, but we were trying to knuckle down and get back to reality.

At 5–237, we were still 125 behind.

Coming down off that wave, we first had to knock off the deficit, then try to build a lead. Hoggard was bowling his first over of reasonably paced outswingers. Stephen went back to defend a short one and as it moved away from him he was lured into following it. He glided it straight to second slip. Pop. It was over. You could feel the entire ground deflate as Tugga departed without making any addition to his score of 102 (off 135 balls).

We were six wickets down with some hard work ahead of us.

Right, I've just got to establish a couple of partnerships and take whatever scoring opportunities come my way.

When I'm the last recognised batsman in, I try to help get the tail-enders established. If they can just get through the first ten balls, they're all talented enough to occupy the crease and then to score runs. Certainly, Bic and Binga are.

Bic was out on the ninth ball he faced. Binga went first ball, caught behind. Suddenly, the momentum was all theirs. Dizzy survived Hoggard's hat trick attempt, but with just him and Magilla left, I had to rethink my plan. *Gotta get some runs while I can.*

Dizzy made it through the first ten balls and proved to be a valuable ally. He held up his end and, in fact, was starting to score well. We managed to work the total up close to theirs pretty quickly.

At the end of each over, the bowlers were trying to keep me on strike so that they could have a go at Dizzy from the beginning of the next over. I must have been 98 or 99 when Harmison was coming in for the last ball of one of his overs. It was obvious that he was going to attempt a bumper to keep me away from the strike. I knew the hook was too risky with their field placements, so I decided to invent a new shot. I was going to squat down and, raising the bat above my head like a two-handed tennis serve, I would flat-bat the ball back past him.

Thankfully, he bowled it where I thought he would. (A yorker would have had me in real strife.) I managed to paddle it back past him and we ran three. It was the ugliest way I've ever seen anyone bring up a hundred, but I didn't care how I got there. It was my seventh Test ton, and I'd kept the strike.

We made it to lunch, trailing by 26. It felt like we were beginning to steal a bit of that momentum back. If Jason and I could just go on and get another 50, it would be a massive psychological blow and really emphasise that aura we'd built up: *No matter what you do to us, we'll always come back at you.*

Soon after the break, I chased a full, wide ball from Harmison and tried to jam down on it. It hit the foot marks and went through to the keeper. I didn't think I'd hit it but they appealed and I was given out. I'd got 133 off 121, but I was intensely disappointed. Dizzy told me later that he was certain I had hit it, so I could understand the umpire thinking I had.

We were still 13 runs shy of England's 362. Dizzy let loose with 13 in the next two overs before Magilla was out for one. We were all out 363, a lead of one.

In the old days, if two teams got scores like that, it wouldn't take much more batting to have the game headed squarely for a draw. England got their 362 off 127 overs at 2.85 an over. We got ours from 80 overs at 4.5 an over — almost three hours quicker. When Vaughan and Trescothick came in for the second innings, the game was poised exactly at the halfway point in the middle day of the Test. The game was there for the taking. It was just a matter of who stepped up to grab it.

They got off to a flyer like we had in the first innings. Trescothick had had a disappointing series by his standards and obviously wanted to come out and dominate to finish on a positive note. When Binga bowled him for 22 (off 21) in the sixth over, they were already 37. From then on it was all Michael Vaughan. He put on good partnerships with Butcher, then with Hussain after tea. He brought up his 100 off 145 balls and England went into stumps sitting pretty at 2–218. They were playing good, positive cricket, but we were still confident we could wrestle this one back.

Arthur Morris tells of how people are always asking him: 'Were you there when Don Bradman got that duck in his last Test?'

'Yes, I was batting at the other end,' he tells them, 'and I was a hundred not out.'

That's how I felt my innings in this Test would be recalled, as a footnote in the Steve Waugh fairytale. And rightly so, such was the brilliance of his effort.

I wrote in my diary that night: 'Happy to score ton, disappointed about being given out, caught behind. Strong feelings on walking, etc.'

With all my thinking about these third-umpire decisions on catches, I'd started to contemplate other issues. *Is it possible to play at this level and be prepared to walk if you nick it?* Like in any series, there had been several times when I'd thought guys from both sides had got an edge but hadn't walked. The seed of a thought had been planted. There was no conscious decision: *I'm going to walk.* It was more a question: *Would I do it?*

But that day it didn't apply, because I really didn't think I was out.

I also wrote: 'I do feel as if something big is going to happen in this game — two tons in a Test at number seven maybe … My 133 was as good as my 138 not out in Capetown.' I rated that innings in South Africa in 2002 as possibly my best Test innings, so after a slightly frustrating series, I was confident of pulling something out in the last days at Sydney.

Vaughan and Hussain got set in the morning. Vaughan just continued to show his class. That guy really has *it*. If you looked at a score sheet, you might not be able to fully understand how important his innings was, but the longer he batted, regardless of how many runs he scored, the more the wicket deteriorated and the harder it was going to be for us to even consider chasing. Every run and every minute brought more negative thoughts into our minds. You have to try to stay positive: *Well, he's playing cover drives and pull shots, so the wicket can't be that bad.*

Indeed, it wasn't a dangerous wicket at first, but when the second new ball came on, it became pretty hairy. Binga got Hussain with the new ball, second-last delivery before lunch, then we got Key soon after, but at 4–344 and with Vaughan still at the crease, they had really done the business. Vaughan was then robbed of a double century by a dodgy LBW decision. But his 183 runs off 278 balls in a crucial six hours and 39 minutes was a superlative performance.

The new ball was exploding through the top of the wicket, giving a totally unpredictable bounce. John Crawley suffered a nasty blow on the arm from one, and watching it was probably scarier for our batsmen than those still to come for England. Still, you try and tell yourself that it's only the odd ball that comes through like that.

Then Dizzy got a boot stuck in the foot holes, which were pretty deep by then. He fell and hurt his elbow and left the field, unable to finish his 19th over. This further depleted our attack and added to the malaise. The wicket had certainly deteriorated more than I'd seen in any Test match I've played in Australia.

Still, we had them at 7–378 just before tea, and even on good wickets their tail hadn't given us much to worry about from there. But the ball was getting old again and the bowlers were weary. The next two wickets dragged out over 20 overs before Harmison came in at number 11. He proceeded to slog them up towards 450, breaking our hearts along the way.

We'd given up on winning the game. My mindset was terrible. I was despondent at having lost the opportunity of the whitewash. It's part of the challenge of these tough scenarios that you've got to keep a level head. And there's no doubt that, after tea, mine was anything but.

Harmison swung at one off Lee and got what I thought was a big nick. Brett did too.

'Howzaaaaaaaaat!'

Not out.

My frustration burst out and I swore very loudly. It wasn't actually aimed at the umpire, but I clearly wasn't happy with his decision. I was really angry. It was the culmination of what I considered to be several incorrect decisions in that game. It's no secret that many people thought the umpiring standard of the two games controlled by those umpires was below par.

Celebrating a ton during the fifth Test at the SCG after an unconventional but effective 'swot' off Steve Harmison.

Something to celebrate at last. The England players pay tribute to the loyal Barmy Army after their Test victory in Sydney on 6 January 2003.

Andrew Denton reckons I have the biggest smile in world cricket. He took this photo of me just minutes after I shared in the emotion of Steve Waugh's brilliant century at the SCG.

The faces of the future. Shane Watson and Michael Clarke will definitely be central figures in Australian cricket's next decade.

Brad Hogg proved his all-round worth with a match-saving innings in the second VB series final at the MCG.

The end of an era? Champion spinner Shane Warne is helped from the MCG after the finals win over England in the VB series.

My right-hand man ... well, lady. Mel and I were stunned to learn that we'd won the Allan Border Medal.

The Allan Border Medal, 2003.

In fact, after the Melbourne Test I'd had a chat with Russell Tiffin and Dave Orchard. I bought them a beer and they seemed very interested to get some feedback and talk about it. I have a pretty good relationship with them and felt that I generally kept a cool head about decisions coming and going. But this day, my frustration had built up to the point where I just exploded.

You just can't go on like that so publicly. It was wrong. And what I said was bad enough, or loud enough, for them to feel compelled to put me on report.

I think Nasser was reluctant to declare. Given our style of play and our record of success, there must have been an element of uncertainty about when it was safe to go. It was that aura at work. But as the wicket deteriorated, it became pretty obvious that it was going to take an amazing effort to bat all day tomorrow, let alone chase the runs. Harmison's little cameo of 20 off 23 must have made him extremely comfortable, and so it was that he called them in at 9–452.

He'd left 20 overs for us to face before stumps.

We gathered quickly before Haydos and JL went out. Tugga was typically straight to the point. 'Look, obviously this is a rare occasion where we've gotta consider not winning the Test. We've gotta consider trying to salvage a draw and seeing what we can get out of it.' The key idea that floated around, though, was that we still had to trust our natural game, and that meant being positive, or even aggressive. We felt no need to shy away from what had been successful for us for so long just because we were in a jam. Who knows, we just might drag this one back.

I suppose we went out with the same attitude in Calcutta two years earlier after we'd made India follow on and they'd gone past us with a big total. Chasing them in the last innings, we'd trusted our natural game and we'd lost. But we were going to try it again anyway. That's the way we do things.

It seemed from our experience out there that the wicket was at its most dangerous while the ball was new and hard and able to break through the surface. It seemed far more docile as the ball softened. So, Stephen, with his extensive knowledge of cricket history, thought back to the days of Victor Trumper and uncovered wickets, when teams regularly had to confront explosive decks. He told us that they used to send their tail-enders in first to blunt the attack. And so that's what he was going to do this afternoon. He decided that Bic would bat at number three and try to see us through the initial tough period if JL or Haydos were dismissed early. It was too early for a nightwatchman, and we don't use them anyway. That's team policy. This was totally different. It showed Tugga's encyclopedic knowledge of the game, and was a strong vote of confidence in Bic. While it was a tried and tested theory from a previous era, the player taking on the role still had to have the skills to carry it off. We knew that if Bic could survive for a while, he was an accomplished enough batsman to have an impact.

We didn't have long to wait, however, for the first impact of the innings. Last ball of the second over, JL was out to a shocking LBW decision. As he headed back towards us, we watched the television replays aghast.

Mark Waugh always used to ask the question, 'Do umpires prepare for the players that they're going to umpire?' This was a case in point. A bowler like Andy Caddick bowls very wide on the crease so that he angles the ball sharply in. It's part of his armoury and it's often difficult to play. But when bowling to a left-hander, the only way that ball is going to hit the stumps is if it pitches outside leg stump — unless it's a really big inswinger. Therefore, if the laws are closely adhered to, LBWs should be very rare indeed whenever Caddick bowls to lefties. Maybe the umpire did factor that in and maybe he just saw it wrong, but this ball from Caddick pitched well outside leg.

I mention these bad decisions as part of the frustrations that built up in this match. Of course, I realise that we weren't the only team to be on the wrong end of the bad ones. There were plenty that went the other way. I'm not blaming the umpires, just making the point that when you're scrambling to save a game, the bad decisions hurt you so much more.

Matty Hayden was out LBW two balls later. He didn't dispute the umpire's call. He was just very disappointed with himself. As he approached the French doors into our change room, one of which was open and the other shut, he kicked the bottom of the closed door to push through it, thinking it would swing freely. The trouble was, it had been latched on the other side and it wasn't going anywhere. The only thing that went anywhere was the glass pane. The kick with his foot had twisted the door and shattered the glass. It made a huge noise and scared the living daylights out of everyone there. The glass shattered pretty much all around myself and one or two of the other guys sitting there. I was right in line with it and saw everything. Haydos went white. He instantly realised how it would look. It was one of those moments where if he could have three seconds of his life rewound, I don't think he'd be kicking any doors. While I saw exactly how innocent it was, I also knew it was going to be portrayed as a dummy-spit. Here we were, going down the gurgler on the field and we had turned into this beast that swore at umpires and smashed doors. It wasn't long before we saw ourselves on the box as the cameras swung in on the action. I felt so sorry for Haydos. He was more embarrassed about that than about having had piles.

Andy Caddick dismisses Ricky Ponting and starts to get a stranglehold on us during the fifth Test in Sydney.

We were soon consumed by more serious matters, however, because Ricky was out three overs later, plumb LBW to a Caddick ball that scooted through. Three for 25.

At least Bic justified Stephen's theory by surviving early and then actually cutting loose, even before the shine was off the ball. Come stumps, he was sitting on 49 at almost a run a ball, being kept company by Marto on 19.

They had steadied the ship to 3–91. That gave us a ray of hope, but sitting in the change room was one very, very disappointed cricket team. We knew that was the day we lost control of our dream. And there were a few of us — Haydos and myself included — who were disappointed in the way we'd reacted under pressure. The first real pressure of the entire series.

We both had hearings looming, but before that, the team sat down and addressed the way we'd handled ourselves. We couldn't use the umpiring decisions as an excuse for our frustration. That's part of the game. We had to be honest about it: it was our poor performance, our lack of ability to claw our way back, and the fact that England was outplaying us, that contributed to us reacting the way we did. We talked about monitoring our reactions in difficult situations. We recognised that we had to stay reasonable. Perhaps because we don't get beaten very often, we're just not used to it. The issue would rear its head again five months later in the West Indies. It's something that we do try hard to control.

The hearings took place that night. Haydos was first. He was charged by the Australian Cricket Board under their Code of Conduct. I think he was fined 20 per cent of his match fee. It might seem odd that the ACB — being our employer and our supporter — would be the one to initiate the charge, but I think everyone realised they had to do something. As innocent as Matt's incident was, it looked so bad they couldn't be seen to be condoning it.

My hearing, which was under the ICC Code, was straight after Matt's. By the time we got in, there was a lot of confusion over exactly what my charge was. We watched a bit of video footage and you could see that I swore and was angry. I had James Sutherland there providing great support for me — which might seem a tad bizarre given that ten minutes earlier he was laying the charges against Haydos — and we spoke with the match referee, Wasim Raja. It came to a point where Dave Orchard, the umpire, actually wanted to drop the charge. He didn't feel that it needed to be continued with. Wasim Raja, who is a terrific bloke, told me he had to charge me with something because it was already on the record, so that was a bit puzzling. In the end, I was told that I was charged with a Level 1 offence and found guilty, but would just be given a reprimand. I knew I had trodden a fine line out on the field and would gladly have gobbled my words back up the instant I said them, but it disappointed me that it was going to go on my record, given that the umpire, in the end, didn't even want to charge me.

The team was long gone by the time my hearing finished, so I had to get a lift back to the hotel with our team manager, Steve Bernard. By the time I got back, Harry was in bed. I'd missed the opportunity to catch up with my little fella. I suppose that, on a bad day like that, I'm even more keen to sit down and take my mind off cricket and appreciate what the important things in life are.

I talked the whole thing through with Mel, who is my closest ally and sounding board. She provides a very good perspective on everything. Rather than talk about whether it was right or wrong to have been charged, she suggested that I try and identify why I'd reacted the way I had.

I felt frustrated by the prospect of our five-nil dream slipping away, and by the realisation that England were comprehensively outplaying us. But at the end of the day, we're all playing by the same rules and have to abide by them. While being frustrated by what I think are inconsistencies in the way the Code of Conduct is administered throughout the cricket world, I had to be honest and admit that I had made a mistake and had let my team down.

I wrote in my diary: 'Day four. Bad day. Our worst of the series.'

I had a good piece of news in the morning when I was told that my reprimand wouldn't be put on my record. However, it also added to my doubts about the consistency of the Code of Conduct. Then again, I had well and truly learned my lesson about how *not* to go about my business on a cricket field. I guess that is the primary objective of the Code and so it was actually working, albeit in a weird way.

Twenty thousand people turned up that day. The last three days of the Sydney Test pulled 95,549 spectators, which exceeded the corresponding days in Melbourne by more than 32,000. In fact, Sydney's total attendance of 181,778 outstripped Melbourne by 4,000. That can't have happened too many times before in games that weren't affected by rain. The construction at the MCG had cut its capacity back to 64,000, but the sell-out first day there still outstripped Sydney's first-day sell-out by 20,000.

The crowds were really good all summer, so I think the lesson is that the Ashes battle still captures the attention and emotions of the public like no other event. The public love to see a winning team, but even more than that, they love to see a winning team under pressure. And no one likes to see us under pressure more than the Barmy Army. As much as I think they are great for the game, adding so much atmosphere and colour, we'd had enough of them by this stage. Like the steel drums at the end of a West Indies tour, we didn't need to hear one more English voice singing, 'We've got three dollars to the pound.'

The majority of the crowd were English on this final day and it didn't take long for them to have something to sing about. Bic was out in the second over, LBW to Caddick again. Tugga chopped one from Caddick on to his stumps a few overs later. Five for 99. His preferred version of the fairytale hadn't quite come to fruition either.

It was Caddick doing all the damage. His stats show that his bowling average for the first innings of Tests is in the high 40s, whereas in the second innings it's in the low 20s. He was certainly the most accurate in landing the ball in the danger area — that zone of uncertainty where you're unsure whether it will pop up or keep low.

Marto lasted another seven overs. Even though he only scored 21, he had at least managed to occupy the crease for 115 minutes. His dismissal brought me to the middle with Lovie. The plan was to just try and stay there, but it's difficult to get a positive mindset when you're going in to bat on a wicket like that. You know that at any time a ball could explode through the top and rear up at your head, or it could just roll along the ground. It's hard to have a clear head and to take each ball on its merits. There was so much racing through my mind, not the least of which was fear. Balls were popping up and hitting guys on gloves and helmets. Even though we're well padded and protected, you can't entirely remove the element of fear on a wicket like that.

I don't want to sound like I'm making excuses. This is all part of the glory of Test cricket. This is what makes it interesting. The challenge of Test cricket is to not be in this position on day five. We rarely get exposed to it because we usually play well enough over the first few days. We were here because of our previous failures.

Lovie and I put on 30 in seven overs before he was bowled, 27, by a ball from Harmison that might as well have been delivered underarm for all it bounced. That brought Binga to the crease.

Right, it's time we have a go. If it's short I'm gunna play my shots. I wasn't just going to die slowly waiting for the unplayable ball. The law of averages said something was going to pop up or skid. Harmison was bowling a spell of short balls and I thought the best way to survive was to go after them. Brett seemed to be of a similar mind.

We added 42 runs in just under four overs.

Caddick had come back on. He sent one down short of a length to me. It looked like it would come up to waist height, but it kicked and headed for my throat. I got my hands up in a reflex defence and it hit the wristband on my glove. Butcher caught it and I was out. I stood there, in a daze, totally stunned at the ferocity of the delivery, and perhaps happy to be alive, before walking off very disappointed that that was the end. I'd made 37 off 29. There were to be no twin tons from me, or anything special at all. I got into the rooms and there was an air of despondency. Steve Waugh came over to console me. 'Well, you probably did well to get a glove on it,' he said. 'Otherwise it might've taken your head off.'

I looked over to the Doug Walters Stand — the bare concrete construction above the old Hill — where the Barmy Army's songs and chants were rising to unheard-of levels. Even though we were headed towards defeat, a part of me felt a certain feeling of happiness for them; that after a long, hot summer, they were actually being treated to a memory they could take home and savour. They loved it and they deserved it.

Binga continued his aggressive swinging, going on to make 46 off 32 balls and becoming the second-top scorer behind Bic in the process. Dizzy dug in with his best Geoff Boycott impersonation and scored three runs off the 36 he faced, but the match was long gone. We were all out seven overs after lunch for 226 — 225 short of their total.

It was a pretty disappointed change room, but not just because we'd missed the chance at a clean sweep. It was the realisation that we'd been outplayed by a better team. They were mentally, and perhaps physically, more up for the game.

It was the first Test I'd ever lost on home soil. Twenty-one straight wasn't a bad record. The team hadn't been defeated in Australia for over four years.

I'm reluctant to say we lost because we didn't have Shane Warne and Glenn McGrath. Of course, being two of the greatest bowlers in Australian, if not world, Test history we missed them, but that wasn't the reason. We would go on to prove in the West Indies that we could win, and win well, without them. Their absence was exacerbated when Gillespie went down injured in the second innings — although Vaughan had already done the damage by then. Even when we've had McGrath and Warne, if we've played back-to-back Tests with long spells in the field, we've shown that we do tire, we do get mentally and physically fatigued, and our performances have dropped off. The Durban Test against South Africa in March 2002 comes to mind. The same in India. So, while Pigeon and Warnie have been a cut above the rest, they're still human.

Having lost this game, the onus was suddenly on us to go to their rooms for a drink, but before we knew it their whole team, Nasser included, arrived in our rooms. Finally, we would get the chance to mix with the lads we'd been battling against all summer.

Player of the series, Michael Vaughan. His batting was on par with any I've seen against us during my Test career.

Although beaten in the last Test, we retained supremacy in the battle for the Ashes.

Chapter Nine

LOWS AND HIGHS

When I first got to know Steve Waugh, he gave me a simple bit of advice: 'Don't get too high when you're on a high, and don't get too low when you're low.'

Once the Sydney Test was all over and we'd had a few minutes to reflect on our defeat, we just tried to move on, and that was helped by the English boys turning up for a lager. As happens when you're in the rarefied atmosphere of the Australian cricket team, the beer seemed just to appear from nowhere. The guys talked about cricket, families, anything. Many of our guys had played county cricket in England, so there was plenty to catch up on. The conversation ambled far and wide, but the one common thread was relief that it was all over. We'd been through so much together, the English and us, and here we were for the first time able to chew it up, spit it out and have a laugh. The pressure and emotion drained away. It was a great afternoon. Brett Lee and Mark Butcher even whipped out their guitars and started jamming.

I remember in the early days of my career, I'd always be thinking about what we were going to do after the drinks: where we'd kick on to; who was keen to do what; how long into the morning we'd be going. I don't know whether it's having kids or just getting older — and the whole team seems to be a good bit older and more settled these days — but I've really come to cherish the atmosphere in the change room. I savour it all. There are very few single guys in the team now, so the desire to go out isn't there. It seems that on good nights, we're staying in the rooms longer and longer. We inevitably end up going out somewhere and kicking on, but by that stage everyone's probably well and truly past their best and going out in public can be problematic. Those hours in the rooms become the precious times. If there's been a midday or one o'clock finish, like in this game, it's not uncommon for us to still be in the rooms at 10 or 11 at night. We stick together.

I think that it shows, too, that the guys have a strong sense of never taking for granted what we are living through. These are special times, indeed. And it's reinforced by guys like Langer, Hayden and Martyn — guys who've been in the team, got a taste of Test cricket and then been on the outer for significant amounts of time, only to have clawed their way back.

No matter what people say about us playing England too often, you'd never hear that opinion from the blokes in that room. The Ashes is the series that you really want on your CV. There may be some room for improvement in the format, but if there had to be changes I'd hope they were minor, because I am someone caught up in the history and romance of Ashes cricket.

To me, it doesn't matter if the actual urn never leaves England. It's always been there. We don't play for it, we play for the *idea* of it. It's all in the rivalry. Even though the results, particularly in the last 12 years, have been very much one-way, you'd like to think that maybe one day the cycle will come around and it'll be competitive again. Just don't let me be in the team to hand the Ashes back.

The amount of time we spent in the change room was totally at the discretion of Ricky Ponting. As the custodian of the team song, no one could leave until he'd called us all together to sing it. That's the unwritten rule. The song was passed down from Rod Marsh, to David Boon, to Ian Healy and then to Punter.

So, there we were. Fully charged up after many beers and another successful series. Punter called us all in to sing it at God knows what time, and off we went. The guys really do treasure the fact that they are part of something that's unique in the modern history of Australian cricket.

As I sat down later to analyse my series, I felt that I'd had a frustrating time with the bat. I wrote: 'I've had three or four chances to nail a big innings and at least two of them I've let go by poor shot selection.' In the first innings of the first Test and again in Perth, I'd let good opportunities go by. At other times I was batting pre-declaration, when you sacrifice your personal ambitions for the benefit of the team. That added to my frustration, because I couldn't get up any momentum.

I also wrote that I'd been disappointed with my keeping throughout the series. Not that there were loads of missed opportunities that anyone else would have noticed, but I knew that there were small technical problems.

Without being a huge analyser of my own game, I do like to clarify my thoughts. I don't really go around telling anyone my conclusions, but I'd have to say I saw room for improvement leading into the World Cup. It was fortunate that we had a one-day series at home first to get the skills fired up.

In the previous few weeks, issues far more serious than cricket had started to rear their heads. The United States was looking increasingly likely to go to war against Iraq, but, more ominously for us, Zimbabwe was re-emerging as a political hot spot. I hadn't given it much thought while we were trying to win the Test series, but after we swung into the VB series of one-dayers, the problems became harder to ignore.

On the last day of the fifth Test, the papers were talking about how Prime Minister John Howard wanted the Australian cricket team to boycott Zimbabwe, but only if other countries did so, too. As if to show what the ivory tower of dictatorship can do to a man, the Zimbabwean President, Robert Mugabe, came out the same day saying that he was happy for us to boycott them, because the English and Australian squads might be hiding assassins. For those of us who were wondering what to do with our lives after cricket, it certainly opened up a few possibilities.

While we were getting public pressure from all sorts of directions, it was nothing compared to what Nasser Hussain must have felt. I didn't talk to him about it, but because of England's historical links to Zimbabwe, he was coming under all sorts of pressure to lead a boycott. It seemed through his comments in the press that he felt he was 'simply a cricketer who's trying to win cricket games. Can't someone who knows a lot more than me make the decision?' But no one would. The pressure stayed on him.

It would have been good to have had a chat after the last Test, but after the stresses and strains of the series, it just didn't feel like the right time to discuss such a serious issue in depth. We were due to fly into that country in seven weeks' time, but it was still a far-off land and first we had a series of cricket games to play.

It was with sore heads that we farewelled the Test players the next day. There's never anything formal to mark the handing over of the reins from Tugga to Punter. When we're on tour, there'll be a dinner or we'll gather for a drink and a chat, but really it's just a handshake and a 'See ya later, boys. Good luck.'

The show rolled on. We woke up the next morning to resume the VB series.

Our first game was against Sri Lanka on 9 January. Two days before that, they'd played Australia A and were skittled for 65 runs — so quickly that they agreed to put on an exhibition match of 25 overs to give the fans some value. They got knocked over just as quickly. They didn't look to be in much form as they came out to bat first against us.

Sanath Jayasuriya was dropped early and then Binga bowled him on a no-ball in the third over.

We paid for that. Jayasuriya went on to play an absolutely phenomenal innings. He went quickly to a century, well supported by Marvan Atapattu who just chipped around and played his quiet hand, until, before we knew it, he had 100 up as well.

We had a pretty off day. I don't think it was any sort of after-effects of the Test loss. I've never felt any continuation of mood between the two forms of the game. It's always a fresh, clean start.

They made 5–343 and when it was our turn, we struggled. I certainly didn't help our chances by getting knocked over early by Chaminda Vaas. There were a few good partnerships and we made it up to 264, but we were never in the hunt.

The game would be significant, not for Sri Lanka's phenomenal turn-around, but as the last game we'd lose for a while.

The next day, Warnie made his comeback for Victoria. It was much earlier than anybody had thought at the time of the injury, so our World Cup prospects were looking rosy. In his second over, JL smashed him for three sixes off four balls and took 26 runs off the over. He finished with figures of 1–53 off eight overs and was run out for a duck. But never before have figures like these been met with such joy. The great man's shoulder was working and that made the day a major success.

We went down to Hobart to play England. We were in trouble early at 3–53. A few more wickets and we could have fallen apart, but Marto rescued the show, scoring a fantastic 101 off 114. With Bevo and Jimmy Maher, he closed us out beautifully to a very respectable 271.

Trescothick and Knight got them away to a blinder. Ricky's use of Brad Hogg was very interesting. Hoggie bowled his first spell and got a fair bit of tap. Ricky took him off after about three overs and held him in reserve. Having worked so hard to get back in the side, I could see Hoggie's mind playing games, as if it was all over for him after one bad spell.

The first English wicket fell in the 32nd over at 1–165. Then, after Marto got the next breakthrough of Trescothick in the 38th, Ricky reintroduced Hoggie. The game was on a knife edge at that point and it appeared to be a risky move, but by showing faith in his player it was amazing to see the confidence that this instilled in Brad. The Poms went after him again, but they paid dearly. He took three wickets in three overs, ripping the heart out of their middle order. Suddenly, they were reeling at 5–211. Ricky's timing had been spot-on. And Hoggie never looked back.

Even with Warnie on the comeback trail, we felt that Hoggie was earning a spot in his own right. Not just as a replacement, but as a great support act to Warnie. It was exciting to see this bloke who had climbed to the top six years before, then fallen right to the bottom, fight his way back into the fold. Warnie's injury was a lucky break, but Hoggie grabbed it with both hands. The most significant thing was his refreshing attitude.

He seemed to have a smile on his face all the time, and he oozed energy in the field and in everything he did. He was like a guy who's died, then been offered a second chance. Asked what he wanted to go back as, he's answered: 'I'll go back as what I was once before — an international cricketer — but this time I'm not going to let it slip away and I'm going to savour every minute of it.'

England, with four wickets in hand, needed 12 to win off the last over and Ricky again showed wonderful leadership in backing yet another new player when he threw the ball to Shane Watson. Shane is a young guy who has shown a lot of potential, but he hadn't quite produced the results people expected of him. Now here was Ricky subjecting him to this. It was very telling. He got Hussain, 43 (off 38), on the third ball and restricted England to just five runs for the over. It was a great buzz for him and the sort of experience he was going to need in the months ahead.

England were always in the hunt in that game. But every time they went in for the kill, we managed to pull away. It was a pattern that was to form in coming games — a winning habit.

We went up to Brisbane to play Sri Lanka, but I was rested. Mel and Harry were there, so after watching the start of the game I took the afternoon off with them. We won a fairly close one with Michael Bevan guiding us past their 211 with seven balls to spare. Next day at the airport, heading down to Adelaide, Boof told me he'd got himself into a spot of bother. He said he'd been really frustrated at being dismissed in a tight situation and, once he was back in the change room, he'd yelled out a racist expletive. He'd had to confront a hearing with Clive Lloyd, the ICC match referee, straight after the game. He apologised profusely to the Sri Lankans, and Clive had said he didn't feel the need to take any further action. Boof thought the issue was closed.

When we got off the plane in Adelaide, however, the questions about the incident were coming thick and fast and it appeared the issue had grown legs. Suddenly, there was a press release saying that Boof was up on a charge and there would be another hearing. The process by which the ICC were handling these types of affairs was again confusing and seemed to be inconsistent. The ICC certainly has a framework for how match referees are to handle the many varying cases, but it seems the referees themselves aren't certain of that process.

Darren felt that he'd already been tried once and now he was going to be judged on the same offence a second time. The Sri Lankans were saying publicly that they accepted his apology and that everything was fine between the two teams. But it seems the ICC weren't happy with that scenario and wanted to pursue it as hard as they could.

That same day, the Sri Lankans' star bowler, Muralitharan, came out and said the Aussie crowds were unfair in their treatment of him and his controversial action. I'd have to agree with him on that one, no matter what my thoughts about his bowling style.

Murali's bowling action was a pretty dead issue by the time I'd been invited to a Carlton Football Club lunch by club president John Elliott, in the winter of 2002. I've been a Carlton supporter since I was a kid living in Deniliquin — which, although it's in New South Wales, is into Aussie rules much more than rugby league.

There were around 200 people at the function. Just before lunch, John Elliott asked if I could get up and do a quick Q&A with him. The questions were pretty standard stuff until he asked: 'Does Murali chuck the ball?'

I hesitated a long while, thinking hard about what I wanted to say before giving my honest opinion.

I went on to emphasise that not for one moment did I blame Murali for the position that he found himself in and that I thought he was one of the more enjoyable blokes to play cricket with and against. I've played with him in a couple of World XI teams. I really enjoy his company. He's a top bloke.

Well, I've answered the question honestly and sincerely. I certainly wasn't looking to make a huge statement and reignite the whole affair.

Late that night, I got a call from the ACB press officer, Pat O'Beirne, who said there had been a female reporter at the lunch who had taped my answers and decided to report them. I felt really disappointed that she hadn't given me a chance to qualify what I'd said, or even just let me know that I was going on the record.

I felt a bit dirty on John Elliott, too, for having dropped his guest into the deep end like that. But he's a larger-than-life character. That's his thing.

Bottom line: I could have said, 'No comment.' There were 200 strangers in that room and I should have been more careful.

After the press officer's call, I spent the next two hours ringing around England trying to track down Murali, who was touring with Sri Lanka. I was desperate to let him know what had happened and tell him the context in which everything had come out. I found him at around 1.30 am Australian time. He was on the team bus. I explained the whole scenario and told him what I had said about his bowling action. I explained that I had no dramas playing cricket against him. And I apologised — not for my opinion, but for the fact that this could inflame the controversy again and I knew that it wasn't something he was comfortable with. He was terrific about it. Then I spoke to his coach, Dav Whatmore, so that he could let the whole team know that I didn't have any drama with Sri Lanka or any of their team members. At around 2 am I finished up and went to bed, waiting for the storm to break.

It didn't. *The Herald Sun* in Melbourne and *The Sydney Morning Herald* ran the story, but very small, tucked away in the back. It looked like the matter would die away. I felt very relieved.

I flew to Sydney that day with Mel and Harry. As I was driving across the Harbour Bridge, James Sutherland, the Australian Cricket Board's CEO, rang me on my mobile. 'What happened?' he asked.

Talking on the phone while driving is not only illegal in most states, it's also not the ideal way to discuss such a delicate matter. I gave my side of the story and the conversation finished with James saying, 'Well, look, if there's any lesson to learn out of this, it's that you've gotta be careful what you say — anywhere. You have a profile, people are interested, and there are people out there who would be happy to use your profile if it's to their benefit.'

'Yep, I totally understand,' I said. 'Thanks very much. See ya later.'

That conversation ended with me feeling comfortable that I had explained myself. James's words and tone left me certain that he too felt the issue need go no further.

A matter of hours later he rang again and spoke with a different tone of voice. He was placing me on a Code of Conduct charge for 'conduct detrimental to the interests of the game' and I had to face a hearing with an independent commissioner.

I was stunned at his turnaround. I lost it. I felt that for something that had caused such a minimal reaction, they were now going to give it legs and make it into a huge story. I explained this to him and we had quite a heated conversation. He said he had no other way to go. I was pretty emotional, and I let him know it. I was very, very disappointed.

A press release went out, saying that I was on a charge. As luck would have it, I was to appear as a guest on the ABC sports program *The Fat* that night. I got a grilling from them about it all, and the next day the headlines were much bigger and more exaggerated. It really gained momentum from there.

If anything, once the press found out the whole story and the context in which I was quoted, they seemed to support me, but in so doing, they created a Gilchrist-versus-the-ACB debate. Next morning at breakfast, I picked up *The Daily Telegraph* at the hotel and the whole back page was devoted to pictures of the ACB board members. The headline read: 'Boring Old Men — These are the people who want to turn our Adam Gilchrist into a cliché-drive robot.' I couldn't believe that the story was getting that sort of coverage and that I was in the middle of it all. The rest of the week I had set aside for sponsors' commitments — most of which was filming ads for Travelex and Orange phones. So, I was trying to commit myself totally to my very loyal sponsors while this storm broke around me. Mel and I had seven-month-old Harry in the hotel with us … It was a tough week, a very tough week.

My manager, Stephen Atkinson, tried to smooth things over. He is a lawyer, so he was preparing my defence for the hearing on the Thursday night, but he was also providing both Mel and me with amazing support, as he always does.

Thursday arrived. I finished filming an ad at the SCG, had a shower there, and Stephen and I then headed to the NSW Cricket Association office where the hearing was to be held. It was pretty quiet and I turned to him and said: 'I can't believe there's no press here, given all the interest in the last three days.' Just as I said this we turned the corner to find six TV cameras staring me down, plus four or five radio and print journos advancing towards us. The full catastrophe.

How did I get myself mixed up in all this? I seriously felt like a criminal walking into court on a murder charge. At the end of the hearing, the independent commissioner, Alan Sullivan QC, said that he found me guilty of 'making public comments detrimental to the interests of the game'.

He, and the ACB representatives laying the charge — James Sutherland and the ACB lawyer, Andrew Twaits, who were on a phone hook-up from Melbourne — very quickly suggested that I be given the minimum punishment, a reprimand, because of my contributions to Australian cricket and the manner in which I handled myself.

To be honest, I found it ironic that just after being told that I had done the wrong thing, I was commended for my behaviour. I became very disillusioned about what it was all about.

Why do I do what I do? I love cricket. I love playing the game. That's why I got into it. I don't need this, and as far as trying to give honest answers when interviewed is concerned … is it more trouble than it's worth?

Anyway, it was over.

The QC asked me for my autograph on his way out.

The preamble to the ACB's Code of Conduct talks about cricket's relationship with our country's identity.

> Cricket has a distinct place in Australian society and history. As an element in Australia's national identity, cricket plays a significant role. This status brings with it particular responsibilities for players and officials to conform to high standards of fair play and personal behaviour on and off the field.

I'm not sure how many players have actually read the preamble, but I certainly had and there was something about the events that had followed on from my comments that left me feeling totally gutted.

Yes, we have to act responsibly on and off the field. I hadn't done so in Sydney when I swore and was charged under the Code of Conduct. Still, to this day, I'm unaware of how I stepped outside the boundaries of 'fair play' by saying what I said about Murali's bowling action. If anything, part of an Australian's identity is the pride we take in our honesty and integrity. I'm not so ignorant as to believe every Australian is an angel and our views are all that matter, but in saying what I had, I felt I'd been honest and balanced.

This might be a bit finicky, but if that's what the preamble is, I would suggest that a right to freedom of expression was pretty fundamental to Australian society and identity.

Darren Lehmann was now facing a breach of the Code of Conduct in Adelaide, but the penalties, if found guilty, were much tougher. Neither he nor I would deny that he had done the wrong thing, but he was being judged with all the same pressures and flawed processes at work.

He was suspended for five one-dayers, which meant that he'd miss the opening game of the World Cup.

The severity of the penalty surprised me. I'm sure the ICC were keen to make a big statement and they were right to do that. There is no room for racism in sport. They had to ensure that no one felt they could act that way and get off lightly. Fair enough, so long as they're consistent.

Boof was very upset about his own behaviour and about the penalty. It was made all the more difficult by the fact that the hearing was held on the day of his twins' christening and it ran hours over time, so they had to keep putting off the christening. Most of the team members jumped in a minivan and headed around to his place in the afternoon, just to see how he was and to let him know that he still had our support and friendship — which he appreciated. There were a lot of friends and family there, so maybe in a way it was good that the hearing happened that day and he got that support.

The worst thing from Boof's point of view wasn't the suspension, but more the fear that he would be branded a racist. He's exactly the opposite. That's something he realised he was going to have to live with. He knew he

Darren Lehmann endured close scrutiny from all quarters after his comments during the one-dayer against Sri Lanka in Brisbane.

had to take responsibility for his actions. He knew he'd done the wrong thing and he stood up and faced it. That is the sort of bloke he is.

Ricky was rested for the game the next day, so I was captain. McGrath, Gillespie and Bichel were all injured, and Matt Hayden was being rested, too. Brad Williams and Nathan Bracken opened the bowling and they did a tremendous job.

Bracken was man of the match with his 3–21, and I gave young Michael 'Pup' Clarke seven overs, too, to get him involved. They all got among the wickets. All except Brett Lee, who was meant to be rested, but was called in at the last minute. In his newfound role as senior bowler, he bowled an outstanding ten-over spell of containment. England was all out for 152.

Our batting struggled early on, but once again Marto stepped up, then Clarke and Shane Watson brought us home with 15 balls to spare. It was a good match to test our depth and the guys came through well. I was very impressed with Pup, who I'd never seen play before. He oozed class; he had such confidence and yet was so keen to learn. He is definitely one of those rare guys who you see play and just know that they're going to make it.

Michael Clarke guides us to victory against England in his debut in Adelaide.

England gained a point from that loss, which was enough to tip them into the finals series against us. We, meanwhile, had a dead rubber to get through against Sri Lanka in Melbourne. They made 214, a total that we knocked over in the 35th, for the loss of one wicket — mine. Punter made 106 and Haydos got 80.

There's this story around about Merv Hughes. I'm sure it isn't true and is just one of those stories where you slot someone's name in to make it relevant to the group you are telling it to.

Supposedly, Merv is at a function and the guest of honour is Frank Sinatra. Merv gets his mate to ask Frank if, at the appropriate time, he would walk over to Merv, tap him on the shoulder and pretend to be old friends, to help Merv impress a few people.

Frank helps out and plays the gag, walking over to Merv who is talking to several attractive young women. With a confident tap on Merv's shoulder, Frank says, 'G'day there, Merv. Long time no see.'

Merv turns around and says, 'Piss off, Frank. Can't you see I'm busy?'

I mention this story because the highlight of that day for me was catching up with Lleyton Hewitt, who was in town for the Australian Open. He came and sat with us and we chatted for about two hours. It was really interesting to swap stories with a fellow sportsman who spends most of his life on the road. Even though our sports are vastly different, there are certain similarities in how we handle the travel, the expectations and the public profile. I've managed to stay in reasonably regular contact with Lleyton since meeting him in 2000. The next day, I gave him one of my playing shirts, which he apparently wore courtside in a Davis Cup tie a few months later. He gave me one of his tennis racquets, so that was a nice touch. I still get a buzz out of meeting people like that.

It reminded me of something I'd read in Michael J. Fox's autobiography, *Lucky Man*. When he had just started to make it big in Hollywood with the films *Back to the Future* and *Teen Wolf*, he'd walk into a restaurant and all these legends of the screen — people he'd looked up to and would have done anything to meet — just came up to him and, without introducing themselves, started yacking as if they were old friends. He called it the 'You're Famous Too Club'.

I suppose you could say that, once you enter the Australian cricket change room, membership of that club is thrown open to everybody. Pop stars, actors, politicians or other well-known sportsmen walk in and you don't introduce yourself, you just talk as if you've known each other all your life. It takes a bit of getting used to. I always used to put my hand out and introduce myself and they'd give me some odd looks. Now I try to act cool and relaxed with it all. I guess part of the bond is that we're all exposed to the public spotlight, so that puts us on a similar wavelength, but I'm not sure I'm totally up there with some of the rock stars and actors I've seen around. Certainly not in my mind.

The next day, we had something of a bombshell dropped. Warnie sat the team down and announced that, after the World Cup, he was pulling out of one-day cricket in order to try to lengthen his Test career.

His announcement came as a total shock and it raised the question of whether we were playing too much cricket — one-day cricket, in particular.

On the other hand, there's a legitimate argument from the Australian Cricket Board that when we are given long periods off in the winter, a lot of our players head to England to play county cricket and earn the big dollars there. Several players had been doing that for a few years.

The first final was the next day. It was Warnie's international comeback in a side that had no McGrath or Gillespie. Shane Watson had pulled out too with a sore back. Brett Lee bowled a terrific opening spell and we had them on the back foot from there. Warnie bowled tightly, but was wicketless going into his tenth over. It was a wonderful over, full of variety and guile. On his final delivery, at the time set to be the last one-day ball he'd ever bowl in Sydney, a beautifully flighted leggie tempted Paul Collingwood to run down the wicket with an almighty swing. The ball dipped and spun right into my gloves and Collingwood was a mile out of his ground. It was a fitting end for a bowler who'd done so much to change the face of the game. Single-handedly, Warnie altered the perception of the spinner from someone who might be used occasionally to tie up an end, to a frontline attacking option in one-day cricket. Few teams now enter one-day games without one. And it's all down to Shane, the Sheik of Tweak.

We smashed England to have them all out for 117. Bic picked up the honours with 4–18.

Haydos and I walked out with no particular plan, but we got to the middle and saw that Nasser had some really odd field placings. No third man, a bloke back deep and straight, a catcher really close at short cover.

Given the small total, they had to try something, but the plan opened up a few scoring opportunities for Matty. He went hard early and that seemed to drag me along. I really can't explain why things happened the way they did. We got some momentum up and decided to keep the foot on the pedal. Everything went our way. Every aggressive stroke hit the middle. Every mishit found the gap. It was just one of those days out. We had

High fives all around. Sharing in a dismissal with Shane Warne on what was set to be his last ball at the SCG in a one-day international.

genuine fun and a good laugh with each other. It was pleasing to be able to put on a show for the packed crowd. It could've been a pretty dull day if we'd chased the runs in 35 overs. We got them in 12.2, at a run rate of 9.6 per over. We'd both faced 37 deliveries and I had 69 and Matt had 45.

We were one-nil up.

Now we had a huge incentive to beat England in the second final in Melbourne. If we won the game on the Saturday night, we wouldn't have to play the third final and thus would get a few days off before the Allan Border medal on the Tuesday night, before flying to South Africa on the Thursday. It was only two days, but I wouldn't get to be alone with Mel and Harry again until after the World Cup.

We arrived in Melbourne to learn that Shane Watson's back injury was serious. He was out of the second final and out of the World Cup. It was another serious blow to our campaign.

Melbourne was hot. Forty degrees. And being Warnie's MCG one-day farewell, it created its own build-up. We won the toss and batted. I was out for 26 (off 32), then Punter and Marto went cheaply. Bevo fell to the ground after a quick single. He was stretchered off with a badly torn groin. For the second time in six weeks, we thought we'd lost one of the key components of our World Cup plans. Andrew 'Roy' Symonds hit just eight off 29 deliveries. When Haydos was out for 69 off 91, it brought the local legend, Shane Warne, to the crease.

A potential World Cup crisis. Michael Bevan collapses after tearing his groin in the second final of the VB series.

As he walked on to the ground, I was sitting up in what they call a coach's viewing box. I cast my eyes around and watched the crowd give him a reception befitting his status. Just in front of our box I could see Warnie's wife, Simone. His daughter, Brooke, raced off down the stairs and all the way to the fence screaming at the top of her lungs, 'Daddy! Daddy! Daddy!' She knew that something big was afoot. The crowd were chanting for her hero.

Once he reached the middle, she turned and came charging back up the steps to her mother. No sooner had she sat down, however, than her daddy was on his way back, with a first ball duck to his name. I'm sure it's the biggest ovation for a duck since Bradman. Brooke shot off back down the stairs, all the way to the bottom, yelling excitedly, 'Daddy! Daddy!' She was oblivious of what had just occurred. It didn't matter. He was still a superstar in her eyes. And in the eyes of the crowd, for that matter.

That wicket, in the 41st over, left us in big trouble at 6–148 (but seven down, in reality, after the loss of Bevo) with Hoggie and Binga at the crease.

It turned out to be a breakthrough innings for Hoggie, hitting 71 off 77 balls, to top score and drag us up to a vaguely competitive 229.

We needed to make an impact early to put pressure on, and Binga did that with his well-directed short balls, giving them all sorts of grief. He bagged both Knight and Trescothick in his first spell. Then Brad Williams got Irani. Three for 20.

But Vaughan and Hussain weathered the storm and started to build momentum. Warnie was introduced in the 23rd over to huge cheers, but it was Hoggie who made the breakthrough in the next over. Hussain for 28 (off 50). Stewart came in and he and Vaughan did the business. They took control of that innings so that, with 15 overs to go, they needed 79 off 90 balls.

That's when Warnie weighed in, taking Vaughan, then Stewart, both on 60. Still, Flintoff looked like he was going to smash them over the line

Brett Lee enjoyed the role as senior bowler in the VB series, and took out Man of the Series honours.

with a couple of nice boundaries — until Binga ripped in and bowled him with a yorker. Seven for 216.

They needed 14 to win with 17 balls remaining.

Four balls later, Binga got Blackwell. Eight for 218. By the end of that over, they needed 12 off 12. It was the closest England had been to beating Australia in a one-day international in four years.

They took six off the next over, and Binga came in for the last six balls with Caddick on strike.

Bowled by a perfect yorker. Nine for 224.

Dot ball.

Anderson swung and missed at the third, but ran anyway. The ball came back to me and I underarmed it and hit the stumps to run him out. We had won the match and secured the series.

Once again, England had blown a commanding position and, through a combination of our efforts and their lack of experience, we came out on top. A couple of the boys picked Warnie up and chaired him off the ground and he got up and said a few words to the Melbourne crowd. Brett Lee was named man of the match for his 5–30. He was also named Man of the Series — a significant announcement, really heralding his arrival as a one-day bowler. He'd been in and out of our team for 18 months to two years. He'd found it hard to maintain a regular spot because of his economy rate. But in McGrath's and Gillespie's absence, he took on the senior bowler's position and relished in it. He really came through and stood up.

Certainly he'd benefited by the rule change allowing bouncers in one-day cricket. That added a major weapon to his arsenal. Batsmen could no longer just go on the front foot to him. It added the fear factor, and we went into the World Cup pretty pleased he was going to be on our side.

The English guys came into our rooms again and everyone mingled really well, but the conversation was more serious this time. Zimbabwe was uppermost in people's minds. I made a point of talking to their guys about it. A few of them said that they had received letters threatening their safety and perhaps their families' safety. 'If you play in Zimbabwe you'll be going home in a coffin' sort of thing. They were pretty worried about it.

That night, I started to appreciate the seriousness of the situation we were about to plunge into, and to consider the issues at hand — not just the security problems, but the moral ones, too.

PART 2
THE WORLD CUP, 2003

Chapter Ten

CAUGHT IN THE WEB
OF POLITICS

While we'd been busy playing England in the VB series finals, the chief executive of the ICC, Malcolm Speed, had gone to Zimbabwe on a two-day, fact-finding mission. During that visit, an opposition legislator had been arrested in an apparent attempt by the government to clamp down on protests during the World Cup.

These sorts of things weren't the ICC's concern, however. It wasn't a political organisation, Speed said, and thus it had no business casting judgment on the country's leader. His mission judged Zimbabwe to be safe, and all games scheduled to be played there would thus go ahead.

The issue of Zimbabwe had been bubbling away for months, with the English players, in particular, coming under pressure to stay away. They had also seemed a bit more keen to address the issue than we had been, but we are all just cricketers and we'd all been far more engrossed in trying to beat each other than in the sorry plight of the people of Zimbabwe.

After the final of the VB series, however, we suddenly found ourselves with some breathing space in which to look at and discuss the issues; quite frankly, I didn't like what I was hearing. It was hard enough trying to figure out if the country really was going to be safe to travel to. The Bali bombings had occurred only three months earlier, so everyone was in a heightened state of wariness. Far more difficult to get our heads around were the moral issues. To sum up my thinking, I was confused.

I felt I had to try to learn as much about the situation as possible, and that while I was trying to make a decision I wasn't going to be put on the spot and say something stupid. The team copped a bit of criticism for not giving opinions, but early on we just didn't have any.

I didn't get to go home after the VB series final because we had the Allan Border Medal presentation coming up, but Mel, Harry and I still got to take it easy for a little while in Melbourne. I used the time to read some of the background material on Zimbabwe that the ACB had provided us.

The ACB did everything that the players requested to help us learn more, and they kept us up to date on unfolding events.

As I read about President Robert Mugabe and the eviction of white farmers from their land, and the complete thuggery with which he was putting down the black opposition, the idea started to crystallise in my head that there were bigger things in this world than cricket. *I'm going to make a stand here. I don't want to go.*

All the other players had flown home on the Sunday, and when they flew back down on the Tuesday morning we got together for a security briefing on Zimbabwe from the Department of Foreign Affairs and Trade. James Sutherland addressed us and asked us how we felt about Zimbabwe; whether it was just security we were worried about, or whether there were moral issues as well.

Publicly, it was being said that the team's only concern with Zimbabwe was security, but I never bought into that. There was a lot more to it, and everyone at some point was talking about the moral issues surrounding the regime. I wasn't alone in my desire not to go. Various players argued that it wasn't our safety, but that of spectators and protesters, that was at risk.

Several times I'd asked myself if I was prepared to make a lone stand. I'm sure that every player asked himself the same question. The topic came up in the meeting, but I don't think anyone really wanted to go it alone. The team wanted to stick together. It was going to be a collective decision.

After our briefing, I was asked my opinion by a reporter and I said there was enough concern to 'warrant assessing it again'. 'It doesn't mean that players are standing up and saying they're not going, but it also doesn't mean we're totally happy with it. We'll assess it over the next few days and learn a bit more about it.'

James had finished our briefing, saying, 'If anyone at any time wants to talk to me personally about this, the phone's there, the door's open.' So, I rang him and we had a good two-hour chat about it. Our conversation gave me a chance to express what I thought the team's views were on the whole Zimbabwe issue, but also my personal feelings. In so doing, I realised I hadn't been totally open and honest with myself.

Often, in a team environment, your mind can be easily swayed to that of the majority and sometimes we don't look at issues objectively. We are quick to decide on a direction, often the most obvious and easy one, and then we go flat out arguing it.

What talking with James did for me was to give me the other side of the argument. The points he raised about our responsibilities as ambassadors for cricket, the importance the trip had for the future of the game, and the commitment we'd already made, prompted me to assess what I really felt, as opposed to the group line of thinking. It also gave me a more balanced assessment of the situation from which I could make a judgment.

To decide not to tour on moral or humanitarian grounds really was moving away from what we do as cricketers and jumping into the political fire. It was here that I began to think that I could go to a country, fulfil my obligations and then leave without even hinting that I was in support of or against the regime. I was truly grateful to James for the time and effort he put into helping me understand this difficult situation.

The English team, at this point, seemed far more set in the path of not going, but their situation was different from ours. Not only were they to play in the capital, Harare, which was likely to be far more unsettled than Bulawayo, where we were going, but those two countries had their whole colonial relationship to contend with, from the days when Zimbabwe was Rhodesia. On top of that, the English players had received death threats from a group known as 'The Sons and Daughters of Zimbabwe'.

All of us were being used as political pawns to some extent, but I felt particularly sorry for the English players. I know that a direct threat to the safety of my family would have changed my thinking.

There were politicians worldwide who were weighing in with lofty opinions about why we shouldn't go, but none acted to make any decisions for which they would be accountable. Understandably, the ICC and the ACB were being extremely careful in not entering into the political debate. It was all left to us.

All the time I was grappling with this, there was also the self-doubt. *What difference does my opinion make anyway?* And there was the feeling that it was out of our control. If the ACB told us we had to go — which the ICC were always telling them — to fulfil our contractual obligations, our hands were tied.

We were certainly up for a bit of light relief that night at the Allan Border Medal presentation. This was only the fourth year of the awards, but they are starting to build up a nice piece of tradition along the lines of the Brownlow Medal in the Australian Football League competition. It's become cricket's glamour night of the year so I think everyone enjoys being there. It's one of the few times when we're all together with our partners and able to kick back, so I was looking forward to having an enjoyable night. I wasn't expecting to win anything. Then the voting started.

They did the one-dayers first. I knew that I'd started the voting period well, because that was in South Africa where I got a couple of man of the match awards. I expected things to quieten down from there, but I had picked up a few points here and there during the Australian summer and, before I knew it, my name was being called as the winner. Richie Benaud was up on stage. I told him how surprised I was and said that, since I wouldn't be up there again that night, I'd thank all the people who were important to me. Richie, as only Richie can, replied, 'Never assume anything.'

They had the vote on the Test-match player of the year and Ricky Ponting deservedly won that after a sensational 12 months. The night went on until the next thing I knew I was up there being presented with the Allan Border Medal, which was a combination of the Test-match and one-day votes.

I was genuinely taken aback. It's a vote by your peers on a 3-2-1 basis after every game, plus votes by the umpires and a media delegate. But the bulk of the votes are by the players, so that made it a special award. To join the three previous winners — Glenn McGrath, Steve Waugh and Matt Hayden — was a huge thrill.

Richie met me at the top of the stairs. 'Respect your elders' points of view,' he said.

I didn't have a speech prepared, but I thanked everyone I could think of. I rattled through my family and my sponsors, and lots of people who have been good to me, but because my mind was racing in front of all the cameras and the people, I forgot to thank one of the more important people in my life. It was only after I came off stage, went out the back, did a press conference, came back in, had a few drinks, and then went to ring my manager, Stephen Atkinson, to let him know what had happened that the penny dropped. I'd forgotten him. I think he was probably a little disappointed, but not half as disappointed as I was in myself. It really sank deep into my heart that I'd let us both down.

Stephen has done so much for Mel and me over the years, both as a manager and, more importantly, as one of our closest friends. Probably the only way that I could wriggle out of my guilt was by pointing out that he is such a good manager, he had taught me too well that I should always think of my sponsors first.

I was up early the next morning taking on the press from about 7.30 am. We were ostensibly talking about the medal, but the interviews usually drifted towards our imminent trip to Zimbabwe. It was a very intense morning of TV and radio, and after having had a few drinks at the awards and a late night, it was tough to present myself in the best possible fashion.

That afternoon I was free to fly home to Perth, where I enjoyed the luxury of a night in my own bed, before we flew out to South Africa the next day.

As I got ready to leave the next morning, Zimbabwe was very much dominating the news. The United States government was urging its citizens to consider leaving the country, and John Howard hinted that the Australian government might pay the $2.8 million it would cost the ACB if we pulled out of playing there.

On the *Today* show, I saw the team going through one of the eastern state airports on their way to Perth. The host, Steve Liebman, asked Matty Hayden if he would shake Robert Mugabe's hand.

'In my opinion,' Matt replied, 'that [a handshake] seriously compromises the values and traditions of what I'm about and I wouldn't like to do that, no.' I could sense that Matt was trying to avoid giving a direct 'yes' or 'no' answer, but then he went on. 'What I'm going to do is rely on the fact that we have a terrific ground staff and support staff behind us to, hopefully, not put us in any position where that can happen.'

Immediately I thought, 'I don't think Matty has meant to say "no" to the actual question.' But it was quickly taken up as a political stance. By the time I got to Perth airport, the media were on to it and it was the first question asked of me. To be honest, I was wavering on which way I wanted to go with the Zimbabwe issue. I was still trying to learn more about it. I said that I had a bit of an opinion but I didn't feel like sharing it because I wasn't 100 per cent sure.

I spoke to Matt about it during the flight. I told him I had been asked the same question and he confirmed with me that he had been trying to say, 'I hope it doesn't come to that.' But from our point of view, even though his comments may have generated a headline or two, we were over the Indian Ocean and leaving that world behind us.

We arrived in Johannesburg and went straight up to our base, Potchefstroom. It's a nice, quiet sort of place — what we'd describe as a country town — about an hour out of Johannesburg. It was ideal for what we needed. Our accommodation was like a country motor inn, where we had free rein. There was a small golf course out the back and a lot of sporting fields. Some of the best sporting facilities in South Africa are in that little town. It's on the high veldt, so a lot of European athletes use it for altitude training in their winter. The cricket facilities are excellent. We settled in well, and while there were plenty of times where we might have liked the attractions of a big city with cinemas or a selection of restaurants, it was a good spot to begin focusing on the World Cup.

Being at altitude, the ball travels a fraction faster. Some of Brett Lee's fastest-recorded deliveries have been in Johannesburg, but it's not all that

World Cup fever had hit South Africa. Everywhere we went the team was welcomed in the traditional African manner.

noticeable. I noticed it on the golf course, though. There was definitely an extra 20 metres on my drive. Unfortunately, that was just 20 metres further into the bush.

The day we arrived in South Africa, we were met by the guy in charge of our personal security, our CPO — Close Protection Officer — Darren Maughan. He is a Zimbabwean, and he addressed us straight away on the state of play up there. He told us that his wife and two little girls were at home in Bulawayo as we spoke and he didn't feel any concern for their safety. He told us about the measures that would be in place for us and he pretty effectively allayed any fears we might have had regarding our own security.

On the more difficult issue of whether our playing there would help Mugabe's regime, he was equally certain. He explained that he was from a fourth-generation white farming family that had been hurt by Mugabe's policy of evictions. He felt that the people of Zimbabwe wanted us to go there and play — they wanted a shred of normality in these dark times.

Darren's explanation really strengthened the way I was thinking after my chat with James. I was leaning heavily towards going.

The next day, the New Zealanders announced they weren't going to go to Kenya because of security fears. Those guys had had an enormous bomb go off outside their hotel in Pakistan the previous year, so I could understand where they were coming from.

Nasser Hussain was still suggesting in the press that the English side

Under the microscope. Shane Warne attends the press conference that revealed the 'biggest cricket story in the world'.

Variety at training is the key to staying fresh. Brett Lee takes time out of the nets in Potchefstroom to work on his speed and power before the World Cup.

The World Cup squad. Bottom row, l-r: Damien Martyn, Glenn McGrath, Ricky Ponting, John Buchanan (coach), me, Steve Bernard (team manager), Shane Warne, Michael Bevan. Middle row, l-r: Darren Lehmann, Andrew Symonds, Andy Bichel, Jason Gillespie, Matthew Hayden, Brett Lee, Ian Harvey, Lucy Frostick (massage therapist). Top row, l-r: Errol Alcott (physiotherapist), Jock Campbell (physical performance manager), Jimmy Maher, Brad Hogg, Mike Young (specialist throwing coach), Tim Nielsen (assistant coach).

The excitement of the World Cup really kicked in once all the teams had gathered in Cape Town before the opening ceremony.

Controversial action? It didn't matter because together with left-armer, Chaminda Vaas, Muttiah Muralitharan formed a lethal combination for Sri Lanka's World Cup team.

was considering a boycott. Echoing what a lot of us thought, he said: 'If nobody has made a decision for us, then we will have to make that decision.'

The night of our first practice match, we were addressed by the Australian High Commissioner to Zimbabwe, Jonathan Brown. He told us quite the opposite story to what our CPO, Darren Maughan, had said. Jonathan claimed that most of the population, particularly the black population, didn't really care for cricket. Even the cricket supporters would love to see us snub the regime, he said.

I was sitting in the meeting feeling really confused. I couldn't escape the irony that if we went up there, we'd have the Australian coat of arms on our chests, representing our country with great pride in a game that the Prime Minister and his representative, the High Commissioner, wouldn't support. That gave me a really hollow feeling.

After Jonathan left, the team went over the problems again and again. The whole squad was there and everyone had their two bob's worth. The meeting was very confusing. No one seemed sure which way they were thinking.

Some of the players were still concerned about what might happen to Australian supporters who were there and who might show support for the protesters. Others in the group were struggling with their conscience, saying they couldn't go because it was supporting the regime. I was still reasonably certain that I would go. Most of the guys, however, just didn't want to stick their necks out. We knew there would be a lot of press coverage about it, and so the players actually asked the ACB to put a blanket no-comment policy on the Zimbabwe issue. We were asking to be silenced.

This really disappointed me. I voiced my disapproval, but I didn't hear or feel too much support around me. Obviously, the guys didn't want to comment and didn't want to be put on the spot, which is understandable, but we were all much more knowledgeable about the issues now and I didn't think we should be silenced as a group.

Aside from the fact that I felt we shouldn't hide from the Mugabe issue, I find the contractual restrictions on our freedom of speech onerous enough without us trying to slap more bans on ourselves.

I thought back to the Murali incident, when I wanted to explain myself publicly, but I couldn't comment because of the Code of Conduct. Now here we were asking the ACB to wrap us up and tuck us away. I think it was naive to feel that we could get by without addressing these issues. If you didn't want to give a comment, no one could make you. We're all grown-ups. Yet, here we were giving up our independence and our ability to make decisions and to think.

The word went out to the media that the players wouldn't be commenting on Zimbabwe any further and that they should refer all queries to James Sutherland or Tim May. It continued to be put out that security was our only concern about playing in Zimbabwe, but the truth was our fears for our personal safety had been well and truly allayed.

It was a week before our first match and the moral issues were still very high in many players' minds. Somewhere along the way, though, I think everyone realised that if we were to go around deciding where we would and wouldn't play on moral grounds, we'd find ourselves being forever confronted with these issues on every future tour. Indeed, some countries may even decline to tour Australia on similar grounds. It opened up a whole variety of scenarios that I don't think we as players are equipped to handle. The feeling among the team grew stronger that politics should be left to the politicians. Also, there was no doubt among the players that just going to someone's country and playing a game of sport doesn't constitute support for that country's government. Nor would it help that government in any material way.

The most important thing I was getting out of all this was an understanding of how to be objective and how to ensure that I could see all sides of an argument. It was really challenging to seek out as much information as I could and to take it all on board while trying to come to an informed decision.

With all this hanging over our heads, not to mention war looming in Iraq, it was good to get a giggle out of one of the local papers. On the front page of a national Afrikaans-language daily they had pictures of the old, well-rounded Warnie next to the new slimline version. Shane had worked extremely hard to shed much of his excess weight leading into his comeback from injury. I firmly believe the new Warnie was a result of plenty of effort. We couldn't read the story, but Warnie got our liaison officer to translate it. It turned out they were claiming that the radical transformation in his appearance was due to plastic surgery. We knew it was a load of rubbish, and besides, he'd never been away from us long enough for the bruises to go down without us knowing. I think Shane got more laughs out of it than anyone else.

The security in South Africa was amazing. I couldn't believe the planning and organisation and how many guards were on duty at any one time. Even in quiet Potchefstroom, there must have been five or six full-time armed guards on duty at all times. If any of us went out anywhere — at night for dinner, to a bar or shopping — security guys would very discreetly follow us. They'd say: 'We don't want to hassle you, we just want you within our sight to make sure nothing goes wrong.' We were all a bit unnerved by it at first: we'd never seen anything like it. But it wasn't long before we no longer noticed it.

All the teams flew to Cape Town the day before the opening ceremony. There was a big reception next morning and a group photo. That was when the World Cup really felt like it was getting under way. Prior to that, we'd been alone in Potchefstroom just training and having practice games. Our minds were on Zimbabwe, and it didn't feel like we were part of a World Cup. Once we started mixing with all the big boys of international cricket, though, the buzz began. Cape Town was alive. The energy was palpable.

For the players, however, the opening ceremony was a bit frustrating. We were all herded into a building out the back of the ground so that we couldn't see the event unfold. There was TV, but it just didn't come up that well. There was no seating, so it was also a bit tiring as the hours went by. I felt for the West Indian and South African teams who were to play the opening match the next day. I also began to understand why many athletes in the Olympics who have competition the day after the opening ceremony decide to stay in the village, rather than expend vital energy.

Once we got lined up and moved into the stadium, the negativity subsided. It felt like we were marching in an Olympics and that was a really proud moment, regardless of whether or not it's thought appropriate for cricket. To walk into a stadium in front of 25,000 people feels quite amazing. The atmosphere was electric, with everyone in South Africa so proud to be showing their country to the world. It made for a wonderful mood. The guys really embraced it and all had their cameras out, having a great laugh. It felt like it was bonding the team. The Cup had begun.

As we had assembled to march into the stadium, I had caught up with some of the South African players, Jonty Rhodes and Mark Boucher. They didn't appear to be enjoying themselves as much as the rest of us. I sensed they were under a huge amount of pressure, with all their country's expectations weighing on them. The impression they gave was, 'It's great, but…'

At a meeting of captains, vice-captains and coaches prior to the ceremony, I'd spoken to the South African captain, Shaun Pollock, who had as good as said it would be nice to be out of the country for a while to take a bit of the pressure off and to get away from the hype so that they could focus on playing cricket.

At the end of the opening ceremony, all the teams were escorted out to a train station next to the Newlands ground. A couple of trains had been chartered to run everyone back into the city, where our buses would be waiting for us. We got in the last carriage, which was occupied by the Dutch

Sharing a proud moment with my West Australian team-mates, Damien Martyn and Brad Hogg, at the World Cup opening ceremony.

team. There were no seats left and one of the young Dutch players stood up and offered Brett Lee a seat, like a schoolkid giving up his seat to an elderly woman. It was part respect and part piss-take, and the Dutch boys loved it. They thought it was the funniest thing they'd ever seen, and it *was* pretty hilarious. We had a good chat to them. They were so excited about being in South Africa to mix it up with the world's top teams, and it was great to remember that the World Cup meant many different things to different sides. We wanted to win the title, whereas for the Dutch it was all about learning, pitting themselves against the 'big guns' and, most importantly, enjoying the ride.

I went into this World Cup having made a conscious decision not to get totally engulfed by it — which is what happened to me in England in 1999. Back then, there was a game or two on television every day, and I'd watch as much of them as I could.

Nowadays, if it's a choice between watching cricket or going to the park with Mel and Harry, well, cricket is a distant second. But I'm happy to sit in front of TV for hours on end if the game's interesting and I don't have other things to do. In 1999, I found myself being a real couch potato. Each night, they had a show called *World Cup Cricket Centre* — a two-hour analysis program. I'd watch these experts and be continually frustrated and angry at them as they wrote us off, then happy if they said something good about me or Australia. I rode it too much.

This time, I made a conscious decision to try not to fall into that trap. Having said that, I found myself glued to the first game of the 2003 tournament between South Africa and the West Indies. *Hey, it is the World Cup.*

It was an exciting game that turned out to have major ramifications for the hosts. With all the pressure that was on them, it seemed that little errors were creeping into their game. The result would still have gone their way if they hadn't been penalised an over for bowling too slowly. The symptoms I'd noticed when talking to the players seemed to be making themselves felt on the field. Rather than revelling in their country's hopes and their favouritism for the tournament, the South Africans took it on as a huge burden. Hosting the World Cup meant so much to them, I was starting to doubt that they would be able to get through it.

Our first game, against Pakistan, was two days away. As equal tournament favourites, we could well have heaped the same sort of pressure on ourselves. But we were relaxed and settled, raring for the challenge. We'd trained hard and got in some quality preparation in our practice matches. So much of our mental energy had been directed at Zimbabwe, we really hadn't been given the chance to be nervous about mere cricket games.

Little did we know, however, that events were unfolding in far-off laboratories that were about to throw our plans into chaos.

Chapter Eleven

'THE BIGGEST CRICKET STORY IN THE WORLD'

I was on the bus going to training. Being an optional session, there weren't many of us there. I was sitting right up the back by myself, when Punter came down the aisle and sat next to me. There was no one else about for six or seven rows. It was 10 February, the day before the first match.

'I've got the biggest cricket story in the world,' he said quietly.

'What?'

'It's easily the biggest piece of cricket news in the world.'

'Bigger than when match fixing broke?' I asked.

'Well, it's got to be on par with it. It'll all come out soon, but I'm going to have to get you to promise not to tell anyone, because we don't want it to go any further just yet. I just wanted you in the loop for when it all blows up. The only people that know about it now are Errol Alcott, Michael Brown, Warnie and me.'

I had absolutely no idea what to expect, but what I did realise was just how serious the issue must be to make Punter so animated.

'Warnie's tested positive to a banned substance on the drug list,' he said.

Bang! I couldn't believe what I'd just heard. And Punter was spot-on; it was the biggest story in world cricket, and we both knew immediately that it was only going to get bigger.

Neither of us said another word for a good few minutes. My mind was racing, trying to come to terms with it all and work out the ramifications. Would Shane Warne be banned from the World Cup? From all cricket? How would the stigma of a positive test play on the rest of his life in terms of sponsors and the media, not to mention his legacy as one of the greats?

Punter and I then slowly started to talk through it. Warnie had worked tirelessly for weeks on end to regain his fitness and form for the World Cup. What was the banned substance? Why was it in his system? We went over these questions during what was surely the most unforgettable ride to training of our careers.

When we arrived at the ground, we got on with training as normal, leaving the rest of the team unaware of the brewing storm. We have optional training the day before a match to give each player the best chance to prepare as individuals. Some like to get into the nets one last time, while others prefer to have a bit of a sleep-in and then do a stretching/pool session sometime during the day. Generally, that results in about six or seven of the boys attending the training session, so things move efficiently to make it short and sharp.

I was able to switch off my mind and focus on my practice with a clear head, but the question lurked inside me; will we as a team be able to do the same tomorrow in our opening World Cup clash with Pakistan?

During the bus trip back to the hotel, we learned of another issue that would spend just as much time in the headlines as Warnie's news. Zimbabwe players Andy Flower and Henry Olonga had entered into the political debate on their country by wearing black armbands in their opening match against Namibia.

Very few details came through immediately, but even with our own issue taking much of my attention, it was easy to see that these two players' actions would have far-reaching effects.

As soon as we got back to the hotel after training, Michael Brown, the Cricket Operations Manager at the ACB, Errol Alcott the team physio, Steve Bernard the team manager, John Buchanan, Andrew Hilditch — the selector on duty —Ricky and myself met in a suite. Michael broke the news to those who didn't already know and we began a process of working out how to handle it.

Warnie wouldn't have known at that time that a couple of us knew, but with so many side issues arising from his scenario, we felt it better to get some contingency plans in place as soon as possible. Could we get a replacement player? When did Shane want to make it public? But probably the most glaring issue was how and when to break the news to the team in a way that would have the least impact on tomorrow's game.

I remember thinking how strong Warnie had been to notify the ACB, because he was quite within his rights to keep quiet. The way it works is that when you test positive with your 'sample A', the Australian Sports Drug Agency (ASDA) sends off your 'sample B' for confirmation. In the meantime, they notify the athlete, but they don't notify the governing body until the results from the second sample come back something like six weeks later. So, Shane could have just kept quiet and played the World Cup. It took a lot of courage and common sense to do the right thing, because it must have been very tempting to sweep it under the carpet. The whole team owes Warnie a debt for that.

A team meeting was called at 6 pm. The whole touring squad was there: our media liaison guy; the baggage handler; our local liaison guy; everyone who was with our Australian campaign.

I think some of the players detected that the meeting was something to do with Shane, but surely none of them could have known what was coming.

Warnie entered the room last and sat in a chair, pretty much in the middle of us all. After an eerie silence while he was obviously going over in his mind how he wanted to start, he began to tell the group the details. As he broke the news, that awful silence seemed to spread his words further and further apart. He basically told us of the contact he'd had from ASDA, and that he'd tested positive to a drug test. He explained to us that he hadn't taken any performance-enhancing drugs. The banned substance was a diuretic to get rid of excess fluid in his body prior to a public appearance. He didn't get very far before he stuttered and stopped, then started again, trying to get it out through some very, very strong emotions. He surprised me because I never thought I'd see Shane Warne show so much of himself to the guys. It's just not in his make-up. In the past, I've found myself in an extremely emotional state in front of the guys when talking through various issues. Some of us are just like that. It was obvious from the very first moment how much it was ripping into Shane. I really felt for him. I sat and looked at him — team-mate, most successful spin bowler of all time, movie-star profile, confident, strong, a larger-than-life character — sitting before us looking like a broken man.

It was tough watching one of the greats struggling emotionally like this. I couldn't help thinking that of all the things that could possibly cause Warnie trouble — all the incidents that have yapped at his heels, all the speculation surrounding his life and what some may call his misdemeanours — who would have thought that taking a diuretic tablet to sharpen up his appearance was going to be the one that flipped his career upside down?

He continually stressed to the team how bad he felt; how much he'd let us down. To see a grown man, such a legend, and particularly someone who wouldn't normally show that much emotion, feel this way was really sad. My mind was rushing to what the public perception was going to be. Because a diuretic could be used as a masking agent for performance-enhancing drugs, the conspiracy theorists were wrongly going to have a field day speculating about whether he was hiding anything, but no one who knows Warnie would believe that for a minute.

Warnie has lived in the spotlight of fame like no one else in the team. He openly admits that he's brought a lot of it on himself, and he's copped a bit of flak over his weight, too. I was sitting there wondering whether it was living in that glare for so many years that had brought this about, creating the feeling that he had to look good. Or whether it was just Shane. Whatever the case, the whole team in that meeting were hurting for him.

He got through telling everyone the news and then gave us a brief summation of his plans: he was heading home tomorrow during our game and he would tackle the problem from there. He wished us all the best and he left the room.

Everyone in the team just looked stunned. I could feel a flood of support for Shane around the room. The guys wanted to show their solidarity, which is a feature of any team I've ever been part of, but particularly at this level.

I was really impressed by what I thought was quite brilliant leadership from Ricky Ponting and John Buchanan. Punter just cut in straight away and said he'd like everyone to go away for a couple of hours. 'Maybe have dinner, do it in groups, do it by yourself, whatever you want, but just have a good think about what you've just heard and work out how you feel, what your emotions are. Then we'll regroup here at 9 pm.'

I had dinner with four other players and it was fascinating to see the mix of emotions the guys were feeling towards Shane. There was great sorrow for him, but that would suddenly veer into disappointment for what they felt was his naivety, and that he'd just have to face the consequences. Then there'd be a welling up of hope that he'd get through it and rejoin us at some point.

When we all got back together at 9 pm, everyone was a lot more settled and had come to terms with what it was all about. Only a few players talked. Matty Hayden spoke really well about how we would, as a natural reaction to the crisis, be drawn closer together.

He was right, and I believe that from that moment on a unique bond started to develop between all of us in the squad.

One of the main things that Ricky and I had spoken about in our earlier discussions on the issue was that just eight weeks earlier we had resigned ourselves to the likelihood that we wouldn't have Shane Warne at the World Cup because of his shoulder injury. Ricky brought it up again now and spoke about how, as a result of that injury, we'd all grown confident in the role that Hoggie was taking on and felt that, although you'd never knock back Shane Warne from any team, we had fantastic cover and could still succeed in the World Cup. After today's news, we just had to keep that belief.

Ricky asked me my thoughts and I was pretty emotional. My main point was that we had to use this as an incentive. Not so much to 'win it for Warnie', but to use it as a reminder of why we were there. That everyone else would be thinking it would drag us down, but that we had to show them that our focus could strengthen.

Whenever I address the guys about anything away from regulation cricket stuff where there's a bit of emotion involved, I have a tendency to choke 'em back a little bit, and this was certainly no exception. I reminded the team of what it was like when the Hansie Cronje bookies scandal broke. We were in South Africa at the time for the Super Challenge 2000. It was a day or two before the first game that the news unfolded. I remember being totally engrossed by the story. It was so hard to believe. I'd watch every news broadcast, read every newspaper, read about it on the internet, just trying to keep up to date. I'd never experienced that with any cricket story before. I've never been the sort to thrive on cricket news, but speculation was swirling around about money and who else was involved. And, if anything, it may have affected our performance more than it did the South Africans'. It seemed to bring them together and gave them a real steely determination. Everybody wrote them off, given that Cronje was such a central figure to their game and so well loved. But they came together and won the series.

So, I guess I just wanted to convey to the boys that we were now in a similar position. The rest of the cricketing world might get engulfed by this news, but we'd already had three or four hours to digest it. We'd let off our steam and formed our opinions. We had the drop on them. So, we had time to wash it out now, forget about it and prepare for the games ahead.

The meeting only went for about an hour, but we left it feeling a lot better than we'd felt after the first one.

Next morning, Shane held a press conference. He announced that he was leaving the country and explained why. There was a firestorm of

Up close and personal. Warnie was extremely emotional when he revealed he had tested positive to a banned substance.

Facing the music. Shane Warne, flanked by the ACB's James Sutherland on the right and Michael Brown on the left, prepares to talk to the press about the ASDA findings.

discussion about it in the media, and even around our hotel and on the fringes of the team, but little was said by the players.

Management was extremely shrewd in taking Shane away from the team, insulating us from the controversy and getting him home as quickly as possible so that all the focus in South Africa was back on the World Cup and not on Shane. Plus, it meant that Shane and his advisers could get moving on dealing with the whole issue without delay.

I didn't see Warnie on the morning of the match, as, like most of the players, I'd said goodbye and good luck the previous night. But on my way to the bus for the game, I slipped a note under his door that I'd written earlier when thinking about his situation. I wanted to let him know that, regardless of the outcome, he had our support and he also had a strong, close family at home that he should utilise as much as possible in these tough times. I guess the truth was, I just couldn't get a grasp of what he was about to go through and I just wanted him to know that people cared about him.

As I looked around the bus on the way to the game, making the same trip I had taken 24 hours earlier when Punter first told me, I felt a calmness within the team about Warnie's situation. We'd dealt with it. Our minds were clear and focused on the job that had to be done that day.

Chapter Twelve

IN THE RING WITH PAKISTAN

I don't think I'd even heard of the World Cup until 1987. And that was only when the news came through that Allan Border's Australians had just won it. I was an avid cricket supporter, but the tournament just didn't seem to be on the radar. It shows the lack of coverage that anything overseas got in those days before pay TV, and even less if you lived in the country rather than in a major city.

For me, the World Cup had none of the resonance of the Ashes or a tour by the mighty West Indies. It was never my childhood dream to play in one.

That 1987 tournament in India and Pakistan was the first time the Cup had been held outside England, but it was more the fact that Australia's struggling team had managed to pull it off which raised its profile in the mind of this 16-year-old. When the World Cup came to Australia, in the late summer of 1992, it was the first time the players wore coloured clothing and played under lights. Its profile was on the rise and it had become a dream of mine to play in it. But by then it was the dream of a young man battling to break into the New South Wales team.

By the 1999 Cup, I'd just cracked a spot in the Australian team. It was the high point of my career. I was playing on the world stage, and in the end I think that overawed me. I averaged 22.4 with a strike rate of just 79.

Leading into this 2003 campaign, I wanted to think I was a better and more developed player. I tried to carry on in a more even, settled frame of mind, and part of that was my decision to avoid watching too much of it.

The memory of the last World Cup was strong in all our minds. We'd played badly in the first few games, losing to New Zealand and Pakistan, and leaving ourselves extremely vulnerable. Basically, it reached a scenario that if we lost another match after our third game, we would have been out of the tournament.

Punter, Boof, Pigeon, Bevo, myself and Warnie were the survivors from the team that won the final, and Marto was in the World Cup squad. None of us wanted to go through that again. But our first two games — against Pakistan and India — were shaping as the hardest in our pool, so there was a strong possibility that we might find ourselves in the exact same hole.

After our initial team planning meetings, the squad came up with the theme of 'intent and intimidate'. We felt that we had the ability to overawe Pakistan and India with our bowling, but we'd carry that theme through to all facets of the game with strong body language and an aggressive, slick approach to everything we did. We would achieve that with an iron-willed intent. We were aiming for physical presence, as opposed to running them down with a verbal spray.

Our opening game against Pakistan was at The Wanderers ground in the plush northern suburbs of Johannesburg. That suited us fine. It was to be the venue for the final in 40 days' time. Known as the 'Bullring' for its gladiatorial atmosphere and steeply decked stands, there was an air of great excitement around the ground as the campaigns of two of the heavyweights in the tournament were about to get under way. There was also plenty of discussion and speculation on the breaking news about Warnie and how that would affect us.

Pakistan won the toss and sent us in to bat. They seemed to have the same plan as us, for they came out breathing fire. Wasim Akram is a terrific bowler and I would say that, over the course of our careers, he's definitely had the better of me. In our 1999 pool game, he bowled me for a third ball duck. There have been a few times I've got on top of him, but the thing is, he really homes in on my off stump and gives me no width.

I tried to move my stance across a little bit. I normally bat on middle stump, but I moved over to cover my off stump and I was just trying to play nice and straight against him. The second ball of his second over was angled at leg stump, so I tried to bang it along the ground through mid-wicket. Being a bit anxious to feel bat on ball and get runs flowing, however, I pushed out at it. The ball held up because the wicket was a little slow and I went through my shot a fraction early, got a leading edge and skied it.

I was out for one off three balls and Australia was 1–10 in the third. It wasn't the start we'd wanted. I was disappointed with myself, but I didn't analyse it too much. The style of player that I am, there are going to be many days like that where it's over before it begins. I was too aggressive too early.

Punter and Haydos kept things moving all right until Wasim bowled Haydos in the 11th. He then skittled Marto's stumps first ball and we were in trouble at 3–52. Jimmy Maher held off the hat trick but was out five overs later. We were staring down the barrel of a very low score with the out-of-form Andrew Symonds heading to the crease in the 16th over, at 4–86. Realistically, Roy was only in the starting line-up because of Michael Bevan's groin strain from the VB series. While he always creates an impression that he's cool and calm, I'm sure that Roy must have been nervous and knew that if he missed his opportunity here, it may not arise again in the tournament.

Punter and he held things together quite nicely. I don't recall exactly when it happened, but early in his innings, Roy hit a cover drive that almost left scorch marks on the turf and a dent in the fence. Suddenly, it felt like we'd stolen Pakistan's momentum. In the 30th over, Punter was out for 53 off 67 with the score at 5–146, but that just seemed to push Roy up a gear and we pretty soon realised we were watching one of the great innings of all time.

By the time he came off, he was unbeaten on 143 off 125 deliveries, and our potentially low score had grown to 310 — the highest by an

One of the highlights of the tour came in the first match. Andrew Symonds, reaching his first century for Australia against Pakistan, shares his joy with Ian Harvey.

Australian team in the World Cup and the highest ever on this ground. The Pakistanis had also given us 31 extras — one-tenth of our score — including 12 wides and nine no balls. That had slowed down their over rate, so they were fined an over. Now they only had 49 overs to catch us.

The change room during the lunch break was alive with adrenaline. Everyone was just so happy to see Roy finally realise the potential that he's shown for so long. He had taken some horrible criticism from several sections of the press leading into the World Cup, and the spirit within the team as a result of his success was at a premium.

Our bowlers weighed in and the four quicks — Lee, Gillespie, McGrath and Harvey — took a steady flow of wickets to make the Pakistani run chase look increasingly hopeless.

Hoggie had just taken his first World Cup wicket when the Pakistani wicket keeper, Rashid Latif, came in at number eight. They needed 186 at better than nine an over, so the game was pretty much in the bag.

Just prior to the match, Rashid had come out in the press saying that we were scared of them. Rashid's a guy that I've always got on very well with. We'll usually chat after games, because keepers always have a bit in common. He came to the crease and looked at my new keeping gloves. He seemed pretty impressed and basically enquired about the chances of my getting him some. We often get guys from the sub-continent sides asking us for gear, as a lot of the top-of-the-range gear doesn't make its way to them. It's quite ironic, really, given that basically all protective cricket equipment is made in India. Most of us try to accommodate these requests and rustle something up for them.

'I'll see what I can do,' I replied.

Hoggie then got another wicket, leaving them floundering at 7–147, but Rashid was still giving it a good shake. He went to cut one from Hoggie and the ball came through to me. I thought he'd nicked it. We went up for an appeal and it looked like Rashid was starting to walk. He looked up to see the Sri Lankan umpire, Asoka de Silva, give him not out. So he stood his ground, which is fair enough, but I thought I'd give him a bit of a razz.

'Rashid, come on, mate. You were walking.' I had a big smile on my face, because it wasn't a big confrontation.

He shook his head and smiled, and mumbled something about never walking. Hoggie bowled the next ball and Rashid was still at my end.

'Well, you know the fella upstairs, it all evens up with him,' I said, and I wasn't talking about the TV umpire. 'You know he watches over it all, and what goes around comes around, so just be ready for the next one.'

He chuckled. It was all in good fun. We've always bantered like that. He hit the next ball away. It was the end of the over and as I walked past to change ends, he said something to me that I didn't hear exactly but which seemed to be much more aggressive than the previous few remarks we'd exchanged.

I turned and told him to save his big-mouth comments for the press. He said something back, and although the blood was starting to rush through my veins a little quicker, it seemed like the end of the issue.

Dizzy bowled the next over with Wasim Akram on strike. Wasim hit a ball just behind square. Damien Martyn chased it and threw it back to me over the stumps, bringing Rashid to the striker's end. Just as I turned to walk back to my keeping position, I was certain I heard him call me a 'white c____'.

I couldn't believe what I'd just heard.

'What did you say?' I asked.

He looked away, and so I went right up to him.

'What did you just say to me, mate?'

Again, he didn't say anything.

I felt I had no choice but to report it to the umpire. I've never had any reason in my whole career to do anything like that before. I've been called a lot of names and been sledged in many different ways, in club, domestic and international cricket, and I've given my fair share back, but I've never had the slightest desire to go to an umpire and make a report before.

I ran straight over to David Shepherd, the English umpire, who was standing at square-leg and told him my version of the events.

As I walked back past Rashid, I said: 'You're gone. You can't say that. It's a racist comment.'

He made a gesture with his hand, saying: 'Be quiet. Too much talk.' And he was gesturing to the umpires. He got a single and went up the other end where he went straight to Punter and told him that I was talking too much. So, I ran up and told Ricky what Rashid had said.

'Make sure you tell the umpire,' was all Punter said, which I had already done.

At the end of the over, Rashid put his hand out and tried to shake my hand, but I just shied away. 'No way, mate. You've done your dash.' I was extremely fired up; stunned at what I was sure I'd heard and confused as to why that sort of comment would come my way.

Rashid hit three sixes in his innings to make 33 off 23 balls. He and Wasim were Pakistan's equal top scorers, but their partnership of 55 off five overs was too little too late and they were all out for 228 in the 45th over. We were pretty happy with the ease of the win, given the shaky start to our innings.

After the match our team manager, Steve Bernard, and James Sutherland came to me and asked to hear my explanation. James basically suggested that I take a few minutes by myself, settle down and have a think

A storm brewing. Rashid Latif chips one away in our opening clash at The Wanderers in Johannesburg. Later, Rashid and I would have a verbal clash that resulted in an ICC hearing.

about whether I was certain I wanted to pursue the issue further. Not for one moment was he trying to influence my decision; he just wanted me to be sure. In fact, he was extremely helpful in letting me know that whatever course of action I chose to take, he and the ACB would fully support me.

I considered the ramifications that would arise; the massive press focus and the pressure it could place on everyone associated with the team. Of course, the fact that it was a huge accusation I was making, and one that I must be confident of, wasn't lost on me either. As I've mentioned, I couldn't for one moment think why Rashid would say anything like that, as we've always got on well and respected one another. But I just felt I had to be true to myself.

I put a written report in to Steve Bernard, who in turn passed it on to the match referee, Clive Lloyd. Ironically, it had been Clive who had handed Darren Lehmann a five-match suspension just a few weeks previously after his comments in Brisbane.

Clive called a hearing immediately. In attendance were Rashid, his captain Waqar Younis, their manager, plus Steve Bernard, Punter, myself and the umpires — including the third umpire. I briefly recounted my version of the incident, then Rashid was given a chance to reply. He asked their team manager to translate for him as he was concerned his English wasn't good enough.

Rashid said that I was one of his favourite players and he had a lot of respect for me. He denied making the comment; in fact, he accused me of making the inappropriate remarks. He claimed that, after he was given not out, I had said that he'd never be given out by that umpire because they were both the same colour — which absolutely floored me. It was probably more distressing than what he'd said on the field.

I hopped straight back in and described exactly what I'd said after the not out. I looked everyone in the eye and said, 'I can promise you I would never have said anything like that ... Why would I bring this up if I'd gone and made a racist comment myself? Why would I report his comment? Why hadn't he reported it if I'd gone on like that? Why was my reaction so strong on hearing his comment if indeed I had already put the wheels in motion?' I was furious to the point of feeling sick in the stomach.

We watched the video and it was clear that Rashid had said something to me, but you couldn't tell what it was.

Clive Lloyd said, 'Look, it comes down to one man's word against another's.' He said he needed to think about it overnight before he made a decision. Next morning, we learned that the ICC policy on hearings hadn't been followed correctly and we would have to have a complete rehearing.

By this stage, the press were all over it. We discussed whether we wanted to go through it again, and James and Steve were really supportive of me. They wanted to make sure that I was doing it for the right reasons. When I'd convinced them that I was, that it wasn't just a knee-jerk reaction after what had happened to Darren Lehmann, they backed me all the way.

We'd secured an audiotape that localised the sound from the stump mic. The technician who had found the tape said that the word 'white' could definitely be heard, but that the other word or words weren't clear. When we heard the tape we thought she was right, though it was difficult to decipher exactly whose voice it was. There wasn't anyone else around the stumps, so we felt it couldn't have been anyone but Rashid.

We went into the hearing that morning and played the tape. The Pakistan members immediately denied that it was Rashid's voice. In fact, they said the tape could have been tampered with. Clive Lloyd said he couldn't decipher whether it was Rashid's voice and discussed getting the opinion of a voice expert.

'Look,' I cut in, 'that could take weeks and I certainly don't want to go down that road.'

I didn't want to have the matter drag out for weeks while the World Cup was on. Although I had felt strongly enough to follow through with a second hearing, I now wanted to clear up the matter as soon as possible and try to limit any damage it might cause to the game in general. While everyone was speculating about whose voice it was on the tape, I started to take a wider view. I'd seen the massive press coverage on the event and realised

Rashid Latif and Waqar Younis awaiting the start of the second hearing regarding comments between Rashid and me.

just how negative for cricket it was, so stretching the issue further would only add to that damage.

I looked at Rashid, who was sitting on the opposite side of the table. I wondered what was going through his mind. I questioned myself. Was he lying? Was he telling the truth? Had it been a total misunderstanding on my part? If he was innocent, why wasn't he up in arms over my accusation? Why, in the first hearing, did he accuse me of having made a racist comment, but now not want to stand by that accusation? I had my version, but so did Rashid.

I said to Clive, 'Mate, you've got all the information. You've got their story, and you've got my story. I think just disregard the voices on the tape, but look at my reaction. Why would I have come here if I didn't have a case?'

To his credit, Clive provided as fair a hearing as he could, but 'through lack of evidence' he couldn't convict. That was fine. I understood that and I had no problem shaking Rashid's hand to put what I thought was closure on the whole issue.

Clive held a press conference and announced his decision. I went out, read my statement and answered a few questions, but consistent with the Code of Conduct I didn't comment on the incident itself or what went on in the hearing. The next day, however, Jonathon Rose, our media liaison officer, told me that Rashid had done an interview with Mike Coward, from *The Australian* newspaper, in which he discussed the hearing in detail. He was now saying that he was going to sue me for defamation.

The ACB complained to the ICC about Rashid commenting publicly on the hearing. Then he turned around and said he didn't want to sue anyone. He said that we had a good relationship and he wanted that to continue. This was another turnaround. He then went on Adelaide radio station 5AA and said that we might have tampered with the tape and that my reaction was an effort to make up for Darren Lehmann's case, but that he didn't want to take any action. I have no idea as to whether the ICC spoke to Rashid or the Pakistan Cricket Board at any stage. There wasn't any mention of any action being taken against Rashid for making comments in the press, and I guess that's why now, several months after the event, I feel justified in making public my views on the incident.

Speaking to the media after the Latif hearing, I was a bit tired but relieved it was over ... or was it?

Aside from these outside issues, I could feel a strong bond forming within the team. We might have lost Warnie and Shane Watson, and we were missing Bevo and Boof, but seeing a guy like Andrew Symonds step up in that game and fill that gap just gave everyone good vibes. Ian Harvey, too — he had taken four wickets. And Hoggie had taken three. Confidence and satisfaction were brewing in this newly mixed unit.

Our team still talked about Warnie. The main issue by this time was speculation about the sentence he'd be given, but it wasn't something the guys were obsessed about. We all rang him at various times, but without luck, so all we could do was leave messages offering support. We read the papers. Stories were faxed from Australia to our media guy and the players would read them, but no one was getting too worked up about it.

Bigger news by then was that England had boycotted their Zimbabwe game, which was scheduled for 13 February. In doing this they gave Zimbabwe four competition points, and so risked their own progression through the tournament. Time would tell how important that might be.

Chapter Thirteen

'INTENT AND INTIMIDATION'

Punter came to me with a plan for the Indians. He said he had an inkling that Brett Lee might be the man to use with the new ball, rather than Dizzy. We'd come through the Pakistan game with a bit of momentum, whereas India had struggled to make 200 against The Netherlands in their opener. Punter thought that a few rockets up into their rib cages would shake them up a bit.

I've got to be honest, my gut feeling was that it wasn't a good idea. I felt that Pigeon and Dizzy would do an equally good job at blasting them, but would be a fraction more accurate at the same time. Punter, however, stuck by his instinct.

We bowled first and Binga came out smoking from his ears, with a really aggressive line and length. He let a few loose ones go, but that led to the Indian batsmen playing wild shots because they were so relieved their bodies were out of the firing line. First, Ganguly tried to smash a widish ball in Brett's third over, nicking it to me, then Sehwag did the same in his next.

At that point, the Indians were still moving it along okay at 2–41 off 7.2 overs, but now they were wounded and nervous. Pigeon produced a string of maidens to tie them right up as Ricky replaced Binga with Dizzy.

Even though the master, Sachin Tendulkar, stayed at the crease, the Indians were restricted to nine runs off the next ten overs — losing three wickets on the way. We could sense their frustration building under the extreme pressure from our attack. Tendulkar looked like he wanted to break the shackles, but there just wasn't any loose bowling to enable him to do that. We continued to contain them, culminating in Dizzy's trapping Tendulkar LBW for 36 (off 59). They were in real trouble at 6–78 in the 28th over. It can't have happened too often that Tendulkar could bat for 28 overs and have so little influence on a game. Their tail gave a tiny wag before it was docked — all out for 125 in the 42nd over.

It was an awesome display of bowling. The concept of 'intent and intimidation' had come to life. Dizzy had bowled his ten overs straight, taking 3–13, one of the most economical spells in World Cup history. Given that Tendulkar took 14 runs off one McGrath over, Pigeon's figures of 1–23 off eight were pretty amazing, too.

Punter's ploy had paid off, and it really confirmed in my mind his wonderful understanding of the ebbs and flows of a game and where certain players can have an impact. It has been really exciting to be alongside him and watch that ability develop.

I've always talked about my consistency in the one-day game, or lack thereof. Ideally, I'd love to be more even and to be able to stack up score after score, but I'm not sure that's the sort of player I am. I'll never be like Matty Hayden, who is a real opening batsman; a great judge of a delivery who lets the ball go beautifully. But that's all right. I've got an impact role and I'm happy with that.

Against India, I set out to take my time and give myself a chance to settle in and build a score the way Roy did against Pakistan. Scoring at a fast rate early isn't a priority for me, but the funny thing is, as soon as I forget about trying to score at five or six an over, the runs just seem to come.

Thanks to our bowlers, there wasn't much pressure. Matty and I took the score up to 100 before I was stumped for 48 off 61. We needed 26 more to win and Punter got 24 of them in 24 balls.

We had won with 27 overs and nine wickets to spare.

The win made us feel pretty good. There was a real tingle from having beaten two serious title contenders in such emphatic fashion. They were always bracketed as danger games, and to have come out the other side with such dominant victories made a statement to the rest of the tournament. It certainly confirmed our status as favourites, given the poor showing of the other pre-tournament favourite, South Africa.

It never felt, though, like we wore that mantle as a burden. The Australian sporting public are a pretty demanding lot, but somehow we've managed to escape the onerous burden that some other countries seem to place on their heroes. The South Africans were a good example of a team not handling the pressure, but the Indians were outright bizarre.

Their billion-odd supporters weigh pretty heavily on them. That became very evident after we beat them. Mohammad Kaif had his house splattered with paint by an irate mob, who felt the team weren't living up to the standards expected of them. I wouldn't say that Mohammad did anything wrong in that game, but the Indian supporters are so wildly passionate about how their team is going that any defeat is taken to heart and they really don't mind showing their disappointment.

South Africa were playing New Zealand in a pretty crucial game for both teams. I caught a bit of it on television, but not much. Herschelle Gibbs made a magnificent 100, thrusting the Proteas up to 6–306. They did everything right. More than enough to win.

The New Zealand captain, Stephen Fleming, however, was mercurial in his charge after the huge total. No matter what they threw down at him, the runs kept piling up as the sky went dark and the rain rolled in. It was an amazing feeling watching the South Africans seize up and lose their grip on that game. After play had been interrupted, New Zealand needed 1–229 from 37 overs to win the match under the Duckworth-Lewis system. You would have sworn that the cricketing gods were ganging up on South Africa. They were now in the same situation we had faced in the last World Cup, but I couldn't help thinking it was just never going to be their tournament. From then on, the local press and the public came down even harder on their team. They could tolerate opening match nerves, but there was a mood around the country that the 'boys' were not going to make it to the finals and gain revenge for that disaster against us back in the 1999 World Cup semi-final.

A couple of days later, Herschelle Gibbs actually came out and criticised his captain, Shaun Pollock, and complicated the matter by talking about Hansie Cronje. It was a huge issue in South Africa and it gobsmacked me. I don't know the full context in which he was speaking about Shaun. Perhaps he wasn't even criticising him, but just fondly remembering the way the disgraced Hansie had handled the team.

It really threw a spanner in their team's works. It seemed that everyone in South African cricket had an opinion on it. Herschelle copped some stern words via the public forum from several former players for bringing Hansie's memory into the equation at such a difficult time. The ghost of Hansie has continued to float around South African cricket. It really was noticeable at the World Cup. There was a lot of opinion that he was terrible for the game, yet some people still held him up as a cricketing god who was responsible for a brief golden age that they were already looking back on through rose-coloured glasses. The type of glasses that rendered confessions of match fixing invisible. Herschelle Gibbs was banned for six months for being involved, too, so you would think he'd be the last person to invoke the name of his late skipper while the world's eyes were upon his country. He did say, however, just how much Hansie had meant to him and that he was staying true to that emotion. It was obvious that the majority of cricket fans in South Africa had forgiven Herschelle for his involvement in the match-fixing scandal. But no one could say that Herschelle was to blame for the Proteas' poor form. After Tendulkar, he was probably the second-best batsman of the tournament.

Rain was sweeping across the country, washing out the game between the West Indies and Bangladesh in Benoni. So, instead of a 'gimme' four points, the West Indies would have to share the points with the lowly Bangladeshis, a result that looked like it might cost them dearly.

Another result of that wash-out was that it saved South Africa from being eliminated. As the Proteas built up to their game against Bangladesh, they started talking about how they had to relax more. I wondered if it was too late. Their crunch match was due in the last pool game against Sri Lanka, but they were already at the mercy of the rain gods. If their upcoming games against Bangladesh or Canada were washed out, they were gone. The weather was already having too much influence in this tournament and I think there is a strong case for reinstating reserve days for rain-affected matches and for continuing games into the second day if rain has stopped the first.

Our biggest fear on going into our next game — against The Netherlands — was the weather. Our spot in the next round of the tournament, the Super Six, already looked pretty safe, but the points we earned now would all go towards carrying us through to the semis.

We were playing the Dutch in Potchefstroom, so it was almost a home game for us. We'd watched the rain sweeping across the veldt for days, but it was clearing on match day so we felt confident the points would be ours. Then, when we got to the ground and the covers were taken off, a huge amount of water was spilt on to the wicket. It was totally unplayable. If it had happened in a third- or fourth-grade game, you would have a good reason to put in a complaint about the groundsmen. To have it happen in a World Cup was inexcusable.

The umpires, Dave Orchard and Peter Willy, weren't overly keen to play. The Dutch coach didn't want to play, but the captain, Roland Levebvre, and his team weren't going to be denied the chance to have a shot at the world champions. Levebvre called for a vote of their entire squad of 15, plus the coach. When he asked who wanted to play, 15 hands went up. Only the coach demurred.

'We're gunna play,' Levebvre said, and apparently the coach stormed off and wouldn't talk to them.

Helicopters were brought in to dry the wicket, and we all sat around and waited until the pitch was playable.

I had the match off because John Buchanan was keen for me to have a rest. I really enjoyed watching the cricket, but also still helping where I could. I realise that that sort of break is going to be crucial in maintaining my intensity for the remainder of my career.

Jimmy Maher took over the gloves and was outstanding. He had put a lot of effort into the wicket-keeping gig since he'd first had a go at it back home during the previous summer. He's been calling me 'Number Two' ever since. He's a funny, funny man. And he'll be an increasingly important player, I think, in both forms of the game in that position as an extra batsman and wicket keeper.

A reliable back-up. Jimmy Maher trained extremely hard to fulfil the second keeping position. In fact, he eventually called me 'Number 2'.

Jimmy opened in my place and made a handy 26. Marto took Punter's spot at first drop to give him some time in the middle and he made a solid 67 off 76. Then Darren Lehmann came in. He'd made his comeback from suspension against India, but hadn't got a bat there, so the 49 minutes he spent in the middle for his 29 were also pretty handy practice time. Because of the accident with the covers, we only had 36 overs to play, so Bevo, making his comeback from injury, didn't get a hit.

The Dutch batsmen all came out prepared to take on our quicks and certainly didn't shy away from the contest. But the wicket remained quite 'sporting' from a bowler's point of view, and our boys managed to secure the win and the four points without too much of a scare.

In the days following Andy Flower's and Henry Olonga's black armband protest, the ICC had decided not to charge them with an offence under the Code of Conduct. They did, however, request that the pair stop wearing the armbands, saying that cricket shouldn't be used as a 'platform on which to advance political agendas'. Fair enough.

The day before we played The Netherlands, Zimbabwe had played India and everyone was keenly waiting to see what they would do. Olonga had been dropped from the side, but they couldn't drop Flower. He came out wearing a black wristband. I thought that was very clever of him. Surely they couldn't ban him from doing that and he was still making his point. A day or two after that, it emerged that Henry Olonga had been suspended by his club side, apparently for his stand. It seemed that the Zimbabwe government had something to do with that. I found it to be an absolute joke that the ICC — the game's governing body — could rule that there was no case to answer, and yet a club side that is way down the family tree could come out and make a contrary decision.

Having said that, it was surprising that as our game against Zimbabwe neared, the discussion on the topic among the team died away to almost nothing. We had made our decision to play there and the guys were reconciled with that. Since the tournament had got going, the political issues had been pushed aside somewhat. Our focus switched to just going up there, winning a game of cricket and getting out.

I don't think that detracted from the issues at hand, and I'm sure that many of us were still thinking about them. I certainly was. I expected it to be an emotional time for all of us when we saw food queues and petrol queues, or perhaps even violence. And while we were united in our decision to go, I still had an anxious feeling, like a knot in my stomach.

Chapter Fourteen

ZIMBABWE

The flight up to Bulawayo was pretty light-hearted and jovial, but as we got closer, everybody became a lot quieter. We spread out through the 150-seat charter flight so we all had a row to ourselves. I didn't talk to anybody.

I felt lousy. My mind was racing with all the issues going back two or three months. The moral issues, the safety issues. *Are we supporting the regime?* I suppose I was hoping that I wasn't letting down the people of Zimbabwe.

I get pretty emotional about this sort of thing and I tried to put a lot of thought into it. I was scribbling in my diary, trying to clarify my opinions. I wrote: 'I want to remain true to the belief that playing cricket here has nothing to do with supporting the regime.'

The night before the flight, I'd received a letter addressed to me in our Johannesburg hotel. The return address was, 'Your Cape Town girl'.

I had no idea who it was from. I opened it to find a handwritten letter accusing me of stabbing the people of Zimbabwe in the back. The letter said that Mugabe was a two-faced backstabber and that, by going to Zimbabwe, I was one with him. 'Next time I see your face or picture I'm gunna spit on it ...'

It was a letter of such out-and-out hatred for what we were about to do that it really got me thinking again about the whole thing. All these thoughts were eddying through my mind as we landed.

There was a big military helicopter parked at the front of the plane. I'm told it had escorted us in. The security looked pretty light on, though, even compared to what we'd had in Jo'burg. I suspect there was more that we couldn't see.

I saw a lot of people on the tarmac and I suddenly felt very vulnerable to a set-up by a government figure or some government newspaper. There wasn't a big chance that Mugabe would turn up, but we'd heard on the way to the airport that one of his close allies, the sports minister, was going to be here.

What happens if I shake some smiling bloke's hand in the welcoming committee, a flash goes off and tomorrow I'm in all the papers shown talking with a government minister?

Our personal security fears may have been put to rest, but there was a definite air of expectancy about what the next 24 hours held for us. We would be safe, but would our fans be? What would happen to anyone who demonstrated at the ground? Would they take them away and flog them, as was reported to have happened in several earlier peaceful protests in Zimbabwe? The whole team was genuinely concerned about that possibility.

I wrote in my diary: 'I hope that in life there is still a reasonable amount of common sense and understanding of the predicament that we are in and that people can make judgment on that. Twenty-minute delay on arrival.'

We sat on the tarmac — the squad, three or four ACB board members, the whole press contingent — and we waited. It got hot and stuffy in the plane. In light of all our fears, the long delay could have been traumatic, but the plane's captain was really good. He came on the intercom and explained that a commercial flight had landed at the same time as us and they were letting those passengers clear customs before we got off. All our documents would be processed on board, so we would be able to walk straight on to our bus.

The immigration officers came aboard. 'Have you heard about Canada?' they asked.

When we had boarded the plane, the Canadian team had just started their innings against the West Indies.

'I'm not sure what they are now,' the official said, 'but I know they were 110 for none off not very many overs.'

What?

'Somebody called Davison's on 70 off 45 balls.'

All the boys had a good reaction to that. Just about everyone knew Davo. I'd played grade cricket with him in Sydney for Gordon in the early 1990s, and he'd played state cricket for Victoria and South Australia before he used the fact that he was born in Canada to get a berth at the World Cup. His form lightened the mood a bit.

Bob Merriman, the chairman of the ACB, had always said, 'I'm going to be the first off the plane in Zimbabwe. I'm going to make sure I'm there to front the whole thing.' We've had other difficult tours with various issues floating around where board members have taken that type of leadership, but I don't think it's ever been as appreciated by the players as it was this time. It helped to create a united feeling. We knew that if we were going to cop anything from the public or press, the ACB were right beside us and would defend our reasons for going. James Sutherland and the ACB's commercial operations manager, Michael Brown, were also in the ACB contingent.

There was a welcoming party with native dancers and drums and a lot of press. We got on our bus and were soon driving along a wide boulevard.

As soon as Jimmy Maher saw the road's name, 'Robert Mugabe Way', he quipped: 'That'd have to be a one-way street, wouldn't it?' It was timely humour from a guy who often reads the mindset of the side well and knows when, and when not, to inject his personality.

A nervous few steps. Arriving to a traditional welcome in Bulawayo, Zimbabwe.

Bulawayo was like a big country town. It's meant to have about 700,000 people, but they must have all been asleep. It was warm and slow, with huge tropical trees all around. There was more scrub than houses. They'd had two or three days' torrential rain and it had been feared the game would be washed out, but it was fine now — a beautiful day, yet somehow dusty at the same time. We didn't see any food queues, but the petrol queues went on forever as people sat waiting for tankers to arrive and fill the station's tanks.

We got to the hotel, where security was pretty high. There were metal detectors everywhere. During lunch, the highlights from the Canada–West Indies game were just coming on the television. Davo had scored the fastest century in World Cup history, off 67 balls. He's a terrific character, so all the boys were really stoked for him. It was a stunning piece of hitting. Amazing aggression. He'd always had the potential to bat like that.

Ian Chappell once said about me that I'm never out of form. I tend either to get runs or to get out before I lose form; I don't hang around, nicking and nudging. I think that's a good assessment of John Davison, too. He's got the potential to play like that in any level of cricket, and hopefully he can use the belief he's got in his own ability now to keep doing it. His bowling for Canada was also outstanding.

That night we had dinner at the home of Darren Maughan, our head of security. He lives just on the edge of Bulawayo in a beautiful house set in large grounds. He put on a big *braai* (barbecue) for us. He'd invited a few friends of his along, too. They were farmers who had all been affected by various groups coming on to their land and trying to claim it. One guy said that as often as once a week somebody would threaten to kill him if he didn't give up something or other. 'We just try to break the issues down and negotiate,' he said, 'but not a day goes by where we're not under some sort of threat.'

It was interesting to sit and talk to them. Amazingly, at the end of each story, they seemed to say, 'But that's life, and we've just got to get on with it.' I expected them to say something like, 'We've gotta get outta here', or be totally belligerent. But they seemed resigned to the fact that this is their life and that they would get through it. Then, they would happily change the conversation back to the cricket or how we were going, and I couldn't help thinking how insignificant our game was compared to their life-and-death struggles.

They all said they wanted the game to take place. They wanted a diversion, a dash of normality in their hard lives. Hearing that made us feel a hell of a lot better about what we were going to do the next day.

We fielded first and for those first 50 overs I found it hard to focus on the game. I was looking to see what the atmosphere in the ground was like. I tried to spot protesters or any outbreaks of violence, but it was quite the opposite. There was a really happy feel to the whole game. The small crowd — of all colours — really got into it. There were some blocks of empty seats and we heard later that the opposition party bought more than 500 tickets

Fortunately, there were no violent protests during our trip to Zimbabwe. Local religious groups spread a peaceful message.

and then didn't turn up. That was their form of protest. In a crowd of 5,000, it was a fair whack.

There were a lot of Aussies who had made the trip, so it was terrific to see them. Some of the crowd scenes were amazing. Australians and Zimbabweans joined together in a giant dancing human chain. I know that a lot of people would say that's an unrealistic image of what life is like in Zimbabwe, but we all understood that people weren't dancing through the streets in conga lines every day. Where in the world are they doing that? It was just a good day out, and I began to feel we'd done the right thing for these people.

We took a wicket early and Andy Flower came out to bat in the fourth over. The reception he got was amazing. There was so much respect for him. The first thing I noticed was he didn't have his black wristband on; he had on a white one instead. He'd come under a bit of heat from the ICC even for just wearing the wristband. He later said that the white one was a symbol of hope for peace and harmony.

Even with all the politics swirling around him, he came in and played beautifully. He hit Dizzy for a few great cover drives and played like the class player he is. *Geez, I wouldn't mind stopping the game and asking him a few questions about what he's thinking; what his prospects in the country are now.*

It seemed that every one of the 5,000 people there adored everything he did. Every single he took got a cheer. Zimbabwe were in a bit of trouble early, but Andy and his brother Grant put together a good partnership. Then, when he reached 50, the crowd went wild. He took his helmet off and signalled quite passionately to all the various sections of the crowd. He held up the Zimbabwe emblem on his helmet, leaving no one in any doubt about just how much his country and its people meant to him. It was pretty emotional stuff. The determined expression on his face made it obvious that he was acknowledging a lot more than just a half-century against Australia. And the crowd, particularly the local supporters, were responding to their hero.

Nevertheless, he looked like he was going to divert some of that emotion to making a big score. That's the other thing — I hadn't really stopped to think about the actual match because of all the other issues surrounding it, but it was a really good game of cricket.

The Flower brothers put on 84, and while they were there it appeared that Zimbabwe would reach 250 comfortably. Then they had a bit of a mix-up. McGrath threw the ball to me and I turned and threw the stumps down at the bowler's end to run out Grant for 37.

We still had to contend with Andy, who's got to be one of the best players of spin in the world, with his freakish reverse sweep. He has scored double hundreds and hundreds against India on the sub-continent.

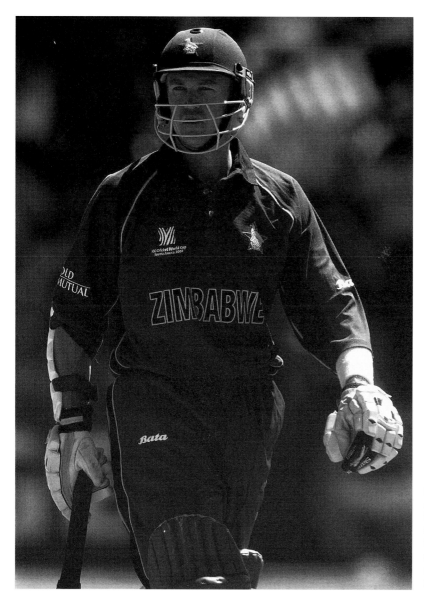

A courageous man. Andy Flower, after being told by authorities not to wear a black armband, dons a white wristband to signify peace.

The night before, in the team meeting, the boys were talking about where to bowl to him because he's a great player who adapts to any situation. Hoggie, in his typical country drawl, said that he'd knock him over with a flipper and everyone sort of ignored that and moved on to the next plan.

But with Andy well set on 62 off 90 balls, Hoggie ran in and bowled a perfect flipper. It was beautifully disguised and had good pace out of the hand. It was short, so Andy went back to cut it, but it shot through, flicked his pad and took his off stump. It was one of the balls of the tournament.

Despite his greatness as a person, from a cricket point of view we were thrilled to have gotten rid of him. The crowd clapped him every step of the way off.

Hoggie bowled a beautiful little spell and took two more wickets in the 37th over. We had them on the ropes at 6–142.

Then Andy Blignaut came in. He'd just returned from taking a year off cricket to pursue a modelling career. It obviously hadn't hurt his eye, because he put on an amazing display of power hitting. All the bowlers had a go at him and they all suffered equally. He hammered 54 off 28 balls before Binga got him caught and bowled. As a result, Zimbabwe got to 9–246 off their 50 overs — a score that was going to be pretty tricky on the slowish wicket.

It was the sort of deck where the new ball came on pretty well, but once it lost its shine and hardness it was going to slow up. So, we wanted to get the run rate up to a reasonable level early. Matt and I got off to a pretty good start. We were 89 when he got out, first ball of the 15th over.

Nothing stands out about my innings except the disappointing way I got out. Dougie Marillier, an off-spinner, was coming over the wicket, aiming at my legs and giving me no room, with his field stacked on the leg side. All I was getting was singles. I don't like to tamper with where I stand on the batting crease. I take block on middle stump and that's where I've always felt comfortable. I'd tried varying it a little to Wasim Akram without success, but for some reason I thought about what Darren Lehmann does if a bowler's targeting his pads. He bats way outside leg, inviting them to bowl at the stumps, and backs himself to hit it through the offside where they haven't got many fielders. *I'll have a crack at that.* For the four or five balls that I faced outside leg stump, I felt so uncomfortable with my stumps being exposed that I ended up doing nothing. So, I moved back to the middle. *Just clear your head and do what you've always done.* Next ball he bowled a rank long hop. Maybe my mind was buzzing a bit too much about too many other things, because I hit it straight down the fielder's throat. Richie Benaud called it a mental aberration, and maybe that's what it was. It was certainly a disappointing end to an innings of 61 off 65 balls and I felt I'd opened the door for the Zimbabweans to get back into the match.

Ricky contributed 38 before he was caught and bowled.

The required run rate drifted up towards a run a ball and it started to look like an upset was on the cards, but then Marto and Boof put together a terrific partnership under pressure, just ticking it over for a while until the boundaries started to come. They guided it home brilliantly with 15 balls to spare, five wickets in hand. It might have looked like a comfortable win, but the scorecard wasn't indicative of the stress they had us under for a long time. It was a solid workout for us, which was quite crucial given the pressure of the Pakistan match and the way we beat them in the end, and then thumping India. The Netherlands hadn't been a tough opponent, so this was very important in applying sustained pressure. We were all tested a little bit and it was good to be reminded that we couldn't slacken off for a moment.

Tony Greig grabbed Andy Flower and me after the game for an interview that went out on the PA. He asked me how the day was and I replied: 'We really, really enjoyed it … And to the people of Zimbabwe — thanks for your hospitality. It's been great. Albeit too quick. But please know that we're all aware of the hard times and we thank you for giving us the opportunity to play today. We really appreciate it.'

The Zimbabweans came into our change room and I made sure I spoke to Andy. I told him how much I respected what he'd done and asked how long he'd planned to make the statement. He said it had been brewing since they were in England — in 2000, I think — when Mugabe's new policies began and the trouble started on the farms with the reclaiming of land. A couple of their players' families were directly affected. 'From that point on, really, we had talked about trying to find an opportunity to make a statement about it, but it was hard to find a way to do it in a manner that would have an effect and was also half sensible so that we weren't going to get in dire trouble.' He said that just a few weeks before he did it, he went to Henry Olonga and asked his opinion. He thought that Henry would say it was a bad idea, because of the trouble it would cause. He was amazed when Henry said, 'Yep, I'm all for it. I want to do it.' They considered trying to take it to the whole team, but then they thought, 'No, we don't want it to become a race thing.' Because most of the team members were white, it might be seen as a white team making a stand against a black leader.

'There comes a time,' he told me, 'when you've just got to say, "Enough's enough!" and make a stand.'

'Weren't you afraid?' I asked.

'Yes, very much. I had a full-time security guard outside my home in Harare. Twenty-four hours a day. But at least I can take some solace from the fact that once the World Cup's over, I'm going. My whole family is going to England. I'm going to play for Essex and then South Australia, so we'll be away for many years now. We'll keep the house in Harare, so we can come back. We're all right, but I'm worried about Henry. I'm really fearful for what's going to happen to him. He hasn't got the money to leave.'

Olonga didn't play against us. The Zimbabwean selectors said he was dropped on form and it had nothing to do with the politics, but, interestingly, Andy said that the selectors and administrators wanted him — the best Zimbabwean cricketer in history — out for our match, too. They cited disciplinary reasons. But five or six of his team-mates said, 'If that happens, we're not playing.' How ironic would that have been if we'd lobbed up to Zimbabwe and they'd forfeited on us? The selectors buckled on Andy, but Olonga was told he wasn't to go on the ground that day, not even as 12th man. He was confined to the change rooms.

Henry was always more of a fringe player, in and out of the team for years, so I suppose that's why it worked out the way it did.

A few of us asked Andy, 'Why doesn't the whole team just make a massive stand?' and 'Why hasn't anyone done it before?' He was just like the farmers back at the *braai*. 'It's not in our nature to stand up against things,' he said. He talked about how the common Zimbabwean isn't an aggressive man by nature. 'He finds it hard to really speak out and protest against anything.'

Andy looked like a man under a great strain. Standing there talking to him, I was surprised at how engulfed by it all I'd become. Not for one moment do I claim any extraordinary knowledge of the politics or history of any foreign country. Far from it, but I did have the feeling while talking to Andy that I was in the presence of someone who was leaving a mark on his world. It was a unique feeling, like I was talking to a great leader from history.

I told him how his actions were inspirational to me and, I'm sure, to many other people. I was disappointed that I didn't get a chance to talk to Henry. I would have loved to have spoken to him to get his feelings on it all.

As we were heading for our bus, an elderly woman approached me in tears. 'Thank you, thank you so much for coming,' she said. It was unbelievable just how emotional she was. 'Thanks for acknowledging our situation, but thank you so much for coming. You've done so much for us.'

On the bus on the way to the airport, I wrote in my diary: 'It was an amazing 24 hours in my career; maybe even in my life for that matter.'

We boarded our plane and flew out. It was over just like that. It had been such a roller-coaster ride from right back at the end of the VB series when I definitely wanted to make a moral stand, through all the heated and tortuous debate, to where I was now, thrilled that I'd had the opportunity to experience this small slice of the world through the prism of World Cup cricket.

James Sutherland, Michael Brown and Bob Merriman were outstanding in the way they handled the whole thing. So, too, was our rep, Tim May, from the Australian Cricketers Association. It was great to have those guys with us all day. The flight back was very entertaining. We sat back in our seats and took a big breath and just went 'Phew!' I think everyone was so relieved that we'd gone there and won, and had done so without incident. There was a real buzz among the team. It didn't turn into a wild party, but the mood on the plane was very buoyant.

I still had a bit of time by myself for quiet reflection. I wrote in my diary: 'I have felt fortunate to have been through the whole process from back when someone first said, "You've got a World Cup match in Zimbabwe; there's going to be problems," right up to the present.'

It was a tough but fulfilling experience. I felt that it had broadened my view of the world and of myself. I learned that you just can't get one point of view and go hard at it. You've got to sit back and be objective and ask yourself questions.

As we began our descent, the PA came on, but instead of the flight attendant doing the full run-down of, 'Please put your tray tables up, bring your seat into an upright position …' it was Jimmy Maher giving the spiel in his Graeme Hughes rugby-league-commentator voice. 'Ladies and gentlemen, as we begin our descent would you please make sure your seat-belts are fastened …' It was absolutely outstanding. I was up the back talking with one of the guys from the ICC and none of the journos or board members back there knew who it was. It was good to be laughing after an intense couple of days. It summed up the mood of the flight.

Chapter Fifteen

RECORDS AND RUGBY PLAYERS

The day after we got back to Potchefstroom from Zimbabwe it was my turn to do the press conference. Punter had a heavy workload, so I tried to help him out where I could. Rotating the press duties was one way I was happy to lend a hand. It just so happened that I jagged a bad day. News had come through that Warnie had been on *A Current Affair* and admitted to taking two diuretic pills — not one, as he had previously stated. The news didn't have any great impact on the team. Without being disrespectful to Shane, we'd left it behind. Still, it was the day's big story, so I thought long and hard about how I wanted to answer the inevitable questions. I wanted to stand by my beliefs and say what I wanted to say, but that certainly didn't include dumping on Shane.

One of the questions was whether Shane's public image would suffer from the new revelation.

'Yeah, of course,' I said. 'I think there's no doubt people don't like being deceived.' I was talking in a very general sense and made it clear that the team as a group didn't feel deceived, or at least that no one had mentioned they felt that way.

I continued: 'I am not saying for one moment that Warnie was intentionally doing that. I don't know the real circumstances surrounding that. I don't know all the fine details, but there could easily be a perception that information had been withheld, and when that does finally come out people can be put off by that and it can [affect] people's judgment.'

To be honest, when the issue first came up and Warnie addressed us as a team, I couldn't remember whether he told us he'd taken one pill or two. Even though I knew the news about Warnie prior to him breaking it to the team, I was still a bit stunned in that meeting. I think we were all trying to come to terms with the big picture and weren't paying much attention to the details. When the second pill theory had first been published a few days before Shane's appearance on *A Current Affair*, we'd asked each other, 'Can you remember what he said in the meeting?' No one seemed to have a clear recollection of it, because it was such an emotional meeting. Warnie was so upset, we were just feeling for him. The way our team reacts when we see a team-mate in a tough situation is to think, 'How can I help? What can I do? What input can I have?'

I explained this at the press conference and said: 'There's only one guy who knows what the truth is and he's got to live with that … I'm not going to lose sleep over it. I'm not going to toss and turn and think, "What else is there?" It's his prerogative to work out what he wants to say. He's got to live with it, whether it's being revealed or not.'

I did say that I had no doubt Shane had never taken a performance-enhancing drug, 'and I'll stand by that. I'll support him as a friend and team-mate.' I also stated very clearly to all the members of the press who were present that I wasn't speaking for the team and that they all had their own views on the subject.

The team seemed to have the attitude that we weren't going to close ranks behind Shane and try to bluff the world that there hadn't been mistakes made and there weren't serious issues to be faced. At the same time, however, we wanted Shane to know that, on a personal level, we were right behind him. Pigeon had already written a column in which he said that Shane had 'brought this on himself'. And in the press conference after the Pakistan match, Ricky had said that Shane had been either naive or stupid. We weren't trying to whitewash anything. We wanted to give honest, realistic answers without hanging Warnie out to dry. Many of us were continually ringing him, leaving messages and trying to get in touch with him to let him know that he had our support through this difficult time.

Because of the time difference, those afternoon press conferences in South Africa were conducted pretty late in the evening Australian time, so the press had a gentlemen's agreement to embargo the stories until the following day. For the newspapers, that meant the story from Tuesday's press conference wouldn't appear until Thursday's paper.

It was on the morning of our game against Namibia that I saw the coverage given to my comments about Warnie. For the most part, it was pretty fair. All the headlines ran with the 'people don't like being deceived' line, and most of the stories were pretty similar. All except one — by Jon Pierik, who writes for *The Herald-Sun* in Melbourne, *The Daily Telegraph* in Sydney, and other News Limited papers around Australia. His lead was: 'A stunned Adam Gilchrist said yesterday Shane Warne had lost credibility with his team-mates by not telling them he had taken more than one banned diuretic tablet.'

It's no secret that over the last 12 to 18 months many members of the Australian team have been unhappy with some of Jon's articles. It really disappointed me to see his perceptions of my comments at the press conference. Jon interpreted the comments in a totally different way to four other journalists. I was disappointed he didn't approach me after the conference to clarify what I'd said. Especially as it was so controversial.

The moment I saw the headline 'Shane loses face with team-mates', I knew it was going to create a lot of concern for Warnie. I tried ringing him that day, but I couldn't get through. I left a message.

Our team manager relayed a message to me that Warnie was pretty disappointed and upset. I still couldn't get hold of him.

At first, I had no regrets about saying what I had said. I thought, 'No, that's the truth. Get on with it.' I was just saying what most people probably felt. A lot of people commented on how open and honest all of us had been, rather than coming out with the bland platitudes we're all taught to spout these days.

But over the following week, as I waited to hear from Shane, I started to have a change of heart. I realised that I should have been more respectful to a team-mate who was going through a very tough time. The more I thought about it, the more I realised I was guilty of not stopping to think what a big issue it was and how my comments might hurt Shane and his family, who were already under a lot of stress. If I had my time over, I wouldn't lie in my answers, but I would be a lot less forthcoming. Shane didn't need me adding fuel to the fire, and for that I began to feel lousy.

The Namibia game was a useful hit-out. Once again we were on our home ground at Potchefstroom. I did very little with the bat, but Bevo was elevated to first drop to give him some time in the middle. It was his first innings in a month, since tearing his groin, so his hour in the middle for 17 runs must have been a good loosener. Haydos top scored with 88 off 73, but just about everyone else got a few. Boof hadn't had much of a hit yet either, but he came in and hit 28 runs off the last over, a World Cup record, which helped us to a tidy 6–301.

The Namibians had it all to do, and they certainly showed their intentions when their opener, Jan-Berri Burger, charged Pigeon first ball. Four. He'd hit 85 against England in their last game, so he was someone to be wary of. Pigeon had him caught at second slip on his fourth ball. Pigeon didn't get a wicket in his next over, but he took one in his third, in his fourth, in his fifth, in his sixth and two in his seventh, to give him figures of 7–15.

Bic had been brought into the team after Dizzy withdrew complaining of heel soreness, so Punter brought him on for the next over. He bowled four dot balls, then took wickets with the last two — finishing with one over, one maiden, two wickets for none. They were all out for 45.

We had a quick chat to the Namibians, before hitting the road for Johannesburg, where we would overnight before heading off to Port Elizabeth, down in the south-east corner of South Africa.

There was no one happier that Pigeon had towelled the Namibians off so quickly than myself and Jimmy Maher. Our wives and children were flying in that day and meeting us in Jo'burg.

In the Australian cricket team, no matter where we are touring, there is no set policy as to when partners or families are permitted to be on tour. However, once a year, the ACB pays for a trip for partners in a two-week designated period during which they cover all the extra costs. So, whether it's internal flights, or breakfast, or any extra accommodation charges in that two-week period, the ACB will pick up the tab. Jimmy's wife Deb and daughter Lily, along with Mel and Harry, were arriving a week prior to that period when almost all the partners would come over.

This whole concept is a major change in the culture of the team. Even as recently as 1989, Allan Border had a rule that he didn't want wives on tour until the Ashes were won. With our ever-increasing travel demands, I don't think you could ask that of a married man these days. But that was a pretty universal mindset back then. The implication was that wives detracted from performance. I believe it's quite the opposite. You let the player and his family work out how he is going to perform best on the tour. And there's no doubt it's a real individual mixture. There are some players in the team who prefer to have a few weeks at the start of a tour just with the team, so that we can get together and get all the momentum going. There are some players who would prefer to have their partners with them the whole time.

It's a difficult life on the road — particularly once children become involved. We are fortunate to stay in nice hotels. We get well catered for and everything is planned for us. Even so, the day-in day-out of packing bags, going to airports, flying and taking bus trips is a huge demand when you have kids with you, and most of that extra work does get foisted on the wives because they know that we've got to be fully focused on the job at hand.

Our next opponents, England, had a no-wives policy throughout the World Cup. I think that was a mistake. I talked to a few of their players — Nick Knight, Steve Harmison and Ronnie Irani — and I detected, without them saying as much, that they were disappointed at the England Cricket Board's approach.

Chapter Sixteen

THEN THERE WERE SIX

The tournament was becoming tense. When Kenya beat Bangladesh, it booked the East African minnows a spot in the Super Six and, short of a miracle, the West Indies would be going home. Carl Hooper announced his resignation as Windies captain. India squared off against Pakistan and were set a hefty 273. India had never successfully chased more than 222 in a World Cup match, but Tendulkar scored a scintillating 98 to help bring his team in with four overs and six wickets to spare. So, Pakistan were in deep trouble and India were shaping as a big threat to us.

The following day, we faced an England team fighting for its survival.

The pretty seaside town of Port Elizabeth had been good to us. A year earlier, we'd played there against South Africa and set a world record in chasing down 326. It had been a perfect batting strip then, but now it looked like it might play a little low and slow.

The psych wars began and Pigeon came out saying he'd go one better than his last game and bag eight wickets against England, albeit a tad tongue in cheek. Ricky declared that we'd be using an at-the-body strategy. Ricky doesn't bother with red herrings.

We were going to try to 'hurry the batsmen up' by bowling an intimidating line and length where they are given no freedom to move their arms. Nick Knight and Marcus Trescothick, especially, were two guys who loved a bit of width to free their arms and swing at the ball. The plan had worked well in Australia, so there was no point keeping it a secret.

While we might have been keen to remind the English of the previous few months, we knew all that had gone out the window. This was a whole new ball game. England were fighting for their life.

We had our own motivations. Mike Young, our fielding coach, gathered us together before we took the field. He knew there was a risk we'd take our foot off the pedal, so with all his American flair, he said: 'This is the first time in this tournament where we've got the chance to send someone home. And it happens to be someone who could give the competition a real shake-up if they start to play well.' That was good motivation. It appealed to our ruthless side.

It didn't particularly work, though, in the first nine overs. Knight and

Trescothick got off to a flyer, racing to 50 at seven runs an over. They flailed away and connected with plenty. Trescothick was hitting the boundary with frightening regularity and he went over it once off Binga. We weren't executing our plan well, and to their credit, they came out prepared to take risks.

It looked like Trescothick had broken his Aussie hoodoo. The Barmy Army had also turned up ready to play, and were going at it in full voice. There was an unbelievable number of English supporters there, but we had a lot of Aussie tour groups as well. Merv Hughes and Allan Border had theirs. And, of course, special mention should be made of Luke Gillian, who we call Lukey Sparrow, from wavingtheflag.com, who had followed us up to Zimbabwe with his backpacker-type tour group. He has seen every game we've played for the best part of a decade. Even though it was a neutral venue, the England-versus-Australia rivalry came on loud and clear.

Dizzy was still suffering from his sore heel, so Bic remained in the team. Punter brought him on to replace Binga for the tenth over. He picked up Nick Knight, 30 (off 33), with his fifth ball, then got Vaughan, two, with the thinnest of edges first ball of his next over. Hussain was walking off five balls later, clean bowled by a ball that shaped away and then cut back in through the gate. As they say, the best way to stop the scoring rate in one-day cricket is to take wickets, and that's exactly what Bic did. The game suddenly had a fresh complexion.

McGrath chipped in with Trescothick's wicket two balls later. Four for 74. Bic got Collingwood soon after. Five for 87.

While we were going great guns, it was becoming obvious that the wicket was becoming slower and more difficult to score on. We knew we didn't want to be chasing much more than 200 to 220.

Flintoff and Stewart put on a good partnership. Like he had in the second VB final, Flintoff seemed to inject some life into the English. He played a very controlled innings and they managed to get England back up towards a strong position as Hoggie and Boof bowled long spells of containment.

After 42 overs, they were 5–177 when Punter brought Bic back on.

He was on fire. Everything he did had a golden glow about it. Flintoff went after him and skied it — straight up and straight down — into my gloves. Bic bowled Stewart in his next over, 7–180, then accounted for Giles in his next.

Craig White managed to scrape them up to 204, but they had only managed 33 runs off the last ten overs, so we went back into the sheds reasonably happy with the way things had gone. Our Mr Fixit bowler had well and truly fixed it, finishing with 7–20. It already looked like a man-of-the-match performance. To see him do so well really lifted the team, in the same way that Andy Symonds' form reversal had done in the Pakistan game.

Our plan was to try and keep wickets in hand. Even if we did let the run rate creep up to a tough ask, on a small ground like Port Elizabeth we knew that we could score at least six or seven an over.

I had all the early strikes and, as ironic as it is, the harder I tried to concentrate on protecting my wicket and not worrying about the runs, the more the runs seemed to follow. I suppose I was also thinking of getting the scoring up to relieve pressure on the middle order.

Caddick, however, bowled very well. He got Haydos caught pulling for one to have us 1–15 in the third.

In his next over, he sent me down a short, wide ball. My natural instinct told me — and will always tell me, regardless of the scenario — that I should have a red-hot crack at it. The situation didn't warrant it. With Haydos just gone, I should have let it go. But I listened to my instinct and all I managed to do in trying to belt it so hard was lose control of the shot and get a big top edge that flew down to Michael Vaughan at third man. He'd had a few fumbles throughout the Ashes series, so as I watched it sail through the air I still had some hope. He fumbled it and gave me an agonising moment of optimism before bringing it under control. I was off for 22 (from 18) and we were 2–33. So much for me helping to get the guys off to a solid start.

I had just plopped myself down in a chair and hadn't even started taking my pads off when I heard an almighty roar go up. It was Marto, LBW, for a duck. A couple of overs after that, Punter was caught down at third man for 18 (off 21). Ricky, similar to me, had scored at a reasonable rate, hitting a couple of fours and a six. The situation probably required us to slow down and take a bit of sting out of their bowling. It was a wicket that wasn't easy to execute horizontal bat shots off because of the variation in bounce — and yet Matt, myself and Ricky were all guilty of trying to play big horizontal shots, looking for maximum runs. We hadn't adhered to the plan, and now we were paying.

Caddick had ripped through and we were reeling at 4–48 in the ninth. I suppose the wicket bore a lot of similarities to one of those second-innings wickets that Caddick is so lethal on. The English really had their tail up, as did the Barmy Army who were winning the war of decibels by a good margin.

But we had Bevan and Lehmann at the crease with Symonds still to come, so we still had hope. Bevo and Boof went about their work in a steady fashion and preserved their wickets like the game plan required. But when Boof was out in the 29th over for 37, it triggered another collapse. Roy and Hoggie fell cheaply, and suddenly we really were staring down the barrel at 7–114 in the 32nd.

It was becoming more and more difficult to score as the wicket deteriorated, but with Bevan at the wicket, you know he's got a cool head and the one thing that wasn't going to worry him was the required run rate creeping up towards six. His philosophy on batting in one-day cricket is that if you've got any wickets in hand, if you can get it down to needing even 7.5 to 8 an over, off five or six overs, you're a genuine chance. What he needed was someone who could stay with him and form a partnership. Brett Lee did that to a certain extent. But then there was a close call on a run-out. The decision went to third umpire and he was given out. I watched the English team's reaction and there was no doubt they felt they had the game wrapped up. Understandably so. No one in our room was openly saying we were gone, but the thought must have crossed everyone's mind. At 8–135, no one was saying anything much.

Nevertheless, that little partnership of 20 had at least kick-started our innings again. The run rate required had continued to increase — from 4.3 when Boof got out, to 5.6 by the time Binga fell nine overs later — but they had bought us some valuable time. And Bic was striding to the crease — the wonder boy from our bowling innings.

No one gave him any advice. At this level, everyone reads the game well and knows what's expected of them. We needed 70 runs off 74 balls with only Pigeon left in the shed with his pads on.

Bic played himself in briefly and then played a few shots. As I've said, if our tail-enders can get through the first ten balls, their natural tendency is towards aggression. Bic started picking up the odd boundary, while Bevo manipulated the ball around the field, picking up twos and ones.

I don't think England necessarily slackened off, but they must have had a terrible feeling as these two settled into a partnership. Slowly, as each over went by and the occasional boundary came up, the mood in our viewing room grew slightly more optimistic. A quiet comment might pass from one player to the next; whispers of 'I think we're a chance here now.' The Barmy Army settled down correspondingly, and the Australians grew louder. The atmosphere thickened and the tension mounted. Every single ball, every single shot, seemed to be the most critical of the match, until it was replaced by the next. One person I was sparing a thought for throughout the partnership was Glenn McGrath, who was sitting quietly out the back with all his gear on. Pigeon's dream in cricket is to walk to the wicket and hit the winning runs for Australia in a tight situation, but I think every time the chance to do that looms up, he wishes it wasn't now.

With two overs remaining, we needed 14 runs to win.

Nasser still had one over left from Caddick, but he chose not to bring him back. Instead, he tossed it to young Anderson. That surprised us a bit — particularly given that Anderson had 0–54 off his first eight, compared to Caddick's 4–35 off nine. I still can't figure out why he did that.

We hoped that we'd be able to get five or six off this one without losing a wicket, so that we'd go into the last with a chance. Bevo was on strike and he took a single off the first ball. Next delivery, Anderson tried a slower ball; it's not the most stupid thing to do on that sort of wicket, but Bic saw it coming, got down and pulled out a slog sweep. The ball sailed out of the ground on to the top of the scoreboard at mid-wicket. There was a lot of screaming and jumping up and down in our room. Suddenly, we needed seven from ten, which is a lot better than 14 from 12. Bic sent the next ball whizzing past Caddick, fielding deep on the boundary, into the fence for four and then picked up a single after that. The game appeared well and truly won.

As Flintoff came in for the last over, we needed two off six. There were a few tense moments, but we got there on the fourth ball of the over.

There were wild celebrations in the viewing room. A lot of hugging and jumping around. It must have really hurt the four non-playing guys from the English team and their coach and management, who were only separated from us by a glass panel.

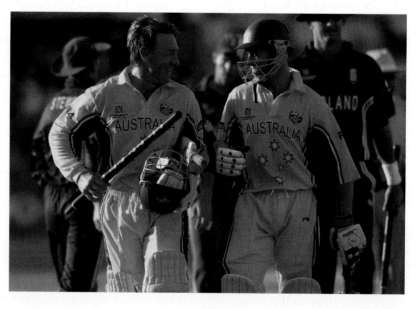

Brilliance times two. Andy Bichel and Michael Bevan grab a souvenir after their heroic fight-back against England in Port Elizabeth.

Bic and Bevo came back in and by the time we got into the change rooms out the back it was just chaos. There was a tremendous feeling of pride in knowing that those guys had dug in at that difficult time, under a lot of pressure to guide us home. For Andy Bichel, surely there could not have been a better day of cricket? Everyone was thrilled to see him announce himself as an all-rounder on the world stage. Within the first few minutes, he wanted to borrow someone's phone so that he could ring his little boy and his wife back in Australia. Heaven knows what the time was there.

Michael Bevan just remained cool and calm. He's pulled off last-gasp heroics for Australia so many times now, he must be struggling to remember all of them.

The English players were staying at the same hotel as us, and I saw them down in the bar afterwards. No doubt they were devastated that it was all over, and that once again they'd let Australia off the hook. They'd had several opportunities through the summer to throw a knockout punch, but they just couldn't quite land it. Why that was, I don't know. Maybe it was a bad decision by the captain on that day not to bowl Caddick in the second-last over. Who knows? There's no reason why Nasser should shoulder all the responsibility. But whatever the reasons were, I felt for those guys at the bar.

There were a lot of wives and partners with us now, so the next day was spent relaxing in Port Elizabeth before we flew up to Johannesburg in the afternoon. One of the first things we saw every time we'd arrive at Jo'burg airport was a giant billboard filled with a picture of the South African captain, Shaun Pollock. It was an advertisement for South African Airways with the caption, 'Polly, we'll get them here — you send them packing.'

That had started to look pretty ironic this day, because South Africa and Sri Lanka were in the middle of a game for their World Cup lives. Moving through arrivals, the whole team drifted over to a TV monitor where the game was on. We were all unusually interested in this one. It was easily the biggest crunch game so far, and all the more interesting for the fact that the hosts were in it. We saw that Sri Lanka had made 9–268 off their 50 and South Africa were in the middle of the chase — about five wickets down and needing close to a run a ball for 25 overs. We moved off to get our luggage under another huge poster with Allan Donald looming out at us and the logo: 'We guarantee some early departures.'

The game was on the bus radio — a crackly thing that kept dropping in and out. We were engrossed as Lance Klusener and Mark Boucher went after the runs. As we checked into our hotel, there was a wide-screen TV down in the foyer. We all gathered around it and watched a couple of balls. It was shaping up as one of the great games. South Africa were six wickets down, needing about eight an over off the last seven. Everyone made a decision to race up to their rooms, dump their gear and meet in the bar to continue watching it on the big screen. My decision not to watch much cricket on TV during this World Cup had to be put on hold. I sensed a big moment about to unfold.

As I went up in the elevator, I thought about what I'd written in my diary the night before about this game: 'Who knows what that result'll be, but as has often been the case with South African sides — they just tense up. And it's not choking but …'

When I got to my room and switched on the TV, I saw Mark Boucher hit a six off Murali. The rain was already falling in Durban where the match was being held. Murali bowled the last ball of the over and Boucher blocked it, just making sure they didn't lose the wicket. The loss of a wicket would have changed the Duckworth-Lewis target and the South Africans had secured the score that they believed would give them victory — 6–229 off 45 overs. The covers were already floating across the pitch.

Neither team celebrated as if they had won, as there was a chance the match could resume if the rain stopped. Slowly, however, it seemed to dawn on everyone, particularly the commentators, that South Africa had in fact only reached the target to tie with Sri Lanka. A tie wasn't a good enough result for them. They needed the maximum four points to go through to the next round. Unless the rain stopped, they were out of the tournament.

I didn't end up going down to the bar, but I certainly monitored the TV in my room as I had a bite to eat with Mel. It was like the South African match against New Zealand, where the cricket gods were up there laughing at the Proteas. As happy as I was to see such a genuine title contender eliminated, I had to feel sorry for Shaun Pollock when the cameras homed in on him as he realised the dreadful mistake he'd made. In the foreground you could see the rain falling, and there he was in the background sitting with his head in his hands. A shattered figure. The dream was over. Not just his dream, but the whole country's.

I don't know who was at fault, but I know that every team in every match, regardless of the weather, gets a printout showing the targets under the Duckworth-Lewis system. On the top in bold print is: 'THESE ARE THE TOTALS YOU NEED FOR A TIE.' So, it's not hard to work out that you need one more run than that. Having said that, if someone had asked me on the day before this, 'Are the Duckworth-Lewis totals for a tie or a win?' to be honest, I probably would have said, 'Win.' We heard a lot of debate in the coming days about whose fault it was and whether it was an acceptable error. I found myself toing and froing. At the end of the day, I think it was a mistake that anyone could have made, but given the importance of the match, it was still unforgivable.

I think from that moment on, every captain had a new degree of wariness about their printout. That mistake wasn't going to happen a second time. There were also complaints that the Duckworth-Lewis totals weren't on the scoreboard. I think that has given the ICC something to work on. There are a lot of grounds around the world that do it. I'd be very surprised if it's not at the next World Cup.

South Africa was in mourning the next day. There was such a huge expectation about the tournament being a showcase of their country and the hope that they would repeat their success at the 1995 Rugby World Cup at home. They had a huge amount of support behind them financially. One must wonder about their World Cup hoodoo. In 1992, their first tournament after readmittance to international cricket, in the first ball of their first game Alan Donald bowled to Geoff Marsh, who got a massive edge to the keeper. Marsh stood his ground and was given not out. Although they went on to win that game, and indeed to make the semi-finals, rain cost them the semi against England where the pre-Duckworth-Lewis system gave them a ridiculous target that saw them requiring 22 runs off one ball. Then, in 1996, they won every game up until the quarter-finals when Brian Lara scored a fantastic 100 that basically eliminated them single-handedly. And, of course, no one needs to be reminded of the drama that unfolded in the famous tied match against us at Edgbaston in 1999. This time around, the whole country was anticipating Australia versus South Africa in a final at Johannesburg, with the chance for them finally to get revenge. That dream was shattered this day against Sri Lanka. From that moment on, every single South African cricket supporter seemed to turn on us and support every team that played against us — which only increased the challenge.

The Super Six was now decided, and it looked nothing like anyone had expected before the tournament. Kenya and Zimbabwe were the bolters, both helped along by boycotts and the weather, but they'd both also played some good cricket. Kenya had beaten Sri Lanka, and Zimbabwe had certainly been competitive against us. A lot of people were critical of the way things panned out, but I don't buy into that. We all started on zero points. We all knew what we had to do to get through to the second round, and some teams managed it better than others. At a big tournament with rain about, there's always going to be a few surprises.

England and New Zealand gave up potential points by forfeiting games. I remember Nasser Hussain saying he didn't regret not going to Zimbabwe because he felt they had made the right stance. If that meant missing the second round of the World Cup, well, so be it. Life goes on. I admired that. Nasser also said there was no guarantee that if they went to Zimbabwe they were going to come home with four points. Zimbabwe showed us what a good team they could be at home.

The rain, however, did have an undue influence. I can look back at the last World Cup and see that if our games against Bangladesh or Scotland had been washed out, we wouldn't have even made the Super Six. But they had reserve days in 1999, and they should have had them here.

Chapter Seventeen

NINETY-NINE

Dizzy's ankle wasn't getting any better. He'd missed the last two games now as a precautionary measure but was still suffering continual discomfort. So, a couple of days after the England game, they sent him off to have a scan.

We were training at Centurion, on the outskirts of Pretoria, the day before the Sri Lankan game when Dizzy started quietly approaching each person. He shook their hand and then moved on to the next. He was saying that he was on a plane home at five o'clock that afternoon. It wasn't a long-term injury, but there was enough damage to require several weeks' rest to ensure that a bone didn't crack in his foot.

It may have been a light-hearted hug from Ian Harvey for the cameras, but we were all saddened by the news that Jason Gillespie's World Cup was over and he was heading home.

His sudden departure came as a huge blow. Aside from the fact that we had now lost two of our frontline bowlers, it was a great loss to the team on a personal level. Jason's a guy you would describe as one of the heartbeats of the team; someone who is constantly involved in so many things on and off the field. He's very aware of his team-mates' emotions and how they're travelling and is quick to sit and talk with someone. He really is a caring guy, if that's possible in the macho world of fast bowlers. He puts the team well and truly before himself, unconditionally. There's no asterisk next to Dizzy's name that says, 'I'll do this, but on these terms.'

Before each series, Dizzy thoroughly analyses our opposition, dividing them into those that get by on natural talent, those who really put in the extra hard work, and the 'consummate professionals' — the one person in every team who is unflustered in times of pressure and who leaves no stone unturned in preparation. It's become a little team joke, identifying the 'consummate' and, at the end of the day, there's no doubt that he is ours. I'm not sure that he knows that, but he leaves nothing to chance in preparing himself.

When Dizzy was selected for his first senior representative game — for the South Australian second XI — he received a letter informing him of the details. The letter included the line: '$80 will be paid per day.' This made Dizzy really nervous because he wasn't employed and had no income. Where was he going to find $80 a day? He didn't realise they were going to pay him, because it seemed natural to him that you'd pay to play this game. And I'm sure that, even now that he's a very well-paid international cricketer, he would still feel the same.

Around this time, a story appeared in the papers with the headline, 'Million-dollar Men'. It was about how Pigeon, Punter and I stood to crack a million dollars a year if we won the World Cup. Whenever this sort of story appears, it unnerves us all. We feel that those sorts of details are private. *How much personal information does the public really need to know?*

The ACB has been very forthcoming in recent years in opening up their books and having a transparent approach to its funds and expenditures, so it's not difficult for someone to sit down and do their maths on our pay packets. I feel that those speculative articles promote the wrong image of what it's actually like. They read as if someone comes along with a briefcase with a million unmarked notes in it and each year we hit the jackpot, but that's certainly not the case. I acknowledge that cricketers today are the best-paid of any era. All the players appreciate that. But there's also a greater level of time and effort and sacrifice that goes into that. As a young man, there's a great deal of risk involved in attempting to commit your life to this game and we all realise the fragility of our status. It can be taken away from us very quickly by way of form slump or injury or the whim of a selector.

There's a memorandum of understanding between the Australian Cricketers Association and the ACB whereby a set amount of money goes to player payments: Test players, one-day players, ACB contracted players, then state players. But if the ACB's revenue exceeds the forecast amount, the players get something like 25 cents in every extra dollar.

So, we benefit from winning tournaments and pulling big crowds through the gate. I think that the current era of players can really feel that they've had a huge part to play in the amount of money that's in the game — along with good administration and marketing. If the team stops winning, however, a lot of the money is going to dry up. Playing attractive cricket doesn't hurt, either. It says something that we can still fill cricket grounds in the fourth and fifth Tests of series that have already been decided.

News came in that Nathan Bracken was replacing Dizzy. Back in the last few games of the VB series, after it was announced that he'd missed a spot in the World Cup squad, he was one of several players that continued to play their hearts out doing all they could to win games for Australia. It was paying off now.

Sri Lanka was our next opponent in the first Super Six game. Even though all the usual stuff about tensions between us and Sri Lanka got trotted out in the press, there wasn't any thought given to that in the team. The most recent entanglement, the Lehmann affair, was long forgotten. I think the press almost feel obliged to wheel these things out for a day, see if they get any nibbles and then move on.

Our focus was very much on the game. Sri Lanka beat Australia in the 1996 World Cup final. A big game. They had beaten us in the Champions Trophy semi-final just a few months prior, and they'd beaten us in a one-day final in Sri Lanka in 1999. They were also the last team to beat us, 13 games and almost two months earlier.

However, as much as the opinion was that the Sri Lankans had the wood on us in big games, those historic defeats were in sub-continental conditions. They weren't particularly relevant here. Centurion, like The Wanderers in Johannesburg, was a bouncy, fast wicket much more like an Australian pitch.

The biggest focus for us was how we were going to play their danger man — Murali. We spoke about him a lot, and various theories filtered around the room when we had our team meeting. But like so many of our meetings, even when we try to get specific, the end result is usually: 'Make sure you have your own game plan worked out. Then execute it.' We can take the field with 11 different plans.

More relevant to me was Chaminda Vaas. He was the tournament's leading wicket taker at this point — a lead he wouldn't lose — so, while all the talk was about Murali, I was quietly thinking that Matt Hayden and I would have to worry about Chaminda first. I knew that if I was still there when Murali or Aravinda de Silva were introduced, I'd be settled enough to hopefully adapt to whatever they delivered.

That's pretty much how it panned out for me. We batted first and Haydos and I took the score to 50 in 51 balls. Murali came on and he got Matt in the 13th over with a little bat-pad catch. But at 1–75, we'd done our job in getting the team off to a solid start. Ricky came in and we made a conscious decision to absorb as many of Murali's overs as we could with zero risk. If it meant scoring at two or three an over, so be it. We could afford to be slow, because the foundation was already there and we knew that with wickets in hand, there were plenty of other bowlers to be attacked later in the innings.

There was a group of Aussie supporters yelling out 'no ball' every time Murali delivered. I didn't like it when the English supporters did it to Brett Lee, and I didn't like it now. It's got to the point where Murali doesn't want to tour Australia any more because of the crowds. That's very sad. I looked over at the Aussie supporters and signalled for them not to do it, which they took notice of and the heckling stopped.

Murali was taken off after a very short spell — three or four overs. Ricky and I took our chances and the runs flowed. The 100 partnership came up in 96 balls. We were achieving what we'd set out to do and it all felt pretty good. When I get up around 80 or 90, I do start to think about getting to the 100. My highest score in a World Cup was just 63 against Bangladesh in 1999, so I was keen on a century. I was on 97 when Fernando bowled a ball that I slashed backward of point in the air to Murali. I was gutted as the ball sped into his hands in slow motion … Dropped. The ball burst through and I picked up a single, so there I was, 98. *How lucky am I?* A couple of overs later, I was still only on 99.

Ricky pushed one out to deep mid-wicket where we'd picked up two runs pretty easily an over or two earlier. There was no confusion, no hesitation from either of us. We ran the first one aggressively and I made up my mind probably halfway through the first run to go for the second. It was a risky run, but the sort that's taken probably 20 times in a one-day international.

Chaminda Vaas was the fieldsman and perhaps I should have factored in his strong arm. But he needed a perfect throw to run me out as he was side on to the stumps, effectively giving him just one stump to aim at. And that's what he delivered. A perfect, direct hit.

The decision went to the third umpire. Sometimes you have a gut feeling and this time mine was that I was in trouble, because so often with a direct hit it looks like the batsman's in, but then the replay shows those last couple of inches take an eternity as the ball screeches in. So it was with me. Run out by an inch for 99 (off 88). It was my first 99 in one-day cricket. I'd got a 98 before, but this one hurt just that little bit more.

As I walked off the field, there was a white marker or a piece of paper on the ground and I swung my bat at it, giving it a smack out of pure frustration. It scurried across the grass. I felt like I wanted to explode. *Cool it. Just walk off as quickly as possible.*

It was a long hike up the steps to the change rooms, and while the great majority of the crowd were supporting Sri Lanka they gave me a warm reception in appreciation of the innings. But I don't remember much of that. I just remember putting my head down and thinking: *Get off before you blow your top and do something silly.*

I walked straight through the viewing area, straight through the bag area where the guys change, put my bat and my helmet down, and walked fully kitted out the back into the showers, where I let out a scream of anger and anguish. Then I screamed again. I didn't want to do it in front of everyone, so that was the way I dealt with it. Maybe I screamed one more time and threw in a few choice words as well. It certainly took longer to cool down than usual, but I soon realised that just two runs earlier I'd been dropped, so it could have happened at any time. And I'd take 99 over a duck any day.

A bit earlier, Ricky played at and missed a delivery off Sanath Jayasuria, and had slipped out of his crease. The wicket keeper, Sangakkara, standing right on the stumps, took the ball and flashed at the bails. All he had to do was knock them off, but his gloves missed. He brought his gloves back for a second swipe, but by that time Ricky was safe. It was a costly mistake. Ricky was about 50 then, but he scored his next 50 off just 30 balls. He hit a few towering sixes off Murali, which launched us along. Marto came in with a great closing overs innings of 52 off 58 and we cruised through to 319.

We were going to be pretty disappointed if we squandered this lead. Our tactics going into their innings were the same as usual — to use the pace and bounce of the wicket to deliver short balls that offered them no width to free their arms.

Well, Binga came firing in and in the first over thundered a delivery into Jayasuriya's arm, which saw him retire hurt. Sanath went for an X-ray, only to find no break in the arm, but a chipped bone in his thumb from a previous match.

Their most lethal batsman was out of the game. Atapattu and Tillakaratne looked solid and took the Sri Lankans into the 40s until Brett picked up Atapattu with a lovely caught and bowled. Jayawardene came in — a guy who ended up scoring about 16 runs from about six World Cup innings. We were out to target his fragile state of mind and so we had lots of close catchers to make sure the bowlers gave him no 'free' hits. Brett got it perfectly right within three balls and had him nicking to me. Pigeon picked up Tillakaratne and Brett trapped Arnold LBW, all in quick succession. They'd lost four wickets for six runs over three overs. It was always going to be difficult for them to threaten from there.

Aravinda de Silva dug in, though, and once he realised the innings was collapsing around him, he hit some terrific shots and took it up to our bowlers. But it always felt like we had it under control. If anything, it just underlined what an outstanding batsman he has been in world cricket. He had announced that he would retire at the end of the tournament, so this was a fine demonstration of his greatness. We were pretty pleased to knock him over for 92 (off 94), but the game was already long since won. We knew that our big challenge against this team would be if we came up against them in the semi-final. Presuming we went through as the top qualifier, we'd be playing at Port Elizabeth, the ground where we'd struggled against England. It was much more like a sub-continental wicket, and if we played Sri Lanka there it was going to be a whole new ball game.

Beating Sri Lanka guaranteed our spot in the semis, but we had to win at least one more to guarantee top spot ahead of India, who were still trundling along undefeated since we'd beaten them in the second game of the tournament.

At that stage, however, it seemed most likely that our semi-final was going to be against Kenya, so we weren't too unhappy about that. To ensure that happened, we had to beat New Zealand in our next game. And if we did that, we'd be helping to put the Kiwis on the plane home. No more incentive was required.

We made a point of celebrating all our wins. It didn't necessarily mean an all-night bar hop, dragging our security guards around with us, but whether it was as a group having a drink in a bar or having a meal together, we made sure we marked each victory. Sometimes it was just an extra hour in the change rooms enjoying the atmosphere. The following day, we'd usually have a free morning before heading to our next destination. Then, after arriving at our new hotel, we'd get the afternoon off and probably the next morning as well, before training the following afternoon. As the tournament went on, it seemed like we got more free time, so it opened up opportunities for the guys to do a few things. Matt Hayden went surfing the day after the Sri Lanka game and the pictures of him flying off the back of a big Jeffreys Bay wave went around the world. Some of the guys visited a game park, or stayed overnight in luxury tents and went on game drives, or did a bit of fishing. Pigeon, Binga and Roy went hunting.

Earlier in the tour, before the Netherlands game, John Buchanan had announced that we had two days free. Some of the guys went up to Sun City, about an hour out of Johannesburg. It's got golf, a casino, tennis courts and game parks. Some others stayed in Johannesburg. A group of us just went to Potchefstroom and played golf and chilled out. But the main thing was, we had plenty of opportunity to get away from the intensity of the World Cup and the touring lifestyle. Buck and the management group saw that as being very important.

Joining in a bit of backyard cricket, South African style. This youngster from Port Elizabeth had plenty of flair.

Buck liked to go for a swim in the mornings. We had been warned that there had been a lot of petty crime in Port Elizabeth and to be careful with our personal belongings when we went to the beach across the road from our hotel. So, Buck was very sensible and didn't take any valuables with him when he went to the beach for a swim. He carefully folded his shorts, T-shirt, sunglasses, joggers and cap in his towel and then went for his swim. When he came back, the whole lot was gone. He'd been totally fleeced. It paints an interesting picture: six-foot-six (198-centimetres) Buck, dripping wet, walking through the hotel foyer in his little Speedos. It taught him a lesson: the next time he went swimming, he took only a hotel towel, his shorts and a T-shirt. When he came back after his swim, they were gone, too. But he's persistent, our Buck. The next time he went to the beach, he had only the Speedos he was wearing. The only thing left to steal was his dignity.

It really showed us that we had to regard security in a whole different way to what we would in Australia. We'd grown used to having our close protection officers with us all the time, especially at night.

Since my first visit to South Africa with the Australian Institute of Sport team in 1992 — then again in 1997, 2002 and now for the World Cup — I've seen a lot more development as the country has reconnected with the modern world. There's been a greater selection of restaurants, bars, and even shopping centres with cinemas or Time Zone-type game parlours. On the surface, the country seems to have come a long way. It's very hard to know how much has changed for the people of the townships, but I remember back in 1992 it seemed that when we drove through or around places like Soweto or Alexandria in Johannesburg, all the houses looked like they were slapped together with pieces of scrap wood or tin. These places had a shanty-town feel to them. Now they are more likely to consist of endless uniform rows of tiny brick cottages. So, the houses have certainly improved, even if the lives lived inside them remain something of a mystery to those of us who are just passing fleetingly by.

Chapter Eighteen

PRUNING THE SILVER FERN

Life on tour without Shane Warne certainly had a different feel to it. I've noticed in the past when he's been injured or away that the attention and focus on the team decreases. This has nothing to do with Shane's behaviour. He slots in as a great team man, but he brings in a lot more interest from outside. It's like touring with the Beatles. He is one of the greatest cricketers of all time. The impact he had on the game in the early 1990s has been unrivalled in this era.

Everything in Shane's life is scrutinised to some extent — whether it's by the media or just by his neighbours. I don't think people can imagine how hard that is. Shane admits that he's brought some of the attention upon himself, but the majority of it comes with his star status. There's no doubt that it has a rub-off effect with the team.

I still hadn't been able to get in touch with him since my press conference more than two weeks earlier. But before each game he'd been sending messages of support to the team via our manager, Steve Bernard, with whom he was in regular contact. It was Steve who told me that Shane was disappointed with my comments.

I had hoped that if he had a problem he would ring me direct so that we could talk it through. I had tried to ring him immediately the headlines appeared. At first, I wasn't backing down from my comments one bit, but then after Mel arrived we talked about it and she pointed out to me the effect that my comments may have had on Shane's family, given the spotlight in which they are forced to live their lives. Even though I had already tried ringing a couple of times, I stepped up my efforts while we were in Port Elizabeth preparing to play New Zealand. I eventually got through to him. I just wanted to explain the situation — how it all came about, what my real comments had been — and to give him a chance to let me know what he was thinking. He certainly did that. There was no arguing and no heated exchange, but he made it clear that he was very disappointed with some of my comments. He said he felt that there were aspects of what I'd said, and indeed of what I'd written in my column in *The Australian*, that were very supportive, and he appreciated that, but he was disappointed with me for saying that people felt deceived by him.

I explained that, unlike the way one journalist had portrayed it, not for a moment had I been saying that he had deceived us or done anything wrong by the team.

He told me what he'd been through in the last fortnight and it sounded dreadfully traumatic. It's often easy to forget that Shane is a normal person like the rest of us. He's just a guy who loves playing cricket and who happens to be extremely good at it. I really tried to look at it from his point of view and I realised that I'd said more than I needed. Maybe I just over-explained my thoughts on the issue, adding some sort of depth to what could be written about him and his family.

I did end up apologising. Not so much for what I'd said, but for not thinking about the potential ramifications of such openness in a press situation. I was extremely sorry that I may have added to the drama in his and his family's life.

The phone call lasted half an hour and we finished it on fine terms.

Having qualified for the semis, we were looking over our shoulder trying to work out who else would be there. India didn't leave much doubt about their qualifications when they demolished Sri Lanka by 183 runs. Tendulkar and Sehwag put on 153 for the first wicket, so it didn't tell us much we didn't already know. Tendulkar was the rock around which everything else was built. He already had an unassailable lead as the competition's highest run scorer. Certainly, Sehwag, Dravid and Ganguly were talented, but we looked at Tendulkar as a player who could win a World Cup single-handed.

I caught a few minutes of him batting, but I didn't want to get bogged down with it. I just wanted to spend as much time as I could with Mel and Harry. I was pretty happy to have four weeks with my little guy and be able to share with Mel the experience of watching him develop while still being involved in some great cricket. I'd already missed a lot of his short life, so there was no way I was going to let watching cricket on TV make me miss more.

In the little bit I saw of the Indians, though, a certain star quality was starting to shine from them. The potency of their fast bowlers was emerging as the surprise of the tournament. You always associate Indian teams with spin, and with opening bowlers who are just there to take the shine off the ball. But here they had three quality quicks — Zaheer Kahn, Ashish Nehra and Javagal Srinath — two of whom were left-armers, which was a unique combination. They were all swinging the ball and they were knocking over everyone in their path. They hadn't lost a game since we beat them. No one had come close.

We, meanwhile, had New Zealand to contend with. They'd knocked us out of the VB series in Australia a year earlier, beating us in three out of four games. It was the series that had prompted the dropping of the Waughs. We knew that the press would really focus on this perception that the Kiwis had the wood on us. It would be the angle of the day, then it would die. So, we didn't pay it much attention. We knew that the circumstances were totally different. We had a very different team and, in fact, we'd won our last two games against them — the last one of the VB series and then when we knocked them out of the ICC Champions Trophy in Colombo.

Having said that, however, we did identify them as one of the very serious title contenders. Like England, we knew that beating them would go a long way towards knocking them out of the tournament. That was all the incentive we needed.

We had a lot of discussion about their main quick, Shane Bond, who had been one of the wreckers in their wins over us. He and Daniel Vettori were the two bowlers we identified as danger men, particularly in the conditions of Port Elizabeth. Nathan Astle, Stephen Fleming and Chris Cairns were all to be feared with the bat.

We got to St George's Park and checked out the wicket. It looked very similar to that of the England match, so we had a fair idea of how it was going to play. We lost the toss, but Fleming sent us in which surprised us a little because we were keen to bat, knowing that the wicket would deteriorate. There was, however, a bit of moisture in the pitch, as though the groundsman had attempted to keep it compact throughout the whole day. That offered a little bit of assistance to the bowlers with the new ball.

The danger man, Bond, certainly came at us hard. He picked up Matty Hayden in the third over with a good delivery that went across him and got an edge. Fleming brought the spinner Vettori on in the fourth over, which looked like a risky bit of captaincy given that the wicket offered something to the quicks. But Fleming is a very astute captain who sums up the conditions well. An innovator. The conditions turned out to suit Vettori perfectly. He bowls quickly for a spinner and the ball just gripped in the moist wicket and really was difficult to play. He tied that end up and built pressure while Bond charged in at the other end.

Bond got me with a fullish ball that swung back in. It was sheer pace that beat me, but the movement he created proved how good his control was. I was plumb LBW for 18 (off 20), and we were already on the back foot at 2–24. He continued to bowl dangerous probing lines, and he picked up Ricky in the ninth. Three for 31. As Ricky was departing, Chris Cairns said a few words to him. I'm not sure what they were. I'm not sure that Punter knew what they were, but Cairns had been on his case, sledging during his whole brief innings. Before the Cup began, Cairns had been quite outspoken in an interview, saying that he felt Ricky's captaincy was untested and potentially fragile; that he hadn't really performed under pressure. I have no idea whether he made these comments in the hope that we would see them, but when they were pointed out to us, Punter just laughed them off.

As the wickets fell, it became harder for us to take Vettori on in that opening 15 overs when the field was in close — another example of Fleming's astute captaincy.

The Kiwis' potent striker. Shane Bond getting the better of me in our Super Six showdown in Port Elizabeth.

Bond was rested after his sixth over, then Lehmann fell to Adams. Bevo and Marto steadied the ship, but as they established the first small partnership of the innings, Fleming reintroduced Bond in the 23rd. He got Marto in his next over. Five for 80. Next ball, Hoggie got an absolute peach — plumb LBW. Six for 80. Ian Harvey survived the hat trick but not much more before his middle stump was skittled in Bond's next over. Seven for 84 in the 27th.

Once more, we were staring down the barrel. It appeared that Fleming had captained a perfect game.

But Ricky had a few ideas, too. Just minutes earlier, he'd come over to me and asked what I thought about promoting Bic up the order above Binga. He thought that Bic was more likely to stabilise the innings in support of Bevo and if he could get through and do that, there might be an opportunity for Binga to come in a little later and play his more natural aggressive game.

I thought it sounded like a great idea and that it really demonstrated Ricky's astute thinking and his ability to adapt to changing conditions.

Bic and Bevo survived Bond's last over. His final spell of four overs had reaped three wickets for three runs, to give him match figures of 6–23. In seeking the knockout punch, Fleming had bowled Bond out early and, while he had us down for the count, he hadn't quite delivered the killer blow.

Here we were, in a disastrous position at Port Elizabeth once again, and once again it was Bevo and Bic who had the job of dragging us off the canvas. It was almost as if they were just carrying on from where they'd left off against England. This time, though, there were 23 overs to survive, compared to 12 against England. They knuckled down and took their time to think through what was required. They were obviously relieved to have seen the last of Bond and then of Vettori.

There were a few lesser bowlers in the Kiwi line-up, and while neither batsman went for the fireworks, they started rebuilding a total. Bevo went through his half-century, the 41st he's made in one-day internationals. Bic then made his maiden international one-day half-century, beating his previous top score from the week before. Soon after, he copped a beamer from Andre Adams that hit him flush on the side of the head and shook him up. It was an ugly incident, but it was evident by the look on Andre's face that it was a mistake. He was quick to see how Bic was and was very, very apologetic. Bic was shaken by it because it was a huge impact, but he was able to get up and carry on.

They put on 97 runs together before Bevo was out with 13 balls remaining. That brought Binga to the crease. We would now see whether Ricky's thinking was going to bear fruit. There were no immediate fireworks, and then Bic got out on the first ball of the last over. Nine for 192 with five balls to go.

That brought Pigeon to the crease. This was Glenn's 25th World Cup match, stretched over three tournaments, and he still had never scored a World Cup run. Having said that, he'd only batted four times, which says something about Australia's consistent batting over that time. With only five balls remaining, there was every chance he'd remain a virgin out there, but instead, from the two balls he faced, he scored three runs. Not a bad strike rate at all. Nine for 196.

Having been 7–84, we were sitting there pretty happy with a score in the mid-190s. It was small, but defendable on a ground like this.

Binga was facing the second-last ball of the innings. It was pitched up and he unleashed an almighty swing that saw the ball disappear over long on and out of the ground. Six. We all jumped to our feet. That got us over the 200 mark and we were still buzzing when the last ball was delivered. Brett wound up again and this time deposited the ball over the cover boundary. Six. We were back on our feet and didn't sit back down until Binga was back in the pavilion.

A score of 208 was such a psychological difference to 196. It was a real shot in the arm for us and must have been a bit of a blow for the Kiwis. You could feel the momentum swing our way.

There was a real vibe in our rooms. We felt like we'd escaped from gaol and collected $200 along the way. Brett had finished with 15 off six balls, proving Ricky's idea to have been a masterstroke.

We took the field fully charged up, ready to take them on. And who should walk out to open the batting, but Daniel Vettori. Fleming is a captain who has always thought outside the square. We were wary of what Vettori could do. He was obviously going to be a pinch hitter who would try to smash our bowlers off their line and length. If he could do that while getting them off to a flyer, we'd be under big pressure.

He got a boundary away pretty early but only lasted nine balls for his ten runs before Pigeon had him slashing an attempted drive/cut shot and he got an edge through to me. That was a big relief, because although he's not a recognised batsman, when a guy has a licence to slog, they can hurt you. It's much better to have him back in the shed and our first wicket under the belt. That wasn't the only positive about getting that wicket. It brought in Nathan Astle. We considered him a danger man, but we wanted to have a shot at him with the new ball. On the last ball of that same over, Pigeon bowled him a beautiful delivery to which he got a big edge to Punter, who took a fantastic catch at second slip. It was a big double whammy. The Kiwis were well and truly on the back foot. Scott Styris was next. He was a bit of an all-rounder who'd occupied a spot in New Zealand's middle order for about 18 months. He had really blossomed in the World Cup, scoring his first one-day 100 against Sri Lanka and was looking to be a threat. He stuck around for a little while, but McGrath picked him up four overs later, so at 3–33 we kept the pressure on. The only worrying factor was that they were scoring at 5.5 an over.

As soon as Chris Cairns arrived at the wicket, Ricky was keen to remind him that it was now his opportunity to perform under pressure. He played a few big shots, hitting the boundary a couple of times and going over it once.

Binga was proving pretty expensive. The Kiwis took him for 31 runs in his first five overs before Punter gave him a break. The fear was that with Fleming still there, if they got through this initial spell without losing any more wickets and with a high run rate, they were going to be able to work the singles and cruise home. Punter brought on Ian Harvey and Andy Bichel.

First ball of a Bichel over, he bowled Cairns a ball that was nothing special. Full pitched, a bit wide. The sort of ball you don't want to give to Chris Cairns too often. He was able to free his arms and take a big swing, but as if Bic needed to demonstrate any more clearly his ownership of this ground he got a thick edge which flew down to Brett Lee at third man. Caught. Four for 66 in the 15th.

Just in case Cairns had forgotten, Ricky helped him out by pointing him in the direction of the dressing room and offering his condolences. We were a bit surprised to see Cairns's reaction. He turned and looked at the umpire with a bewildered expression. He must have forgotten he'd thrown a bit of fuel on the fire himself.

Obviously, Cairns's comments about Ricky's captaincy and his sledging earlier in the day hadn't fallen on deaf ears. But there was nothing out of the ordinary about Ricky's reply. It was just a bit of verbal tit-for-tat that you see on any cricket field at any level.

What it did for us was inspire us to keep the pedal down. Harvs picked up Vincent a few overs later, but we still had Fleming there who was now pushing up towards 50. He'd been having a terrific World Cup and we'd seen his magnificent century to sink South Africa under real pressure. It felt like he was in the middle of the same sort of match winner.

Ricky took a punt and brought Binga back on. We needed a break-through, in much the same way that Fleming had needed one when he'd reintroduced Bond in our innings. Brett came in bowling at absolute express pace. Once again, they took him for a few runs — until the second-last ball of the second over of the spell, when he had Fleming caught behind for 48 (off 70). The Kiwis were 6–102 in the 25th. Brett kept steaming in, shaking them up with an aggressive short length and stirring them with brilliant Yorkers. In his last 15 deliveries, he took five wickets for three runs and suddenly the game was over. He had just routed their bottom order and it was so abrupt as to take us almost by surprise. He'd bowled us to a win.

Everyone was noticeably pumped on the adrenaline of having escaped another close call. In the end, it looked like a flogging. They were all out for 112 in the 31st over. Anyone who saw the game knew it was much closer than the score indicated, but we also knew it sent a statement to the rest of the teams in the competition. No matter what you do to us, we've got depth all the way down our batting and the bowlers to barrel you. We'll always come back.

Chapter Nineteen

PRE-FINAL TUNING

Kenya had sprung a surprise win over Zimbabwe, which ensured that they would finish third in the Super Six. Our hopes of meeting them in the semi-final were dashed. Then India thumped New Zealand, ensuring the Kiwis were headed home and leaving fourth-placed Sri Lanka as our semi-final opponent.

The Sri Lankans would be the first team to have the opportunity to put us on a plane home.

In the meantime, however, we travelled to Durban to play Kenya in the last Super Six game. It was a good opportunity for us to fine tune everything in preparation for the semi.

We had been facing the prospect of playing Kenya twice in a row, but now that that wouldn't be happening there was the potential for a lot of disappointment at losing what was perceived to be the easy route into the final. John Buchanan, however, was quick to knock those thoughts on the head.

The night before we played Kenya, Buck called us in to a team meeting. He had a few notes written large on butcher's paper. Two or three points per page. I whipped out my notebook.

The *last* thing we wanted, he said, was an easy route into the final. Our ultimate goal was to play the perfect game in the World Cup final. And the route to that summit wasn't by winning easy games. It was by climbing the mountain. Playing Sri Lanka at Port Elizabeth was going to be tough, but it would lift us to our ultimate goal.

I think there was a public perception that we were the ones under pressure in the lead-up to the Sri Lanka game. The reasoning was that, because we'd won so many games on the trot — 14 one-day internationals since Sri Lanka whipped us on 9 January, and 15 World Cup games going back to when Pakistan beat us in the third game of the 1999 tournament — we were due a loss. And what a horror time for it to happen, in the knockout stage.

I've got to be honest and say that the thought had crept into my mind as the tournament went on. We'd got ourselves through two very tight situations in Port Elizabeth against England and New Zealand, so there was a natural tendency to start to wonder whether we could keep winning these 50/50 games.

Buck got stuck into that idea. It was a myth, he said, that you had to have a bad game eventually. He asked: 'Is anyone feeling that? And if so, how do we deal with it?' He didn't wait for anyone to reply, thankfully. 'Yes, there's a myth around, but that's what it is — it's a myth. There's no rule that says you have to lose a game.' He stressed that we managed our own destiny. 'We're the ones that are in control of how we play, how we prepare and how we think.'

From the beginning, John had broken the tournament down into segments. The initial two matches, against Pakistan and India, were the launching pad; then we had the rest of our pool matches. Having won the first Super Six match, we were guaranteed a semi-final, so the next two Super Six games became preparation for that semi. We weren't relying on results, we weren't going into every game saying, 'We have to win.' We were just trying to get our minds focused and build our technical skills so that we were playing our best cricket come the semi-final.

Because the competition had been broken down into segments, the Kenya game wasn't going to be our 15th win in a row; it was the second game of a small segment focused on getting us ready for the next segment.

John flipped over his butcher's paper.

'Having played the way we've played in the World Cup,' he said, 'we've earned the right to play in a semi-final without doubt, but that's all the competition owes us at the moment. We've still got to earn the right to play in a final. The work we've done so far owes us nothing more than a chance at a semi-final.'

This touched a chord with me, because when those fears of a bad match started to creep into my head, I was thinking, 'Hang on, it's not fair if we lose this semi-final. We've been the best team by so far it would be unjust if we had one bad day and got booted.' John's talk addressed that feeling perfectly. *This tournament owes us nothing but a semi-final berth.*

There have been many times in the four or five years that Buck has been coach where he's had what I thought were really insightful meetings which have had a huge impact. This was one of them. I sat there and looked around at the team wondering if they were all feeling the same motivation from Buck's messages as I was.

Am I just romancing myself, thinking, 'Wow, this is a key moment in our World Cup campaign?'

At the end of the day, the results prove that even if he wasn't reaching the other guys the way he got to me, he touched them in some way. Everyone's got their own way of perceiving things and of taking key points on board. I might have been the only one taking notes, but Bevo went up and asked for a copy of Buck's notes, so it had obviously struck a chord with him.

Any cricketer who has played enough cricket at a standard that warrants sitting down and planning for a match knows that, at the end of the day, you walk out and the old terms — 'bowl top of off stump', 'tight corridor', 'bat without risk' and 'build partnerships' — are pretty much what the meetings come down to. There's a lot of theories that you can talk about for hour after hour, but it always comes back to the basic formula. Occasionally, though, we'll have a meeting like this one where there's been an inspirational message to keep us going forward, rather than going through the motions.

Because the Kenya game was seen as a rehearsal for the big games ahead, we played a pretty much full-strength side against the erstwhile minnows. But the look on Ricky Ponting's face was priceless when he came back from the toss and told us that the Kenyans were resting their stars, Maurice Odumbe and Thomas Odoyo. It seemed ironic at the time, and gave us all a bit of a giggle, but I suppose it made sense, given that they were due to play India in a semi in five days' time.

Kenya won the toss and elected to bat. They didn't do much in the first couple of overs. Binga was bowling with a lot of pace and it was obvious that the Kenyan top order just weren't familiar with that type of speed. None of them shied away from the responsibility, but Brett was too quick for them. The fourth ball of his second over was a brute of a delivery. It rose up at Otieno, who tried to leave it, but it hit his elbow on the way through, at serious pace. It ricocheted on to his stumps. He jumped around and

A knockout blow and Brett Lee is on his way to a hat trick against Kenya. The first wicket not only bowled Kennedy Otieno Obuya, it also gave him a nasty knock on the elbow.

stumbled and fell to the ground writhing in pain. He had to be assisted from the field with a suspected broken arm. It was a pretty nasty blow and he would've definitely had to retire hurt if it hadn't hit his stumps. (X-rays later showed his arm wasn't broken.)

Brett was pumped up and keen to do a bit of damage. Next ball he bowled a perfect out-swinger to their number three, B.J. Patel, who nicked it. Ricky took the catch down low and Binga was on a hat trick. Ricky brought in four or five close catchers and a packed slips cordon. Binga bowled a fullish ball that David Obuya jammed out, but the sheer pace of the ball squirted it into the pitch and back towards me, clipping a stump on the way through. A single bail dropped off, but that's all you need.

Binga tore away down towards fine leg and gave Pigeon the big high five and maybe even a little cuddle and everyone chased him down there. The way he ran to Pigeon shows the respect all the quicks have for Glenn McGrath. They look up to him and his achievements. And while it's not all compliments and cuddles — there's a good bit of verbal jousting — they're like a band of burly brothers.

Brett's figures for his last 27 deliveries going back to the New Zealand game stood at eight wickets for three runs. It was an amazing sequence of deliveries spread over two games and showed his strike power. The Pakistani quick, Shoaib Akhtar, had come out before the tournament trash talking about how Brett wasn't as good as him because Brett wasn't a match winner. Well, Shoaib was already home. If he had seen our last two matches, he might have had to change his opinion.

At 3–3 in the fourth over, it looked like we were going to knock them over in record time. But Ravi Shah and Steve Tikolo showed some dogged defence and a real defiance of the aggression that was served up to them.

The last time we had played Kenya, during the previous winter, was in Kenya. We'd rested a few players and had Matt Hayden and Damien Martyn batting at ten and 11. In chasing a total just over 200, we were very nearly bowled out. If it hadn't been for an innings of 70-odd from Shane Watson, we could have lost. So we were well aware of what they could do. The fact that they'd made it this far in the World Cup showed they had a lot of ticker. They certainly stood up and took whatever we served up to them after Brett's hat trick. Just surviving the full 50 overs was a feat after that, but they did it and put on 174 runs.

It was our only match of the tournament under lights. In Durban, it is well known to favour the team bowling second, because dew comes in from the ocean and it really livens up the wicket. There was quite a controversy around it because a few crucial games — most notably, England versus India — were played there amid complaints that it was unfair. The history of the ground shows that any score of 230–240 takes a lot of chasing under lights.

But the moisture also meant that the ball was coming on to the bat quite nicely and the Kenyans didn't have the type of bowlers to exploit it, so we started with a lot of aggression. Haydos and I reached 50 in 5.4 overs, so we were travelling all right, but Haydos was dismissed next ball after looking to hit over the infield.

The Kenyans introduced Collins Obuya, their World Cup find. The young leg spinner had bowled them to victory against Sri Lanka and they would have wanted a breakthrough from him here. I decided to put a bit of pressure back on him, given that he was inexperienced. I got him away for a couple of sixes in a row. One hit the roof of a tall stand, and the next went over it. A lot of people have commented to me about the size of those hits because the stand was pretty high, but unless you were there you wouldn't know that the square boundary at Kingsmead is very short, so the hits looked bigger on TV than they actually were.

Then I got out. Caught behind for 67 (off 43). Coming off, I was pleased to have had a bit of fun. I'd hit a few balls in the middle and felt like I was in good shape for the business end of the tournament. We were 2–98 in the 12th over, so once again it looked like the game was going to be over quick-smart.

When I got back in the rooms, Andy Bichel was looking terrible. He'd taken ill with a stomach complaint and was in the process of leaving the ground. Management had told him to go back to the hotel and get some bed rest because we weren't going to be needing his services this evening.

The Kenyans introduced Asif Karim, the 39-year-old stalwart of the team who they'd dragged out of retirement for this tournament. He bowls an innocuous little left arm finger spinner that doesn't seem to turn very much. But in his first over he bowled a great ball to Punter that looked like it would spin away. It skidded and darted back. A bit of an arm ball. Punter was trapped in front. Three for 109. Then Karim had Boof caught behind in his next over, and Hoggie caught-and-bowled three balls later. He used the conditions remarkably well, bowling with accuracy and patience. From 1–98 before I got out, we'd collapsed to 5–117 and we just couldn't get any runs off Karim.

A stunned feeling came over the dressing room. Perhaps even a mild panic, made worse by Bic's absence and by the fact that Marto had suffered a nasty blow to his finger while fielding which would later be assessed as broken. He wasn't in much of a state to bat and had slid down the order. Roy and Harvs were out there now, but after the fifth wicket had fallen Marto padded up and was ready to go in next.

Kenya on a roll. Brad Hogg is dismissed for a duck in our final Super Six match and the Kenyans can smell an upset.

No sooner had Bic arrived at his hotel room than they rang to call him back to the ground. The hotel was only five minutes away so he was back there pretty quickly and ready to do his thing. But Roy and Harvs were digging in. They didn't get many off Karim, but he didn't get them out, either. By the time he finished his eighth over he had figures of 3–2. It really was a pleasant sight to see a guy who has given so much to Kenyan cricket over the years put on a display like that on the world stage.

We were, however, getting a few runs off the other bowlers and as Karim began his ninth over we only needed two to win. Unfortunately for his figures, he went for five runs off the first two balls, giving him match stats of 3–7, with six maidens. I can't imagine there'd be too many better spells than that in the record books. He was picked as the man of the match, which was debatable given that Brett Lee had taken a hat trick and set up the victory, but I don't think anyone was complaining. It was a proud moment for him. He came and asked us all to sign the ball that he'd used.

That night, I was thinking about the upcoming tour of the West Indies. While Steve Waugh had just announced his intention to tour, I was thinking about the natural progression of the Australian captaincy once he was gone. It was pretty obvious that Ricky was going to get the job, given how well he'd done in the one-day role. So, I fronted Punter that night and suggested we recommend him as vice-captain in the West Indies so that he could tie in with Stephen and learn as much from him as possible. Ricky was quick to dismiss the idea. He didn't see any need for it, he said, but I'm sure it was more out of courtesy to me than logic. It wouldn't have been in his nature to say, 'Great idea. I should be in the job. Let's do it.'

Coincidentally, Trevor Hohns rang me the very next day to warn me that the selectors had decided to make the decision for us. Ricky was the new Test vice-captain. Trevor explained that it wasn't because of the job I'd done; it was just that it was the direction they felt they were probably going to go in the future.

I can honestly say that there has never been a time in my life when I coveted the Australian captaincy — or captaincy, for that matter. I've always been happy to play and just get into teams. As a kid, I wanted to play for Australia, but I don't remember having a desire to lead it. Through junior cricket those positions of responsibility came my way, and then I was thrown into the Australian vice-captaincy when Shane Warne was deposed following the mobile phone incident in England. At that time, Ricky was still a bit young. Glenn McGrath and Mark Waugh were certainly candidates, but it fell to me. I was honoured to take on the role — and it was only then that I started to wonder if the captaincy was something I wanted. I was lucky to captain Australia on a few occasions because of injuries to Tugga, but I suppose the passion for the job never did burn as brightly within me as in a few other players.

Those opportunities made me realise that it was a full-on job. It takes a lot of time and effort. It was a big ask when combined with my responsibilities as keeper and batsman, and my life away from the game. I'm not saying a keeper–batsman can't do the job, because I believe that a keeper can be a very good captain. But I just didn't feel I could commit to all that was required to fill the role. It takes so much to give myself totally to the team in my two roles, I think it would have been stretching it to try and be full-time captain as well. My son Harrison had just come into my life, too, and that started to take a lot of my attention away from the game. After thinking it through and discussing it with the people whose opinions I valued, it became apparent around the time the one-day captaincy was given to Punter, a year out from the World Cup, that Ricky was the man for the job. He has an amazing understanding of the game, and his appetite for the responsibilities of captaincy is unquenchable. Darren Lehmann is very similar to Punter in his ability to read a match and predict which direction it should take. Of course, it goes without saying that Tugga is exceptional in this area as well.

I do, however, find the vice-captain's role interesting and enjoyable. But all our senior players are constantly asked for their thoughts, so you don't need a letter next to your name to feel that you can have input on or off the field.

I didn't ask Trevor if I'd be reinstated as vice-captain when Tugga retired, and I wasn't given any guarantees. I wouldn't expect any, because who knows when that transition will take place. Only Steve Waugh knows when he's going to finish up, and by then, there may be a much better, younger candidate to fill the position and learn from Ricky. I was still going to be in the leadership group and that was fine by me.

The next day, Steve Bernard gathered us together in our team room and announced the West Indies squad. It was a potentially testing time for a few of the fringe players. A couple were a bit disappointed, but certainly the grin that appeared on Brad Hogg's face was as wide as the West Australian wheat belt. Everyone was pleased for him and very sincere in their congratulations. His tally of one Test appearance was set to rise.

I was doing my regular reports back to radio station 2UE in Sydney, talking to their morning show host Steve Price, when he informed me that Henry Olonga had fled the Zimbabwean team, fearing for his safety. Henry had learned that some Zimbabwean police had been sent to East London to arrest him immediately after Zimbabwe's last Super Six game. If this was true, one would assume that they were doing it because of Henry's black arm-band protest. It was all very hazy as to what was the truth, but I felt terribly disappointed for him. My mind raced back to my conversation in the change rooms with Andy Flower, one of whose biggest worries had been for Henry's safety after the World Cup. It all seemed to be coming true. It was so sad that this celebration of cricket could have such negative undercurrents.

We waited to see what unfolded. Over the course of the next few days, it became apparent that Henry was hiding in South Africa and that talks were under way to get him to England or Australia.

New South Wales beat Queensland in the Pura Cup final that day. Whenever the national team is together, we always keep a close eye on the domestic competitions. The New South Wales–Queensland rivalry was very strong because we had quite a few players from each state. There were verbal barbs being fired back and forth as the game unfolded and as New South Wales dominated the match and went on to a crushing victory.

The guy that took it hardest was Jimmy Maher, who is Queensland's captain and has had a lot to do with the development of that side over the last few years. Being the captain and such a competitive guy — it doesn't matter whether it's a game of cards or a Shield final — Jimmy wanted to win it and was happy to talk it up. Bevo, Binga and Pigeon gave him heaps.

Meanwhile, there was carnage among the failed World Cup captains. Shaun Pollock was sacked as South African captain the next day, following in the path of Nasser Hussain who'd quit as England's one-day captain a few days earlier.

I felt for those guys. Shaun's sacking was the hottest topic in South Africa for many days to come. I think his ousting was an over-reaction. A captain is only as good as his team. I don't see why, when a team doesn't achieve a certain goal, the captain should be the one that has to take the bullet. There's a great deal more that goes into a team than just a captain's abilities.

X-rays had revealed the break in Damien Martyn's right index finger, so he was ruled out of the semi. He took it very well. He's not a guy who will outwardly display his feelings to a large group. He prefers to talk more with individuals and discuss issues one on one. He rose to the top at a very young age and then sort of fell away just as quickly, so in rebuilding his career and his life to where it was now he probably became quite conscious of not being over-the-top. He plays his cards close to his chest. The other reason for staying upbeat on such things is that you don't want to drag down team morale. He just wanted to stay involved with the team and commit to helping in any way possible. It must be tough to put on the happy face when you are feeling so frustrated, but Marto was terrific support for us as we headed into the next stage of the competition. The diagnosis was that if we got into the final there was a chance that he'd be fit to play, so he desperately wanted us to win this semi.

Chapter Twenty

'GO. WALK.'

We had already survived two big scares at Port Elizabeth. We realised the conditions there were probably going to suit the Sri Lankans because of its likeness to a sub-continental pitch. A lot of people were saying it was going to be a bigger challenge than the final at The Wanderers.

Buck pulled us in for a talk and reiterated what he'd said before the Kenya game: that the tournament owed us nothing more than the right to play in this game. We had to earn the right to play the final.

All the pundits were saying that we had to learn from our two previous escapes at Port Elizabeth, and of course we knew that. The question was, what did we have to learn? The wicket was slow and easy to get out on. All we had to do was not get out. Simple. That was our plan: keep wickets in hand so that we could attack the bowling at the end of the innings. We knew Vaas and Murali were their dangers and we wanted to lighten the impact they could have.

The pitch at Port Elizabeth was going to favour their type of cricket. There was no secret that they were plotting our downfall with spin bowling, and so we were doing all we could in our preparations to take that on. Still, each player had to work out his own technique for nullifying the spin.

Their paceman, Vaas, was again my main focus.

If we lost three or four wickets and exposed ourselves, that's when Murali, Jayasuriya and de Silva could come on and bowl a tight line and length, drying up the scoring knowing that our batsmen couldn't take a risk.

Before taking the field, we got one of our regular talks from our fielding coach, Mike Young. John Buchanan first got Mike in to help with our throwing techniques, although in the last 12 months he's had more of an involvement in the general fielding. He's spent a lot of time with the guys in short, sharp fielding exercises and we were all benefiting from his work. He has brought new ideas to the game from baseball. Obviously, it's different with a glove, but he has challenged us to look at whether we can do things differently: to not always get our bodies behind the ball in a traditional cricket way; to back ourselves, spin and throw. It's riskier, so you've got to have your fundamentals right.

On top of his coaching skills, Mike's a great motivator and assesses individuals well. He played a huge part in this World Cup in keeping the guys focused and upbeat over a long period of time. He knows when to rev up, he knows when to be quiet. He's grabbed guys individually for a talk. Sometimes he does massive rev-up talks to the team that come out of nowhere. He's a typical American, and really entertaining. He knew nothing about cricket before coming into our set-up, but we felt he had so much value to add that we fought long and hard to get him to the World Cup. We had to convince the ACB to fund his trip, which they did in a very reduced manner. The player group actually helped fund the expenses for Youngie's rooms in most of the hotels, such was our keenness to have him with us. His fresh ideas added a lot to our campaign.

There were a lot of Australian supporters in the ground at Port Elizabeth, but there were plenty of Sri Lankans, too. Plus, all the Indian fans were going for Sri Lanka. They didn't want to meet us in the final. And, of course, there were the ABBA supporters — the South Africans who backed Anyone But Bloody Australia.

We won the toss and elected to bat, so I kitted up and was ready to go in, but first there were the national anthems and then some tribal dancers right in front of our change room for pre-game entertainment. I knew I had to go through all these activities, so the best way to stay relaxed and not get too hyped up was to enjoy it and not think about batting. That's when I play my best cricket.

I felt comfortable going into the middle, as I had for the whole tournament. I was repeating my catch words 'Test match, Test match' in my mind, trying to get myself playing more like I would in a five-day game where preserving your wicket for the first ten or 15 balls is the main priority — even if that means letting some balls go that you might want to hit over the fence.

I played and missed the first few from Vaas before I took a leg bye off the fourth. The ball was keeping low, but it seemed like a better wicket than our first two games there. Gunaratne came on for his first over and he wasn't as controlled with his opening few balls as Vaas. I found myself going for them. Suddenly, I had a four and a six under my belt.

Matty Hayden came down at the end of the over. 'Did you pre-plan that?' he asked.

'No, I had no idea.' I was just trying to watch the ball. When things like that happen, it tells me I'm thinking the right things and I've got a clear head. It felt good.

Vaas was bowling tightly, so we had to be wary of him. And Murali was still to come, but you try not to bat against the other bowlers with those things in mind, because if you do, you'll start premeditating shots and going after balls that aren't there. We didn't plan an assault on Gunaratne. He just gave us scoring opportunities.

After we plundered his second over, we had the satisfaction of seeing him taken out of the attack. They used their usual tactic and brought on a spinner — de Silva. I wanted to be careful and wait for the opportunities. I was going well on 22 off 19 balls, seeing it like a football, when he came in for the second ball of his first over. He pitched it up and I went for an aggressive sweep, trying to hit it behind square leg. I got a thick, loud bottom edge. It bounced off my pad and I had no idea where it went.

'Catch it! Catch it!' I heard. I stood and turned to see that Sangakarra had it. I knew I was done. It was so obvious.

Then, to see the umpire shaking his head, meaning 'Not out', gave me the strangest feeling. I don't recall what my exact thoughts were, but somewhere in the back of my mind, all that history from the Ashes series was swirling around. Michael Vaughan, Nasser Hussain and other batsmen, both in my team and against us, who had stood their ground in those 'close catching' incidents were definitely a factor in what happened in the following seconds. I had spent all summer wondering if it was possible to take ownership of these incidents and still be successful. I had wondered what I would do. I was about to find out.

The voice in my head was emphatic. *Go. Walk.* And I did.

It was a really weird sensation to go against the grain of what 99 per cent of cricketers do these days, and what we've been doing for our whole careers. I was annoyed because I felt like I was batting well and had the chance to lay the foundation for a big team score — and it was me taking that away from myself.

Of course, the guys back in the viewing room were a bit stunned at what I'd done. Flabbergasted, really, that I'd do it in a World Cup semi. While I sat there, thinking about it and being asked about it, I kept going back to the fact that, well, at the end of the day, I had been honest with myself. I felt it was time that players made a stand to take back responsibility for the game. I was at ease with that. The more I thought about it, the more settled I became with what I'd done. *You did it for the right reasons.*

That was on a personal level. But what about my commitment to the team? I couldn't entirely keep a lid on the negative thoughts. *If we lose this game, how am I going to feel?*

We were 1–34 in the sixth when I came back into the sheds. But suddenly Ricky had scooped one up from Vaas in the next over and we were

An underestimated man. With so much focus on Sri Lanka's spinners, Chaminda Vaas quietly went about becoming the tournament's highest wicket taker.

2–37 in the seventh. It was the sort of wicket that was difficult to play big shots on. Playing through a ball a bit early encourages it to pop up, and that's how Vaas got Matt Hayden in the twelfth. Three for 51.

The nerves were so intense at that point, my self-doubt was mounting. Even if I'd been bowled middle stump, I still would have been kicking myself for having lost control of the game.

Roy and Boof settled the middle of the innings. They kept Murali wicketless for his ten overs as they ground out a stand of almost 100.

Everyone started to relax and to unwind the knots in our stomachs. It looked like a total of 240 was well within reach. We don't like to set targets for an innings, preferring to see how things pan out, but given our experiences on this ground we knew that would be a winning total.

When Symonds was on 33, Sangakkara should have had him stumped, but he spilt the ball and we had a reprieve. It would prove to be a costly miss.

Boof was bowled by Jayasuriya on the last ball of the 35th over and Bevo was out first ball of Jayasuriya's next. Five for 144. We could see the expression on Bevo's face from the television replays. 'Oh, no!' He couldn't believe it. He came into the rooms pretty pissed off. He's not a guy to carry on, so he just went into the change room out the back and let off some steam before rejoining us to watch the game in silence.

That was when I really started to doubt what I'd done. I was looking around at the guys: *I wonder if they're thinking, 'Jesus, Gilly, what'd you do that for?'* Bevo showed perfectly why you don't walk — because you're likely to cop a rotten decision like his and you don't get to walk in reverse.

Nevertheless, I made a decision during our innings. *If we lose this game, it's not because I walked.*

Hoggie and Harvs went cheaply, but once again, Roy stood firm and Andy Bichel came in to score a quick 19 off 21 to close us out at 7–212.

The way Roy played for his 91 off 118 was so controlled and symbolic of the belief he gained during this World Cup. It was such a mature innings, defending at the right times, seeing off Murali without trying to dominate him, then leaving his assault until the last two overs because we'd lost too many wickets to do it any earlier.

We were still 20 or 30 short of what we would have liked, so we were pretty nervous. When we'd got to 208 against New Zealand on this ground, it had felt like 308 because we'd been seven for 80 before the momentum swung back our way. But this day we didn't have that surge behind us. It was a hard slog all the way and the wicket was better than the one on which we'd played New Zealand.

No one said it, but there was a feeling that 212 wasn't enough. We knew that Jayasuriya could have an impact early with the bat. Would we get him quickly, or would he get away and go at six an over like he did when they inflicted our last defeat on us? It was only going to take one good innings to sink us.

There was a lot of talk in the break. Punter addressed the team and then threw it over to me. I wanted to reiterate John Buchanan's theme. 'Just remember that this tournament owes us nothing more than the chance to earn the right to play in the final.'

I'd like to think the guys carried something of that on to the field. You could see from the way we defended the total that we were taking nothing for granted. We weren't nobbled by the fear of losing. Of course, that fear had entered all our minds, but we weren't going to let it affect us.

I was concerned that my walking might have embarrassed the umpire Rudi Koertzen by going against his call, so when we took the field I made eye contact with him at square leg just before the first ball was bowled. He nodded his head and sort of clapped his hands. That made me feel a bit better.

We expected Jayasuriya to come out with fireworks and to have Atapattu just keeping him company. But the understudy began in commanding style. He hooked Pigeon for four in the first over and played some big drives off Binga.

Brett copped a hiding in his first two overs, but his pace was steadily building — each ball a little faster than the last. Those balls that reached me started thumping into my gloves. I'm not sure about the accuracy of speed guns. There are days when Binga will bowl a ball that almost burns a hole through my hands and I've been certain it's the quickest he's ever produced. I'll look to the scoreboard and it'll say 147 km/h. Other times, a ball will seem slow, yet show up at 158 km/h.

No matter how fast he was going this day, however, the batsmen were using that speed to their advantage in timing several shots to the boundary. The first few overs of an innings can be so crucial and the Sri Lankans were starting to get on top when Atapattu smashed one from Binga in the air to Brad Hogg at cover. It was sizzling, but you would expect Hoggie to swallow it nine times out of ten.

It went to ground.

That sort of thing can establish patterns. Build momentum. I just knew that everyone was thinking: 'If we're going to win, we need those chances taken.'

Next ball, Brett slammed down a lightning bolt that started to shape away, but then hit the seam and straightened. Suddenly, off stump was ripped out. Atapattu wasn't just out, he was out in the most emphatic manner. I'm sure it reverberated through their change room and it certainly pulled our spirits back up.

We went into a huddle to gee ourselves up and as we came back out, I turned to Punter: 'Mate, that ball must've been pretty quick. Did you see the speed?'

'Yeah, it was 160.1,' he said.

To bowl one of the quickest balls ever and to put that accuracy and movement on it, was a beautiful thing to witness.

Pigeon was still the leader of the attack, but he was injured a lot during

Stretching myself in our World Cup Pool A match against England in Port Elizabeth. This photograph appeared in the US edition of *Sports Illustrated* in March 2003.

The weight of a nation was perhaps too heavy for Shaun Pollock and his team, sitting in the Durban rooms after rain washed away South Africa's hopes during the Pool B match against Sri Lanka.

The World Cup final and a fly-by tribute from South African Airways. Though spectacular, the sight provoked an uncomfortable feeling inside me.

Engaging in a polite chat with Sourav Ganguly during the World Cup final, after he appealed for a catch that bounced well in front of him.

An unfortunate incident. After a short verbal clash with Rashid Latif, I felt all I could do was report it to umpire David Shepherd. (*Photo by Phil Hillyard, News Limited*)

The unique feeling of success in a team sport is something I wish everyone could experience. Enjoying our World Cup win on 23 March 2003.

the one-dayers in Australia and now, with Dizzy gone, Binga had to step up. I think he enjoyed that responsibility.

Atapattu's dismissal slowed the Sri Lankans. Pigeon was doing his usual workmanlike performance, pinning them down, building pressure, until Jayasuriya (who was carrying the broken thumb from that previous game) tried to break out. He was caught at square leg. Two for 37 in the ninth.

Pigeon's performance went a bit unnoticed because Binga was in such a brutally fast groove at the other end. But that was probably the most important wicket of the day.

The Aussies in the crowd started singing *Waltzing Matilda*. We were giving them something to sing about, but it was a two-way street. In these little South African grounds, we'd been able to hear what they'd called out all tournament, and we'd fed off their enthusiasm and pride in the face of an otherwise negative crowd.

There was certainly a feeling of desperation from everyone non-Australian wanting to see us get taken down and to see our campaign crumble. The crowd was picking up on every little thing we did, trying to use it against us.

On the flipside, let's face it, a lot of Australians aren't exactly supportive of the teams we play against, either.

Brett's general plan against the Sri Lankans, as it had been for the entire Cup, was to be a bit short and intimidating, to get up into their rib cages. Then, in the tenth over, Ricky sent a message to Boof to pass on to Binga that he wanted him to start coming through what we call the channel — a good length just outside off stump — to try to get the batsman on to the front foot, opening the possibility of a nick.

The very next ball was an absolute peach. I don't know how fast it was, but it really belted into the channel and Tillakaratne got a good edge which flew through to me. They were 3–37 in the tenth. It was extremely exciting to see things being planned and executed so precisely.

Tillakaratne is the sort of guy who could have held us up, blunted our attack and enabled others to score around him. They feed off his experience and his solidity. His exit brought their biggest last hope, Aravinda de Silva, to the middle. With him there, anything could still happen.

Binga kept steaming in, and Ricky picked up a great catch in gully to dismiss Gunawardene. But de Silva had hit a couple of fours and looked pretty solid. It was still only going to take one big innings to swing the game back to the Sri Lankans.

Ricky rested Binga after his sixth over. Since copping the hiding early, he had turned the game around to finish his opening spell with the figures of 3–30. The ball was tossed to Andy Bichel. I suppose we shouldn't have been at all surprised at what happened next, given what had already gone before in this tournament. First ball from Bic, Sangakkara pushed it into space at short mid-wicket and set off for a single. It looked like a good piece of running, but Bic went at the ball like a bullet. He fielded with his left hand, turned 180 degrees as he transferred the ball to his right hand, and threw the stumps down from 15 metres. De Silva was gone. Five for 51 in the 14th.

Everything Andy did at Port Elizabeth turned to gold. They might as well have named the joint after him. By this time in the tournament, he was averaging 117 with the bat there and 4.5 with the ball. This is someone who might have hardly got a game but for injury, and that's very typical of Bic's career. He's always been a guy who's been on the edge, always been part of the squad, yet not quite in the starting team. But whenever an opportunity has come up, he's taken it and done so with good grace and humour.

Now his little flash of brilliance generated so much excitement within the team it was extraordinary. Like Atapattu's stump cartwheeling backwards at 160 km/h, it was a match-winning moment — totally symbolic of the team's ability to produce results when it counted. I'm sure it sent a further shudder through Sri Lanka's change rooms.

They still had Sangakkara, Russel Arnold and Jayawardene to come — three blokes who had all done good things in the past but none of whom had got many runs this tournament. Hoggie got a ball to lift a bit and got a bat-pad from Jawardene which popped neatly into my gloves. Six for 60.

The momentum was all ours and we were able to continue building the pressure. Bic bowled four maidens in a row. After five overs, his figures were 0–1. Yep, 'Andy Bichel Stadium' did have a certain ring to it.

The ABBA crowd had gone awfully silent. The required run rate crept ever upwards, but even so, it was still only about five an over. The frustration started to get to them and Arnold — on three runs off 26 deliveries — lashed out at Hoggie and was caught at deep square leg. Seven for 76 in the 25th.

That brought Chaminda Vaas and Sangakkara together. They started to play a few shots and got the Sri Lankan innings ticking over again. I looked across to the west and saw some really bleak, dark clouds. *That looks like it's heading over here*. My eyes went to the scoreboard and I saw that 25 overs had been bowled. *That's great, we've got a match on our hands, we don't have to come back and start again tomorrow*.

Ricky had the Duckworth-Lewis printout in his pocket and I saw him checking it out. He relayed the message that we were way in front.

Vaas and Sangakkara were going along steadily — four or five an over as their partnership neared 50. All the momentum was with us, but each boundary they found was a significant little milestone as the wind picked up and the first spits started to fall, sparse but hard. Then, all of a sudden, it

Brad Hogg celebrates the wicket of Russel Arnold in the semi-final. Brad, along with the rest of us, could sense a World Cup final approaching.

was a deluge. We ran for it as the groundsmen came the other way with the covers. They were 7–123 off 38.1 overs. The printout in Ricky's pocket told us they needed to be 7–172 to tie.

The minutes went by and the rain never showed the slightest sign of letting up. I was sitting in the viewing area thinking it might have been nicer to be out on the field to win the game and win it 'properly'. I was wondering what the feeling would be like when the umpires came in and called it off. A World Cup semi isn't a match you get to win very often in a career and I feared a big anticlimax. We sat for over an hour in limbo. The televisions mounted high on the walls of the viewing area were showing a replay of the 1999 semi-final, which was one of the greatest games in one-day history. We were all sitting there watching with our heads tilted back when the umpires came in and announced that the match was over.

The boys erupted. It was a white-hot feeling. There was no anticli-mactic let-down. It was pure relief and satisfaction. We'd won and now we were going to a World Cup final. The goal that we'd had in our minds for so long had been achieved.

As the celebrations got under way, I sought out the umpire, Rudi Koertzen, to tell him that I hoped I hadn't put him in an awkward position with my walk. 'No, no,' he insisted. 'Quite the opposite. Congratulations. It took a lot to do what you did and we'd all be better off if there was more of it.' It was something of a relief to have that confirmed for me.

Back in the change rooms we were enjoying the moment and getting ready for a ritual that we perform after every game — the rock-paper-scis-sors tournament. The stakes were high. The loser would be lumbered with the CD player, the 'rock box', until the next game. There have been vari-ous techniques used on different tours to judge who carries it. Sometimes it's the youngest, sometimes the most inexperienced player by number of games, or it might be the person who got the last duck or had the worst bowling figures, but we try to steer away from those sort of result-based deci-sions. The reason it's such a hated job is that when you're on the road for two or three months, you build up a lot of luggage and to have to carry this thing through airports and on to buses isn't something you want to be lum-bered with as well.

This tournament, the rule was that anyone who had been late at any stage of the tour was fined — the money going into a kitty for the end-of-tour party — and they became a candidate for the rock box. Rock-paper-scissors was played on a best-of-three basis, with the loser going into the next round, culminating in a final. The tension that would build up made for some hilarious contests. Those who hated carrying the rock box or who had an extremely competitive streak — guys like Jimmy Maher — made for the best matches. The pool grew larger as the tour went on, and by this time, every player except Damien Martyn was in it. He was joined by the assistant coach, Tim Neilson, the physio Errol Alcott, and our massage therapist, Lucy Frostick, who had all been perfectly punctual.

The tension was mounting as we prepared for that big showdown, when word came through to Steve Bernard from the ACB that we had to make a decision on a homecoming if we won the final. It was a delicate issue, because most of us were only going to get five days at home before we had to fly out to the West Indies. We still had to win the Cup, of course, but they needed to have plans in place.

After the last World Cup, they'd given us tickertape parades in Melbourne and Sydney, and it was quite mind-blowing. But the guys wanted to have as much time with their families as possible. The Board was keen for us to do something, but they left it open for us to decide. I stepped in and said, 'Look, I know we're all tired and will be keen to have time at home, but from the perspective of a guy who's been fortunate to have been through one of these parades, it really was one of the great moments of my sporting life. And one of the great moments of my life to that point.'

I tried to explain how I would never forget sitting on the back of the car being driven through the streets of Melbourne, while 100,000 people with joy written on their faces clapped and cheered us. Kids, 80-year-olds, suits, all so happy and proud. I wanted the guys to think about it before we dismissed the idea. They tossed it around and it was decided that we'd have a civic reception in the mall in the centre of Perth. The ACB and the Australian team's major overseas sponsor, Travelex, were also very aware that war was looming in Iraq, so we didn't want anything too big and brassy.

I think Jock Campbell, our fitness trainer, lost at paper-rock-scissors, so the blokes were pretty pleased about that. He's the giver of pain.

Meanwhile, the rock box was pumping out the music. Binga and Bic are the two who police the music the most. Anyone can put whatever they like on, but how long it stays on is a more open question. With Dizzy gone, the chances of it being heavy metal had subsided somewhat. Matt Hayden and myself are into more mellow stuff or even classical music. Steve Waugh has left a permanent legacy with his John Williamson albums. Andrew Symonds is very much into country. If he had the chance, I'm sure that Slim Dusty would be on all day. But Brett and Bic are the two guys that seem to love a constant run of good music. Their tastes run to AC/DC- and Cold Chisel-type Aussie rock, although Brett might also put on Boyzone or those sort of boy bands. It raises a few comments from the other quick bowlers, suggesting that he's a bit, how would you say it … he's showing his softer side. Occasionally, too, Brett will try to slip on a Six And Out CD — the band that he and his brother Shane are in — which I'm more than happy to listen to because they're pretty good (for cricketers), but he cops an earful from the rest of the team.

Aravinda de Silva came into our rooms. He had earlier asked me to swap a shirt with him, because he was retiring. I got a bit of a thrill that he'd asked me because he's had such a wonderful career. We had a good chat there, and then saw each other again at breakfast in our hotel. It was as if he was trying to soak up every last piece of atmosphere before the curtain came down. It certainly made me think: *Why didn't I talk to him more throughout his career? Why don't we talk to opposition players more?*

You don't want to leave it until it's all over. I know the schedules in this day and age are tough and you're on planes straight after a game, but there are still opportunities to mix and to find out more about these people and their extraordinary lives.

Aravinda said that he wanted to stay involved, but he knew it was time to give it away because he'd had too much time away from his family. I think the fact that Harrison was sitting there with us may have prompted him to touch on his family life, given that he'd missed so much of it over the years.

By breakfast the next morning, I'd done a couple of radio and press interviews about my walk. I was surprised by the degree of interest. I was told it was all over talk-back radio in Australia. People seemed more interested in that than in the game itself. I suppose that everybody expected us to win, but no one had expected a member of this hard-bitten, win-at-all-costs team to give himself out. Man bites dog. That's news.

Sachin Tendulkar, a pure genius who once again dominated bowling attacks throughout the tournament.

People were asking: 'Why that stage? Why a World Cup semi?' and I could only say that I didn't plan it.

'You've set a precedent, you're gunna have to do it for the rest of your career,' they'd say. I could only answer that I hoped I would. And if I set a precedent … well, if that was all I achieved in my career, it wouldn't be a bad career.

It was probably a good thing that I never actually saw any of the quotes from various ex-players who came out saying I'd joined some sort of morality police. It seemed as if it was now a world where doing the right thing was not the right thing. While I heard about these comments, I never heard them from the horses' mouths, so it was easy to ignore them.

The issue was already taking up more time than it should have. George W. Bush declared war on Iraq that next day, 20 March. India flogged Kenya in the second semi and we were being quoted at $1.36 favourites to win the final.

I didn't watch much of the India–Kenya game. I didn't expect there to be any surprises and I was more keen to spend time relaxing with Mel and Harry. It was appropriate, though, that we were playing India in the final. The form showed throughout the tournament that we were the two best teams.

Chapter Twenty-one

THE BULLRING

The war in Iraq didn't seem as big an issue in South Africa as it did in Australia, probably because they weren't as directly involved as we were shaping up to be. Word filtered back from Australia via our media manager, Jonathan Rose, that there was speculation Channel Nine wouldn't show the final live because they would be covering events unfolding in Iraq. That was pretty disappointing. All the inevitable death and destruction of war seemed bad enough, but now it was going to take a little bit of the gloss off what could be our greatest moment. Of course, a World Cup final is insignificant in the bigger picture, but cricket does play an important part in people's leisure and provides some light relief, so a lot of people were going to be upset if it was affected.

For us, the big question hanging over those few days was Damien Martyn's finger. I had a chat to him and it was clear he thought he could play, but he had to wrestle with the fear that he wouldn't be able to commit to all the obligations that a game of cricket entails. He had to be able to field and catch and throw. He didn't want to let the team down. He talked a lot to Ricky about it and was having plenty of physio from Hooter. I later learned he'd also spoken to Ian Healy, who had played with broken fingers for much of his career. Heals's fingers are atrocious now, the worst-looking hands I've ever seen. But every craggy digit is testimony to his courage. I think Heals went a long way to convincing Marto to declare himself available. Heals made him realise that it was psychological, more than physical. It's just accepting that it's going to hurt, and if you can endure that then you're going to be able to do everything that's required.

But he still had to pass the fitness test.

Twenty-four hours before the game there was an optional top-up session — optional, that is, for everyone but Marto. He was put through the mill. The bulk of it was batting in the nets — showing that he could hit the ball hard and wasn't too shy of that delivery rising up at his bottom hand. Then he had fielding drills and all the facets of the game that he was potentially going to face.

Marto knew he would be able to bat — obviously, there was going to be an issue if he was hit on the finger again — but his fears were about fulfilling his duties in the field, so Errol went through a rigorous test there.

He had no splint on the finger, just a protective wrap. His fingers were taped together, so that had an impact on his throw because you'd normally spread your index and middle fingers around the ball to grip it, but he managed okay. He passed the test and that had a really positive effect on the side. Everyone was relieved to know he was going to be able to take his spot.

The Indian team was staying in the same hotel as us in Sandton. We would see them at breakfast or in the lobby, and they looked nervous. They had the weight of the world on their shoulders. Their bowler, Javagal Srinath, looked as if he was literally being crushed under it.

The Indian team get the red carpet treatment from fans as they arrive in Johannesburg for the final.

The hotel was like the home base of the Cup. Just about everybody there had some sort of connection to the tournament, so you couldn't escape that feeling of being at the centre of the universe. There were a lot of Indian supporters hanging around who were just passionate about glimpsing their players, or any players. On the night before the final, we had to go to a conference room in the hotel that was set aside as our team room, next door to the Indians' room.

We came out of the lifts and turned the corner to walk down the corridor and there were hundreds of Indians all crammed into this space. Their response was overwhelming. They were cheering almost as if we were their team. That's the great thing about Indian cricket supporters: they do love cricket and they're quite generous in their offerings of goodwill. Their immense noise was shotgunned down the cordoned-off corridor as we made our way to our room.

Traditionally, the night before a big game was always a team dinner. But during Steve Waugh's time the thinking changed, because we might have gone to a restaurant that didn't have the type of food some players wanted, or some of the guys might just have wanted to be alone. So, we've found it works best to leave everyone to their own devices.

But Ricky wanted to bring us together for a quick meeting. Because training that morning had been optional, many of us hadn't seen each other all day. He just wanted us to touch base, continue the focus and enjoy each other's company.

Once inside, there wasn't much to be said. Everyone had a fair idea by that stage of what the team was to be, but Ricky made the official announcement of the final XI. Ian Harvey and Jimmy Maher had obviously held out hopes of getting a start if Marto's finger was no good. Punter made a special mention of the four guys who had missed out, and thanked them for their input. 'Please know that regardless of the result, you've had a huge impact in this World Cup,' he said. Even Nathan Hauritz, who hadn't played a game, got special praise for the way he handled himself around the team, his willingness always to contribute at training, and to do whatever it took to have us ready and playing. They are little things that can often go unnoticed, but Ricky was quick to compliment them all on that. No one showed any disappointment at missing out and certainly didn't let it overtake the team's focus on the events ahead.

'Has anyone got anything they want to talk about?' asked Ricky. 'Anyone nervous? Anyone scared of the result? Is there anything that anyone wants to say that hasn't been said in preparation for us to try 'n' play our perfect match in the final?'

I put up my hand. I admitted that I was getting nervous even though we'd prepared in every possible way, but I was comforted, I said, by the fact that there was nothing left undone.

That prompted a few similar comments. Ricky said he was getting anxious, too, and was just keen to get into it.

I thought it was good leadership to go through this, so that we all realised we were on the same wavelength. It created a good feeling within the team and I think everyone appreciated it. We knew that from the moment we got on the team bus tomorrow morning, events were going to whirl by and we probably wouldn't have a quiet moment as a team again — perhaps ever again.

As we sat there airing our feelings, we heard a number of roars from the crowd outside, but when an incredible frenzy erupted there was no need to guess who had turned up. Sachin Tendulkar.

We knew that a billion people were barracking against us, but that just reinforced that we had a small band of passionate supporters to whom the game meant just as much.

There was no change in our game plan for the Indians from the one we'd used at Centurion in the pool match. The wicket at The Wanderers stadium suited our intimidating style of bowling. Batting, we again wanted to keep wickets in hand going into the last 15 overs.

There was a lot of hype about the showdown between the master batsman, Tendulkar, and Brett Lee. Binga had left a huge impression on the semi-final. Yet, I wasn't so sure that we could discount the impact of the old pro Glenn McGrath, or even Andy Bichel, given the effect he'd had on the World Cup so far. Nor did I think Tendulkar was the only danger man. Virender Sehwag was getting some runs. Sourav Ganguly had had a good World Cup, although most of his runs were against the lesser teams, so we wanted to test him out.

I raised the point that John Buchanan had made in the meeting before the Kenya game. 'And remember that we've earned the right to get into the final, but we haven't earned the right to call ourselves world champions. This tournament owes us nothing but a place in the final.'

We couldn't afford to get carried away with thinking about the result, what we'd do if we won or the injustice of it all if we lost. 'We've still got a process to go through, and we've still gotta go out there and achieve the result.' There wasn't too much more said in the meeting. Someone brought up the 'myth' that you had to lose one eventually.

It was a special feeling within that huddle. We knew that we were all embarking on something unique. As I looked around knowing that we were sharing the same emotions, I started to choke up. I thought about all the issues, such as Zimbabwe and Warnie and my business with Latif, and how we'd managed to put them all behind us to be here facing the ultimate challenge. We had a special understanding with each other, a bond which I'm sure would be hard to achieve in the normal world.

There were many people who we could have dedicated the game to. Let's go and win it for Dizzy or Warnie or whoever, but we just wanted to win it for ourselves. 'Let's go out and enjoy it. Enjoy the moment — with each other.' We'd worked so hard to get here.

Mel, my manager Stephen Atkinson and I went out to dinner at an Italian restaurant. We left Harry with Mel's younger brother, Phil, who had come over to be our nanny. He'd managed to combine the role superbly with exploring the surf breaks and nightlife of South Africa. He's a terrific guy and very helpful to us, allowing Mel and I to spend time together by ourselves.

Dinner arrived and we were just starting to eat when an Indian supporter who'd spotted me from outside the restaurant came rushing in to get my autograph. I don't normally mind doing it, but all I wanted this night was to sit and unwind. The tension was mounting as the final neared and I really wanted to be left alone with my meal.

'Look, I'll happily do it after dinner, but at the moment I'm just trying to relax,' I told him.

This young guy wouldn't take 'no' for an answer. He didn't appreciate our privacy and tried to force the issue. The manager of the restaurant came over and asked him to leave. The manager offered to move us to a table in the back corner, but I just turned around so that my back was to the window. Apart from that incident, it was a lovely meal spent with two people who have been most important in helping me to get where I am.

I flew Mum and Dad over for the final and they arrived looking bleary-eyed at ten o'clock that night, so we went and caught up with them for about half an hour. It was very important to me to have these most special people around me at this time.

I slept like a baby, although I did wake a bit earlier than usual. I tried to maintain the routines I had kept for the whole tour. Harry woke and I had a bit of a play and a wrestle with him before going down for breakfast. All the guys filtered in and it was just like any other morning as they filed around the buffet. Everyone was keeping a level head.

The bus was leaving at 8 am, so I went back to the room, got my gear and returned to the foyer. That's when the buzz began. The lobby was packed. There were still a lot of Indian supporters, and because everyone in the hotel was there for the cricket, the anticipation was thick in the air. The staff lined up along a walkway and clapped us out to our bus. The cleaning women wore African-style print dresses, so it was quite colourful as they cheered and wished us well. The Indian team came out at the same time, so there was a strong sense of the occasion.

Our partners came on the bus with us because all the roads within kilometres of the ground were going to be closed off. Mel was sitting next to me. We'd left Harry at the hotel with Phil, who was going to give him his morning sleep and then bring him along to be part of it all.

Our police escort fired up their sirens and flashed their lights, adding urgency to the occasion as they cleared a path through the traffic. It was an amazing trip and I loved the fact that our wives and partners were there to share it with us. I got my phone out and rang Shane Watson, the young all-rounder who should've been here with us. He was on his way to a mate's place to watch the game. He seemed pretty thrilled to hear from us. I rang Warnie. I didn't get him, but I left a message: 'We're all thinking of you. You'll never know how much of a significant part you've played in helping us get to this position.'

We rang Dizzy. The Consummate was getting primed up to go to a pub to watch the game with Damien Fleming, a veteran of the previous World Cup final.

When the stadium came into view, everyone went quiet. *What does this day hold in store for us?*

The bus got a mixed reception from the crowd moving towards the ground as they spun around to see the sign on the front of the coach telling them who we were. It sent the Aussies into a frenzy and the Indians into an even bigger one. The Indians would wave and then give us the thumbs-down, which is about as aggressive as Indian cricket fans tend to be and isn't overly offensive.

We pulled into the ground where we said goodbye to the non-team members. I said goodbye to Mel and walked into the change rooms. That's where we clocked on for work. It was a big, open room fringed by lockers. The nerves were hanging there and you could feel everyone was just mad keen to get on with it. We walked down through a little dining room and then up the steps into the viewing area where we could see the sweep of the stadium filling early.

The Indian team was already warming up as we walked on to the pitch. A roar went up and Ricky pulled us together in a huddle. 'Everything's been done and said,' he told us. 'Now, it's time to just embrace what the game is. Enjoy it for what it is. It's a World Cup final. It's a special moment in your lives. Let's just go out there and give ourselves the best chance.'

We went through our stretching and jogging, then went over to look at the wicket. You could see it had spice in it and there was a little bit of cloud cover, so there was a real temptation to bowl first. The core group of senior players — Ricky, myself, Darren Lehmann, Matt Hayden, Damien Martyn, Michael Bevan and Glenn McGrath — stood there throwing opinions around in an open forum.

The problem with bowling first was that it went against our ingrained philosophy of one-day cricket — bat first, get the runs and put the pressure on the opposition.

I told Ricky, like I always do, to go with his gut feeling. He's the man who'll be credited with the great call or brought undone by a bad one.

Ricky went in and changed before coming out for the toss. I was back in the change room when the coin went up ... it came down ... we could see from Ganguly's reaction that he'd won. The message went up on the scoreboard that India had elected to bowl.

'Well, that's the first mistake you've made for the day,' Pigeon commented in the change rooms. It was just light-hearted banter, and it cracked us up. Even though Glenn would have liked to have had first crack at the wicket himself, he saw the need to put a positive spin on it. It's amazing how, when you get put in like that, all of a sudden everyone's saying, 'Oh, there's not much in the wicket. It's flat as a tack. It's gunna be a beauty. Get through the first five overs, we'll be home.'

If they'd batted first, we would've been saying, 'Beautiful! We're gunna tap into the moisture and have it zingin' around everywhere.'

I'm sure that's what the Indians were saying. I wasn't that bothered. I went back to the belief that it didn't matter what you did first, you just had to do it well.

John Buchanan went around and shook everyone's hand. 'Have a good day,' he said, as he has done every match that I've ever seen him coach. Over the years, some players have started to do the same — certainly Roy and Bic do it, as does Jimmy Maher. It must be a Queensland thing. But that morning, everyone went to everyone else and wished them all the best. We were all a little more hyped than usual and the adrenaline was flowing.

I was feeling fairly settled. I was really trying to keep a lid on it. *Don't be over-awed by the situation. Just look forward to it.* I was excited by the fact that Haydos and I were going to go out there and have the chance to set up a successful day. To be ring-masters again. I felt a great bond with him, much the same as I felt going out with Mark Waugh in the big games.

The sky was still grey and it looked like it might rain. But as we walked on to the field for the anthems, the clouds parted and a ray of sunshine broke through.

I was trying to be conscious of relaxing and soaking up the moment. The stadium was full and the noise level was rising. It's a pretty noisy place. When you're playing South Africa there, it's an intimidating ground. They call it the 'Bullring' because of the way the stands crowd in on the field. And there were definitely more Indian supporters crowding in on us than Australians.

The anthems finished and we headed for the players' race where Haydos and I had our bats and gloves. We already had our pads on, so we didn't need to go back up to the rooms. The boys filed by and gave a quick word of support, then Haydos and I walked on to the ground. The crowd had worked itself into something of a frenzy. There was a lot of support for us. A tour group from Australia called the Fanatics were all in yellow.

The wavingtheflag.com group were in their combination of yellow and blue. Allan Border and Merv Hughes both had huge groups all in white. What staggered me was the number of Australian flags there compared to any other game. They were still outnumbered by the sky-blue of the Indian supporters, but it made for an amazing sight. Aside from the spectacle, it gave me a real buzz walking out there.

The huge weight of support behind the Indians brought home to me the pressure they were under. I could see it in their demeanours. A real desperate nervousness. It made me realise how important it was to survive those initial few overs in order to keep them nervous.

Zaheer Khan measured out his run-up and stood there at the top of the corridor. The umpire's arm came down and the Bullring erupted as Khan ran towards me with a determined grimace on his face. I had to block out everything. *Clear your head and watch the ball.*

My world went silent.

Chapter Twenty-two

THE FINAL

Ole! I let it go as it flashes by outside off stump. The roar of the crowd closes back in upon me, filling my helmet with all the senses of the real world. 'No ball,' the umpire is saying. *Well, that's good. We're off the mark.* Suddenly, Khan is down the wicket and in my face saying something I can't make out amid the noise. His body language is that of a man who wants to make a statement. He wants to intimidate me.

Gee, that's interesting … the Indians don't normally carry on like this.

The speed of the ball was quite a shock, too. Quicks usually take a couple of overs to build up, but that ball was solid adrenaline.

Next ball is much the same, only this time I slash my bat in a clean air swing. A nervous shot. *There's a bit of life in the wicket. Be careful. We've gotta really knuckle in here.* The crowd is roaring at this small Indian victory and Zaheer is following through towards me again. I can't make out exactly what he's saying, but this time I can hear the expletives. They always seem to come across louder and clearer than other words.

I hold his gaze while he talks. *Just ignore him. Concentrate on your job.* I turn away.

Next ball gets a thickish outside edge and runs down to third man. It is never in danger of being caught and it gets me off strike. That's a nice release. It's good to get away.

He dishes up another quick one to Haydos, and yet again he follows through with a spray. Matty stands tall, looks him in the eye and gives him some curry back. Unlike me, Haydos is always happy to return these serves purely as an exercise in getting himself hyped up to his desired tempo.

If you're going to give a verbal dose like that, you've got to back it up and I'm wondering how soon it will be before the balls start whizzing by our ears. But Zaheer serves up a half-volley and Haydos creams it. A perfect straight drive that never leaves the ground.

Zaheer is like a yacht whose spinnaker and every piece of available sailcloth is flying in a stiff breeze. Suddenly, someone has hit a button and cut off the wind. He is totally deflated as his once-majestic sails flap listlessly. For the first time, he has nothing to say.

The rest of his over is a disaster. He bowls another no-ball and two

With all the work done … let the celebrations begin. (*Photo by Phil Hillyard, News Limited*)

Sharing the spoils with skipper Ricky Ponting, whom I'm sure will lead Australian cricket well into the future.

Returning to the hotel in Jo'burg with Jimmy Maher, and possibly the Worst Hat award.

Along with the rest of my family, these few people are the most important in my life. It was the crowning moment of the World Cup to have them all with me to share in the achievement.

With Mum, Dad and Mel.

With Harry, only just standing taller than the trophy.

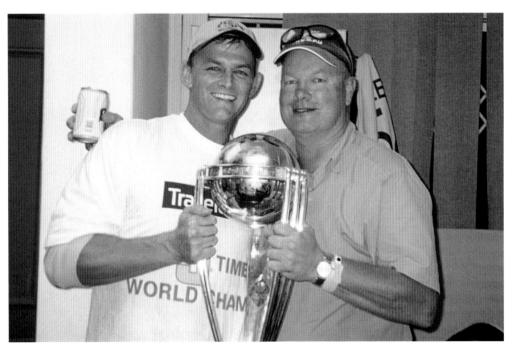

With my manager and great mate, Stephen 'Axe' Atkinson.

The best supporters in the world, Mel and Harry.

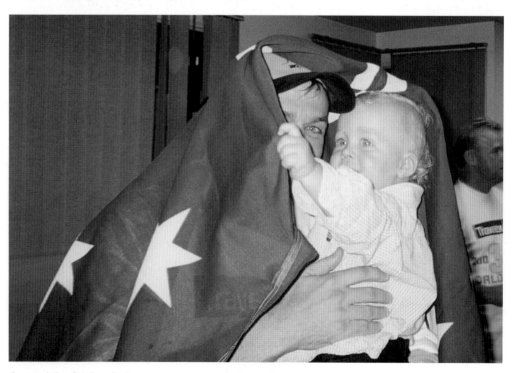

A proud day for Aussies!

wides, one of which evades the keeper and goes for four byes. The over lasts eight or nine minutes. At the end of it, we are cruising on 15 runs while the Indian fleet wallows becalmed somewhere behind.

The significance of that over isn't lost on me. *That really is going to be important to the outcome of this game. Keep the pressure on.* I find it hard to understand how a bowler of such stature can come in and bowl so badly. As he walks down to fine leg, he looks like a beaten soul. He'd come out with so much intent, so much huff 'n' puff, that to see his expectations reversed so boldly has affected his whole team.

Next over, however, Srinath shows what life there is in the wicket and what can be achieved with a good line and length. The way he bowls, he angles it across us left-handers. *He's going to be very difficult to score off here. We're gunna have to bide our time.*

At the other end, however, Zaheer can't get his line right and he gives us a couple of boundary opportunities. Ganguly takes him out of the attack after his third over with figures of 0–28. He is quiet now.

Their spinner, Harbhajan Singh, is happy to keep the talk going as he walks by at the end of each over. He's a fiery character, a good, aggressive cricketer whose stoushes with Haydos go back to the magnificent duels they fought on our tour of India where they were the two stand-out performers. Their chat this day is nothing outrageous, just two guys pumped up on adrenaline, but Harbhajan shows he isn't going to take a backward step.

Ganguly brings Nehra into the attack. He's had a good World Cup as part of this surprisingly effective Indian pace attack. He settles things down at his end with a reasonable line and length, but we cruise through the 50 partnership off seven overs. Next over, Srinath decides to change his strategy and comes around the wicket at us. Right from the first delivery it seems that he doesn't have a plan. I can't understand why he's changed. The different angle opens up some scoring opportunities. I get a square cut away for four and then another boundary through the on side. He comes in tighter, shorter at my body and I pull it over mid-wicket for six. He has played right into my scoring zones and the run rate goes up a notch to eight an over.

This is living.

Srinath is removed from the attack and Harbhajan is given his chance to back his words. Haydos is facing. Chest out. He sweeps one away like an absolute bullet. He's making the same statement he made to Zaheer in that first over. More verbals are exchanged at the change. Heated stuff. The temperature is rising. I say a few words too, now, caught up in the emotion of it all.

I make it to 50 off 40 balls and our century partnership comes up at the same time. It feels good to have got through the tough period. We've laid the foundation. Perhaps I should be thinking about consolidation, but the excitement is dragging me on.

I'm facing Harbhajan and I go for a slog-sweep against the spin trying to get it over the fence, but I find the top edge. The ball falls safely out in the deep and we run two, but it unnerves me. *What's the best way to go, here? Should I slow down and try to just knock some ones around? ... Nah.* If the momentum keeps running the way it's going, the outcome could be catastrophic for India. *Keep it going. Keep the hammer down at least to the end of the 15th.* Next ball, the last of the 14th, Harbhajan bowls the same sort of ball, an offspinner (a leggie for us left-handers) that doesn't have a lot of loop about it. I go for the same slog-sweep and proceed to get the same top edge. I'm immediately angry with myself. It was the wrong shot. And as it falls towards the earth I no longer have control over my destiny. Sehwag holds the catch and I'm on my way.

They're making me leave the party early, just when it's getting to be fun. I'm furious with myself. When I walk up into the rooms, though, everybody seems elated. They're all slapping me on the back. 'Well played.' They seem thrilled by the foundation we've laid, so I sit down and start to think that maybe 57 off 48 isn't too bad. There had been a lot of life in the wicket, so the scenario could have been quite different. We are 1–105 off 14 overs chugging along at 7.5 runs an over. I find myself becoming quite pleased with the impact I've had.

Only later will I realise that my score in this game is pretty close to the previous World Cup final where, chasing Pakistan's small total, I hit 54 off 36.

My exit from the middle slows our run rate, as the loss of a wicket so often does. Then Haydos follows me into the sheds, also caught off Harbhajan, for 37. We are 2–125 off 19.5 overs. The run rate is still a respectable 6.3.

It rankles to see Harbhajan get the both of us after our chatter out there. *Oh, well, he's won the battle.* We are, however, secure in the knowledge that we've inflicted a lot of damage.

That brings Marto to the crease with Ricky, who has been moving along at a pretty regulation pace. There's a lot of nerves up in our rooms. The Indians have snatched back a bit of momentum and we are all keenly watching to see how Marto's finger holds up. The Indians have Srinath back on, trying to put a bit of pressure on Marto's hands, no doubt. Srinath bowls a shortish wide one on the off side and Marto steps back and plays a cavalier back foot slash over cover-point. One or two bounces into the fence. It makes a statement. He's up for it.

That gets him going and he takes the initiative in the partnership, quickly passing Punter's score and keeping the run rate up at a run a ball.

Marto's always had something of an identity crisis in one-day cricket when it comes to scoring rates. He's always had this light-hearted gripe that if he scores 20, it's off 22 balls. If he scores 50, it's off 60 balls. He'll look at me and my 20s off 18 balls, my 50s off 40. 'Where's the justice?' he'll say.

So, it's something to see that he pushes through his 50 off 46 balls and soon after brings up the century partnership with Punter. Marto is on 56, while Punter is in the back seat with just 39 off almost 70 balls.

The run rate dips below six for the first time in the innings and Ricky sends a message to us that he's going to start to have a dip. Suddenly, he whips out two sixes in a row off Harbhajan as he climbs over into the driver's seat. Suddenly, he's taking them on everywhere, going over the top.

Boof, Bevo and myself start discussing the advantages of lifting Roy up the order, to give him as much time in the middle as possible. We get Ian Harvey to run a message out to Ricky, asking what he thinks. He says to do whatever we reckon. So, we have Roy padded up and ready to go as our score swings through 250 in 40 overs.

While Ricky's first 50 took 74 balls, his next 50 takes 29. He's only hit two fours at this point, but five sixes. Marto just seems to get left behind. His run rate doesn't drop. He just can't get on strike as Ricky dominates.

Through the middle overs we have our eyes on the magic 300 mark, but as we have one good over, and then another, we start to think more like 320, 330. As Ricky's hitting display reaches new levels of power and timing, the mood in the room builds and builds. We realise we are witnessing something special. The longer any partnership goes on in a game, the more relaxed the mood becomes. This is one chilled-out viewing room.

The Indians are looking ever more flat. Every time Ganguly tries to get Zaheer back into the game, he's hammered out again. All their part-timers get wheeled out for a few overs — Sehwag, Tendulkar, Mongia and Yuvraj Singh.

The Aussies in the crowd are making a lot of noise, but the general noise level is still high. I'm sure the Indian fans, being great lovers of the game, are getting some pleasure out of witnessing something so extraordinary.

The 200 partnership comes up off 173 balls, with Ponting on 105 and Martyn on 86 in the 48th over. At 325, we already have a huge total with two overs left to bowl. Ricky, still dominating the strike, whips his own score up to 130 with two balls left in the innings. He hits his eighth six of the innings off the second last, and on the last ball of the day hits what is only his fourth four. He is not out 140 (off 121), having hit his final 40 runs off just 18 balls.

After Marto had dominated the first century of their partnership, he'd only faced about another 30 balls and hit 32 more runs to take him up to 88. Ricky had faced about another 50 balls and hit 101.

Ricky Ponting salutes the crowd after completing one of the all-time great knocks in one-day cricket history against India in the final.

They come back in and are exhausted from swinging the bat so hard. They've just hit the biggest one-day partnership ever by Australians, 234, beating mine and Punter's from Melbourne only a few months earlier. Only 98 of those runs were from boundaries, so they've also been doing a lot of running in pretty warm conditions. There's a wonderful feeling of excitement and awe for what we've just been part of. No one is happier than Marto. He's quick to point out to everyone that his 88 came off just 84. He's beaten the hoodoo.

We know we have to contain our excitement. It is now a beautiful batting wicket and India are a dangerous batting side. If we've got this many, so can they. We have to bring our thoughts back to the processes required to finish the job.

We settle in for lunch, and keep an eye on the heavens. The forecast is for showers later in the day. It's clouding over a bit, but there's nothing to worry about yet.

We run out on to the field and again the crowd is in a frenzy. But coming up over their roar is an even louder howl. I look up and three South African Airways airliners are doing a fly-by. The noise is astonishing. We're throwing the ball between us as they circle and come around in single file. A chill goes down my spine and for some reason I think of New York's World Trade Center and the unforgettable images of those planes flying into the towers. Thankfully, we know that this is planned, but I hope that everyone in the ground and nearby knows the same. It's amazing how big those things are and I'm awed by the impact they could have. I just can't imagine what the survivors of September 11 must go through whenever they see a plane. It creates an eerie feeling, a funny thing to have in your body in the middle of a World Cup final.

The departure of the jets leaves the crowd still roaring. They've just seen one of the great innings of all time and now they have one of the all-time greats coming to the crease in an attempt to make an assault on it. Tendulkar has scored 669 so far this tournament, easily the most runs ever by a batsman at a World Cup, averaging 66.9.

Game on.

McGrath opens the bowling. Fourth ball is a typical McGrath delivery, just short of a length, and Tendulkar makes his intentions clear, hoiking it over mid-wicket for four.

Tendulkar knows he has to get on top early, and next ball he plays the same shot, but the ball is too tight and it shoots straight up. Pigeon claims the catch. One for five in the first.

After a wonderful series with the bat, Tendulkar leaves the field in the final after being snapped up by McGrath for just four runs.

All the build-up has been Lee versus Tendulkar, and yet Binga never even gets a shot at him. Don't ever discount the old experienced head; a guy who so often gets the big wickets. Our biggest danger man is out of the way, so like the first over of our batting, we've got the perfect start.

But Sehwag is a very dangerous player, too. He and Ganguly start to show their intent. In the fifth over, they get two sixes and a four to take 19 off the over. They go through 50 in 52 balls. They are going for it.

Ganguly holds the record for the second-highest World Cup score ever, 183 off 158 against Sri Lanka in 1999. In scoring that, he and Dravid put on the highest World Cup partnership ever — 318 — in taking India to a total of 373. With Dravid still to come, the Indians have plenty of firepower left.

They are having a go at everything now, but we know that if they keep it up, they'll offer us a chance sometime. They have to score at a run a ball for 40 overs and then accelerate to two a ball for the last ten.

Ganguly attempts to pull Lee, but lobs it to Boof at mid-on. Two for 58. Kaif comes in, but Pigeon bags him caught behind four balls later. Three for 59 in the 11th.

No matter what the next partnership does, we know that losing those two wickets is going to build pressure on their ability to lift their tempo later on.

Some nasty black clouds appear out the back of the stadium, obviously heading our way. Ricky and Boof and I get together and pull out the Duckworth-Lewis printout. We have to get to 25 overs to make a game of it, at which point India would need 157 for the loss of no more wickets. Every extra wicket is going to add another 20-odd to their target.

We feel we should squeeze through a few quick overs to help us get up to that 25-over mark, because the last thing we want after an almost perfect start is to have to come back tomorrow and do it all again. It's a sickening feeling that it could all be for nothing. *Where's the justice in it?* We have to get to that 25-over mark.

Punter brings Hoggie on in the 13th to lift the over rate, then Boof bowls the 14th. No one spends less time than Boof sending down six balls. But Sehwag takes a liking to him and belts three fours off his first over. That gives them a little bit of momentum and Hoggie goes for a four, then a six in the next over. Three for 88 off 15.

Suddenly, there's the equally sickening prospect that they could make another 69 runs off the next ten overs and steal the game. After seeing the way they are dealing with the spinners, we decide we're not going to think about the weather. It's out of our control. We'll just play to our game plan. Punter brings Andy Bichel and Pigeon on to steady the ship as the rain comes down in the 17th. The score is 3–103. The Indian fans all around the ground seem ecstatic, dancing and celebrating in the rain.

It's unpalatable that it might end this way. Fat chance of us coming out and hitting 359 again tomorrow.

But even as we make it to the change room and as the covers go on, we can see brightness out the back window. There is blue sky off in the direction from which the rain has come.

The bowlers stretch and try to stay warm.

We are back on the field after 25 minutes, spot on 4 pm. No overs have been lost. But the weather still looks ominous. The fear is that we'll make it to 25 overs and more rain will come. A run rate of 6.75 an over for just eight overs could win them the game. Provided they don't lose any more wickets.

The adrenaline is pumping. The drama is real. We *can* lose this unlosable game. Like we always do, we fall back on plan A: bowl line and length and restrict their scoring.

But Dravid and Sehwag keep the run rate ticking over ominously, taking their partnership through 50 off 48 balls. Sehwag has the momentum and Dravid is working the ball around nicely. After 20 overs, India are 3–122, compared to our score of 2–126 at the same point.

Sehwag, on 72, slashes one to backward point where Hoggie puts down a very tough chance. Soon after, he puts a ball from Hoggie into the car park and follows it up with a four to have India right on track at 3–145. They need only 12 runs in two overs to be in front when the Duckworth-Lewis system clicks in.

They take an aggressive run and Boof fields it at short mid-off, throwing the stumps down. Direct hit. Sehwag is caught short. He's hit the pressure valve. The release is amazing. India's Duckworth-Lewis total for the 25-over mark blows out by 21 to 178.

Still the Indians keep coming at us. They can't slow down. It's death or glory.

Marto gets under a high ball from Yuvraj Singh, which he'd catch nine times out of ten but it just doesn't go into his hands right. He's not too happy about that, worrying that we think his finger might have let us down.

There is thunder off to the east with the Indians at 4–178 in the 31st, just 20 runs behind on the Duckworth-Lewis.

It is surreal. This storm looks bigger and darker than the first, full of rumblings and anger. It gives the Indian supporters hope and lifts their noise level while the air swirls with the smell of rain.

Dravid has kept things ticking over without playing any big strokes. But Bic gets him. Bowled for 47 off 57. Their rain-affected target blows out by another 20 and the game slips further away from them.

The temperature is falling as this storm-to-end-all-storms rumbles closer. It feels like the World Cup is building up to a final eruption. At the

Self-doubt? No, after dropping this one off Yuvraj Singh in the final, Damien Martyn would later take a brilliant catch to prove he was up to it, even with a broken finger.

next break in play, Marto swaps positions with Brett Lee to avoid the same sort of high ball.

Mongia is not laying down and lets loose a few fours before Yuvraj Singh skies Hoggie down to Brett Lee right where Marto had been standing. Six for 208. Three balls later, Mongia skies a ball past Marto who I'm sure is still uneasy about the last one he dropped. He runs backwards, turns and chases, makes great ground and holds it. The excitement on his face says it all. He's proven that he is up to it.

Harbhajan Singh is at the crease now and he gets a pretty aggressive welcome from the boys, but there's a light-hearted tone to it, because we know he's got Buckley's of turning it around. He has a huge swing and miss off Hoggie. I want to keep him aggressive and swinging like that so I take the opportunity to ask if he realises the position he's in and that it's the World Cup final. He turns to me. 'Oh, don't worry, I stuffed you. I got you out.'

'Yep, correct. Well done. But I suspect that in the context of this match it's the best thing that I could have done because Ricky Ponting came in and tore you to pieces.'

The stump mike apparently picks up that comment and beams it around the world. Two balls later, a ball shoots through my legs and goes for a couple of byes. It may have been a stumping chance. He tells me I'm a hopeless keeper. More like a soccer goalie, or something. It continues back and forth like that until he whacks a ball from Roy to McGrath at mid-off where Pigeon takes a low catch. Eight for 223.

Lee bowls Srinath next over. Nine wickets down, we're just one wicket away from being world champions. I look around to see how everyone's travelling. They're all lively and on their toes, looking at each other, laughing. We are enjoying the moment. Buzzing. The bond between us as teammates is so apparent at this moment.

McGrath bowls to Zaheer Khan, who skies it. Darren Lehmann runs around and latches on to it. The Cup is ours. Boof finished the last World Cup with the bat, now he's ending this one with his hands. And I don't remember him letting go of that ball, either. Everyone races in. I make a beeline for Ricky, who is on his knees with his arms raised. I just want to grab him and share this instant. Everyone comes together into a huddle. I'm pretty emotional. Tears well up. I look around at all the guys who I've been through so much with. Roy's tearing up, too. The realisation of what we've achieved overcomes me. It's a unique feeling that only us blokes can share. One moment in time.

After the initial embracing, our thoughts go to the rest of the team — the guys who didn't play — and the support group. We go to share it with them and after that we break off to connect with the people who are most important to us. In my case, Mel and Harry, Mum and Dad, and Stephen my manager. They were all in various sections of the stands, but I was able to wave to them and share that moment.

Chapter Twenty-three

THE STORM

The change room is filled with solid elation. We've achieved what we set out to achieve. A lot of hugging and screaming and yelling is going on. It's just the players, initially. It's the first time it's been just us since the meeting the night before. Then the entire support group — coach, assistant coach, manager, fitness trainer, the fielding coach/motivator, masseuse, physio and our media representative — piles in. Roy is spraying the champagne around. *This isn't gunna slow down*. It's a terrific moment that we'll all savour for the rest of our lives; the culmination of so much effort.

But we pretty quickly have to turn around and head back out on to the field for the presentations. The media liaison, Jonathan Rose, had the idea to give us little Australian flags and we don't need any encouragement to pick them up.

As we stand, waiting for the presentations to start, our shirts sticky with champagne, the storm is coming closer and closer. It reminds me of the movie *The Never Ending Story*, which I saw as a youngster, about a kid who flies around on a big dog and has to save the world from The Nothing — a storm that threatens to wipe out everything.

Our storm here on this day is brewing like it's the storm to end the world. Thunder and wind and darkness close in on us.

We're all saying, 'Come on, get it under way!' They introduce the dignitaries and there are speeches by Malcolm Gray and Malcolm Speed of the ICC. Then, finally, it's the presentations. The Indians get their runners-up medals. Sachin Tendulkar is announced, deservedly, as Man of the Series, and then one by one we go up on to the podium to collect our winners' medals. It's a real high point for me. I turn and look up into the boxes and see Mel and Harry waving. Harry looks about an inch tall. It's a very special moment. Ricky is presented with the World Cup and all the boys are up there. That's when the celebrations begin. To me, the feeling is even more special than the 1999 World Cup. It's hard to put a finger on why, but I think it's because of my greater involvement in the team, my more senior role and my contribution throughout the campaign. And the victories are so different. The last one was such a seat-of-the-pants, adrenaline ride after our shocking start to the tournament. We'd clawed our way back and

A wonderful feeling when a plan comes together. Enjoying a victory lap with the lads after a great win.

snatched a draw from the jaws of defeat in the semi and then won the final in a cakewalk. This one has been much more methodically executed with a huge build-up at the end, and here we are again.

We go for a victory lap, hurrying more than we'd like, as the first spits of rain start to hit. We'd love to stay and mop up the atmosphere, but we at least reach most of the supporter groups that have stayed on. As we pass the section where Stephen Atkinson and Ricky's manager, Sam Halvorsen, are sitting, we give them a big hug. It didn't go unnoticed by Ricky and myself that, after all we'd been through together as captain and vice-captain, our managers had watched it unfold together.

Winning the World Cup is such an emotional time. I think about the special people who have helped me, but there are a million thoughts racing through my mind. I head back out to the middle of the ground by myself. *I just wanna stop and look and really take it all in and make sure that I never, ever forget this moment.* I stand there, and it might sound a bit cornball, but I have the Aussie flag and I'm wearing the Australian uniform and it's one of the proudest moments of my life. The stadium is clearing, but the people who are still there are the Aussies. It's like my day is flashing before my eyes. Breakfast, getting on the bus, the air of uncertainty, my nerves, the switch that was hit when the wind fell out of their sails. All of these images flash through my mind. I know that I've just been through an amazing little part of sports history and a huge part of my own life.

There are photos taken down on the ground and then the rain starts to come in. We race back to the change rooms where the door is open for whoever we want to join us: all the Australian Cricket Board reps, the CEO and chairman of Travelex — our major sponsor for the tour — and various other sponsors. Mum and Dad, Mel and Harry. Our security officer, Darren Maughan, who's been with us day-in, day-out. Our liaison officer, Colin Dettmer. Our baggage handler, Lucas. Everyone's there.

Binga or Bic must be floating around the rock box, because Cold Chisel's *Khe San* comes on. Loud. The passion and the emotion in the room is hard to describe. It's all the clichés. Champagne is flying. But it's not out of control. There's a certain calmness about the whole thing, as opposed to 1999 at Lords where all the tension exploded into a wild party. It's calm here, but emotional all the same. John Williamson's *True Blue* comes on. It seems like everyone at some stage speaks to everyone else in the room. There must be 50 or 60 people there.

The Indian team doesn't show up, but in this case I wouldn't expect them to. The hours tick by. All the cameras come out; everyone is having their pictures taken with the Cup. Harry can't walk yet, but he can stand. I look down to see him sort of leaning on the £30,000 World Cup, which he's crawled over to and used to pull himself up to his full height. I marvel at how fortunate I am to combine such a wonderful family with achieving what I've achieved and being paid well to do it.

Gradually, the friends and families fade out of the rooms and it comes down to our tour group — players and staff. We have a bit of time for a drink together and I whip out a box of cigars. It's a contentious issue as to whether it's promoting the right image, but I like to have a cigar when I'm celebrating and no one's going to stop me. Everyone seems to stick their hand in and light one up. Even guys that hate them have a go. It's just another bit of the bond between the group in wanting to share everything.

And then I decide that it's time for the team song, of which I'm the custodian in one-day cricket since Punter passed it to me when he got the captaincy. For some reason, it's felt that the captain shouldn't be the one who leads the song. It's now about 9 pm. The ground is silent and dark but for our room. Traditionally, the song is sung in the change room, but in 1999 Punter led us out on to the Lords pitch to sing it and it was a memorable experience, so I decide to follow suit.

We traipse out on to the dark oval. The guys are fully pumped by this stage. Everyone's had a few drinks and the excitement is rising again as we reach the centre. We form a circle around an Australian flag laid down in the middle. 'Let's just really, really embrace this,' I say. 'This is a unique time in our lives, and let's never, ever forget that.' We launch into the song, and the way the guys sing it shows that they appreciate what a wonderful time this is. Whenever we get to sing that song, it's a special occasion — either a Test win or a one-day series victory. But this is more special than most. As we leave the ground, we realise that a few security guards and some corporates who have been up in the boxes have snuck down on to the pitch for a look at our little ceremony.

Whether it means anything to them, I don't know, but not many people get the chance to witness the team song being sung.

From there, it's back on the bus. It's a great bus ride, with lots of laughter. Back at the hotel, everyone races up to their room to change and then we all get back on the bus to head off to a party put on by Travelex for our invited guests. It's a good night, but again it's not out of control; everyone is just enjoying what's taken place and realising how fortunate we are to be involved.

The celebrations well under way, Andrew Symonds still makes sure that no one else gets their hands on the World Cup.

Slowly, guys disappear at different times, conking out, but Mel, Stephen and Phil — the babysitter for whom we'd booked another babysitter so that he could come to the party — are in the last batch to leave with me. We get back to the hotel at about 5.30 am.

We order some food and the others crash out at about 6.30, but I know that Harry is due to wake up at any moment so I figure I'll push on. I sit on the lounge and run through again what's happened on the wonderful day just gone. Right on cue, Harry wakes with a little squawk. I get him up and we spend the next few hours playing.

EPILOGUE

While I was standing in the middle of the ground, taking in the sights and sounds of my second World Cup, a thought hit me: *I wonder if I'll be around for the next one?* In 1999, there was no such question. I knew that if my form and fitness held up, I'd be there. But this time my future was shrouded in uncertainty.

Sitting on the floor playing with Harry, the thoughts of my own cricketing longevity came back.

Only six of the 1999 squad made it to this year's tournament. I wouldn't expect there would be too many more than six coming back to the next one.

I'm going to be 35, around the age at which the Waugh boys were shunted off. There's going to be a whole bunch of us hitting that wall together. I don't think age will rule any of us out, but the way the cycle operates, it's going to make it harder. Particularly in the one-day game, given the way it has evolved over the last ten years, getting quicker all the time. There's a core of young players that will definitely be there. Guys like Andrew Symonds, who will be 31, Brett Lee, 30, and Nathan Hauritz, 25. Ricky, 32, will be there, while Jimmy Maher, 33, and Michael Clarke, 26, may well make up the core of the batting.

There's a little bit more uncertainty about the rest of us. Dizzy will be 32, so we'll see if his body holds up. Haydos, Marto and Ian Harvey will be 35. Bevo, Pigeon, Hoggie and Bich will be 36, while Boof will have just had his 37th birthday.

I haven't decided yet whether I want to be there. But matters may well be out of our control. In sitting back and savouring the win, I must say I felt thrilled for the Australian selectors, particularly Trevor Hohns. Regardless of what mine or anyone's thoughts were about their selections, they had proven that they were prepared to back their judgment in trying to keep Australian cricket at the top and I think they deserve a lot of credit for that. Those hard decisions aren't going to go away.

Mel woke up and the focus of the day became packing up. Being on the road for two months with a baby, we'd accumulated a lot of stuff. I did what I could to help between phone interviews and going downstairs for the signing session. At the end of any tour, we have a session where all the guys get out shirts, bats, pads or flags to be signed as memorabilia. It was due to take place at noon, but the guys filtered in as they woke up and dusted off the cobwebs. There was an awful lot of stuff there, but we got through it.

All of a sudden, we were on the road and flying out. I was looking forward to crashing out on the plane and having my first sleep since the night before the game, but Harrison had other plans. He decided that he was wide-awake, so I had to keep him entertained. I ended up getting an hour-and-a-half's sleep near the end of the nine-hour flight.

We landed in Perth at about 8 am. We had a press conference involving the whole team and were then taken to Forrest Chase shopping area in Perth, where about 5,000 people were waiting at a reception for us. That was really exciting, especially for Hoggie, Marto and myself, being local boys. Perth doesn't get the opportunity to have a bite at these cherries too often. It was a beautiful day and it was good fun to get back and start sharing our win with the rest of Australia.

And that was it. It was a pretty emotional time saying goodbye to everyone and knowing that the journey was over. I'll always feel a special bond with that group of people, and that's something that will never be taken away. It's the same with the 1999 group, too.

All the guys flew out to their home ports.

We had about five days off before regathering in Sydney when the Test team was to fly out to tour the West Indies. The World Cup guys had one more reception, a short cocktail party put on by Travelex and the ACB. Then we took off to the Caribbean, via London, that night.

It was frustrating, given what we had achieved, that there wasn't the time to celebrate and enjoy the win for longer. We should have had some time off to enjoy our success. Immediately our thoughts had to turn to a new tour and that took away a lot of the sparkle. I think the scheduling devalued the win. I don't recall the Brazilian soccer team going off on tour a week after their World Cup win. I think any team needs to be given a chance to revel in the moment. The schedule didn't give the ACB a chance to show off its great achievement. And the sponsors didn't get a chance to leverage their considerable investment.

It was very disappointing.

Punter and Buck both came out after the win declaring that this team could take the game to a higher level still. I don't necessarily disagree with that. You can always look to improve in anything. And knowing John Buchanan the way I do, even if we don't get better, he'll at least explore ways of doing things differently to seek that improvement. He won't sit back and let us slide down the other side of this peak. That's the challenge that he throws at us.

We won the Tests in the Windies 3–1, and it was pleasing when the one-day squad reassembled for a seven-match series against the West Indies that it was the World Cup squad — minus Marto, whose finger ruled him out — with Dizzy back in. To bring that group back together was terrific and something that everyone was really pleased about. It gave us a chance to see if we could challenge ourselves to stay up on that high plateau.

I'm sitting here in Grenada now, writing this with the Caribbean just 20 metres away lapping gently on the beach outside my hotel window. The World Cup, only eight weeks gone, seems like three years ago. We were able to come here and respond to the challenge and continue that level of excellence. We wrapped up the series by winning the first four games, taking our world-record winning streak to 21, before crashing back to earth in Trinidad. We've just lost two more games here in Grenada as well.

Maybe it's not a myth. Maybe you do have to lose one … eventually.